The Fairy Tale
and Anime

The Fairy Tale and Anime

Traditional Themes, Images and Symbols at Play on Screen

Dani Cavallaro

McFarland & Company, Inc., Publishers
Jefferson, North Carolina, and London

LIBRARY OF CONGRESS CATALOGUING-IN-PUBLICATION DATA

Cavallaro, Dani.
    The fairy tale and anime : traditional themes, images and
symbols at play on screen / Dani Cavallaro.
        p.   cm.
    Includes bibliographical references and index.

    ISBN 978-0-7864-5946-9
    softcover : 50# alkaline paper

    1. Fairy tales in motion pictures.   2. Fairy tales —
Film adaptations.   I. Title.
    PN1995.9.F34C38   2011
    791.43'6559 — dc22   2010052296

British Library cataloguing data are available

Cover art © 2011 ATOMix/Shutterstock

Manufactured in the United States of America

*McFarland & Company, Inc., Publishers
  Box 611, Jefferson, North Carolina 28640
  www.mcfarlandpub.com*

To Zia Serena, fairyland muse;
to Paddy, unique friend;
to Betsy, furry sibling

Contents

In a place far away from anyone or anywhere, I drifted off for a moment.
— Haruki Murakami

What the caterpillar calls the end, the rest of the world calls a butterfly.
— Lao-Tzu

Preface •

Deeper meaning lies in the fairy tales of my childhood than in the truth that is taught in life.
— Friedrich von Schiller

Nothing can be truer than fairy wisdom. It is as true as sunbeams.
— Douglas Jerrold

As an art form of widely acclaimed autonomous caliber, anime has consistently come into fruitful collusion with themes, images and symbols (archetypes included) associated with the fairy tale tradition. This phrase does not, it must be emphasized, allude to stories that literally feature fairies but rather denotes, in keeping with contemporary scholarship in the field, stories where a prominent place is accorded to otherworldly phenomena, where the boundary between reality and fantasy is boldly and even grotesquely transgressed, and where the capriciousness of human destinies is repeatedly exposed — it is no coincidence, after all, that the word "fairy" is derived from the Latin *fatum*, or "fate." This book seeks to both document and pay homage to the time-honored discourse of the fairy tale tradition by exploring in depth the appropriation and articulation of its materials in an apposite selection of shows.

The analysis is not principally concerned with interpretations of famous fairy tales in anime form, even though some of these are incorporated in the discussion where appropriate. In fact, its focus is on the strategies by means of which certain fundamental principles of the fairy tale tradition are deployed, and hence come to manifest themselves narratively and cinematographically, in anime. These embrace storytelling, aesthetic, dramatic, ethical, psychological and social considerations. The themes, images and symbols on which they depend, relatedly, can be treated as versatile tools for the orchestration of allegorical commentaries on particular cultural and historical scenarios. A variety of Western and Eastern

1

perspectives on both the fairy tale itself as a form and theorizations thereof by recourse to various philosophical positions provide the project's critical frame of reference. The discussion therefore invokes numerous scholars and artists engaged specifically in the fairy tale tradition or, more broadly, in the investigation of folkloric, rhetorical and pictorial trends pertinent to the study of the field. Relevant voices from the domains of Japanese aesthetics and cultural history are also brought into play to document the fairy tale's relationship with two influential discourses emanating specifically from anime's indigenous milieu.

The book's opening chapter, "Theoretical Foundations," looks at a selection of critical and philosophical positions on the fairy tale in order to contextualize it in relation to an appropriately broad frame of reference. Each of the ensuing chapters engages with specific anime titles, considering their use of themes, images and symbols embedded in the fairy tale tradition with reference to narrative examples gleaned from both Eastern and Western lore. Chapter 2, "Alterity," explores the incidence of fairy tale elements in the art of anime as pivotal to the orchestration of dramatic narratives centered on varyingly perturbing encounters between Self and Other. In Chapter 3, "Voyages," the analysis concentrates on literal and figurative journeys of exploration, search and discovery, requiring their actors to suspend all familiar certitudes in the face of the inscrutable. Chapter 4, "Creativity," looks at the processes through which anime appropriates and relocates certain fundamental features of the fairy tale tradition specifically in order to dramatize a character's expression of creative urges and, ideally, artistic talent. This, in turn, can be seen as instrumental in the achievement of self-understanding and maturity. In Chapter 5, "Dystopias," finally, the focus is on anime's constellation of worlds where practically all of the darkest connotations of the fairy tale tradition are brought to the fore as a means of reflecting elliptically on the eternal evils of political corruption, absolutism and iniquity.

Anime and the fairy tale tradition have interacted over several decades. Some titles have adopted fairy tale materials to construct alternate worlds and the epic sagas unfolding therein, while others have turned to the fairy tale as a repository of convenient character types, actantial relationships and yarns. Others still have capitalized on the form's knack of boldly transcending, or indeed subverting, the dictates of logic and the laws of physics to weave entertainingly preposterous dramatic tapestries. Furthermore, countless anime titles have relied on classic "hero-versus-villain" (or "white-hat-versus-black-hat") typologies of an unmistakably fabulous stamp. The two interconnected aspects of the Western fairy tale — at least in its mellowed-down and ideologically massaged incarnations — for which anime has by no means invariably exhibited unequivocal respect are the "and-they-lived-happily-ever-after" formula and the dishing out of a tight moral. This is feasibly a corollary of the medium's proverbial cultivation of inconclusive endings and eschewal of stark binary oppositions in the distribution of good and evil.

While several contemporary shows still evince the preferences delineated above, it is nonetheless noteworthy that recent anime has often opted to draw from the fairy tale tradition specifically for the purpose of elaborating the sorts of allegorical commentaries that were alluded to earlier. This shift in emphasis arguably corresponds to a general intensification, within many of the more intelligently conceived anime of recent years, of the proclivity to engage with acute psychological analysis — and accordingly nuanced character development — and with dispassionate meditations on the human condition. A parallel increase in the penchant for ambiguous resolutions is concomitantly observable. For this reason, this study concentrates on shows released almost exclusively over the phase of anime history approximately coinciding with the past decade as more relevant objects of scrutiny in terms of their cultural weight as allegorical interpretations of reality and, relatedly, of their greater amenability to theoretical investigation: a clear priority in a book of this nature.

CHAPTER 1

Theoretical Foundations

For those who immerse themselves in what the fairy tale has to communicate, it becomes a deep, quiet pool which at first seems to reflect only our own image; but behind it we soon discover the inner turmoils of our soul—its depth, and ways to gain peace within ourselves and with the world, which is the reward of our struggles.
— Bruno Bettelheim

Independently of the curious circumstance that such tales should be found existing in very different countries and languages, which augurs a greater poverty of human invention than we would have expected, there is also a sort of wild fairy interest in them, which makes me think them fully better adapted to awaken the imagination and soften the heart of childhood than the good-boy stories which have been in later years composed for them.
— Walter Scott

In a characteristically sprightly account of the dynamics of transmission of the fairy tale over time, Angela Carter has commented: "The chances are, the story was put together in the form we have it, more or less out of all sorts of bits of other stories long ago and far away, and has been tinkered with, had bits added to it, lost other bits, got mixed up with other stories, until our informant herself has tailored the story personally to suit an audience ... or, simply, to suit herself" (Carter 1990, p. x). Few words could provide more auspicious a point of entry into a study of the fairy tale tradition's molding by another art form — in this specific instance, anime. The impressive adaptability intrinsic in that discourse to which Carter refers — and which makes it amenable to ongoing transformation and repositioning by another form — is largely a corollary of its sprawling and haphazardly documented history. One of the principal reasons for this nebulousness is that the fairy tale tradition encompasses both orally divulged narrations, presumably ascribable to anonymous and collective authority, and literary texts with identifiable singular authors, and that only the latter are available for perusal and systematic study even though oral and written fairy tales have promiscuously traded plots and themes with one another both within the remit of individual cultures and across disparate lands for a very long time.

While the tension between oral and written traditions remains something of a conundrum, scholarship is also hazy in dealing with the relationship between the fairy tale and the folktale. Thus, some critics tend to conflate fairy tales with particular types of folktales, such as beast fables and stories dominated by the marvelous. Particular themes are often singled out as distinctive markers of the fairy tale, with the topos of transformation and the quest motif in conventionally privileged positions. At the same time, specific storytelling ploys stand out as clear generic definers. These include the use of indefinite, vague or patently unreal settings evocative of a never-never domain; humble protagonists capable of prevailing over their powerful (and often evil) antagonists and of winning the day; axiomatic characters and symbols; the violation of taboos and prohibitions as a crucial narrative trigger. The narrative cement holding these various elements together consists of one crucial event and its repercussions: the encounter between a human — or otherwise mortal — character and the fairy world, resulting in varyingly radical disruptions of the status quo. Relatedly, special prominence is typically accorded to fantastical, otherworldly and make-believe situations and incidents, alongside wizardly people, animals and props, as well as magical practices of both beneficent and destructive kinds. In these scenarios, problem solving frequently operates as a major plot activator. Happy endings and moral lessons may be included but these often result from post-hoc editing and adaptive moves rather than original narratorial tactics or ethical priorities. The fairy tale recipe is vitally abetted, on the semiotic plane, by memorable language distinguished by the assiduous use of repetition, rhythmic patterns and rhyme, archaic or regional vocabulary, formulaic phrases (especially in the tale's opening and ending) and a subtle differentiation in the styles and registers associated with human beings and characters from the fairy world.

The worldwide recurrence of certain narrative materials is itself a complex phenomenon open to variable interpretations. Some view it empirically as a product of gradual improvements in global communication and the dissemination of ideas, whereas others ascribe it to the existence of an underlying universal imaginary. Whatever the causes underlying the fairy tale's culture-hopping migrations, it is patent that the adoption of recurrent factors in disparate contexts is never conducive to pure repetition.

In fact, it demonstrates that there can be no such thing as straightforward and undiluted reiteration for the simple reason that meaning is notoriously prone to slippage, forever in the process of sliding, erring, taking detours and getting stuck in blind alleys. Therefore, tales produced in different geographical and historical milieux but evincing analogous ingredients should not be approached as replications or simulations of one another but rather as parallel interpretations of those core elements. Accordingly, in examining the relationship between two tales exhibiting thematic or formal affinities, we should not presume to peel away at their figurative layers and contingent culture-bound accretions in order to reach some ultimate urtext but rather accept that the materials at our disposal are only the surfaces of representation themselves, and that these very surfaces deserve credit as autonomous realities in their ability to both entertain and stimulate reflection.

Additionally, fairy tales have time and again tended to overlap with myths and legends with a grounding in historical reality. This factor has further problematized the task of demarcating the fairy tale's territory and chronological scope. At the same time, numerous critics have called attention to the importance of disassociating the fairy tale tradition from the figure of the fairy per se. J. R. R. Tolkien, for instance, has stated: "fairy-stories are not in normal English usage stories about fairies or elves, but stories about Fairy, that is Faërie, the realm or state in which fairies have their being. Faërie contains many things besides elves and fays, and besides dwarfs, witches, trolls, giants, or dragons: it holds the seas, the sun, the moon, the sky; and the earth, and all things that are in it: tree and bird, water and stone, wine and bread, and ourselves, mortal men, when we are enchanted." By severing Faërie from the fabulous creatures reputed to inhabit it, Tolkien is in a position to propose that any cogent "definition of a fairy-story — what it is, or what it should be — does not, then, depend on any definition or historical account of elf or fairy, but upon the nature of Faërie: the Perilous Realm itself, and the air that blows in that country. ... Faërie cannot be caught in a net of words; for it is one of its qualities to be indescribable, though not imperceptible. It has many ingredients, but analysis will not necessarily discover the secret of the whole. ... Faërie itself may perhaps most nearly be translated by Magic — but it is magic of a peculiar mood and power, at the furthest pole from the vulgar devices of the laborious, scientific, magician. There is one proviso: if there is any satire present in the tale, one thing must not be made fun of, the magic itself. That must in that story be taken seriously, neither laughed at nor explained away" (Tolkien). Faërie's defiant rejection of neat labels does not only expose humanity's inadequacy in the face of worlds that elude its comprehension. In other words, it does not merely tell us that we are powerless to name it. In fact, and more crucially, it emphasizes that we should not even attempt to name it. Were we to do so, we would be disregarding its principal attribute and, ironically, would end up being further away from any prospect of grasping its reality than we were when we first embarked upon our vain quest for definitions.

What can hardly be called into question is that fairy tales have been around for thousands of years: many illustrious anthropologists, folklore scholars and literary critics would readily defend such a hypothesis, grandiose though it may sound. The term "fairy tale" itself is quite a recent invention, having reputedly been coined in 1697 by the French fairy tale author Madame d'Aulnoy (Marie-Catherine Le Jumel de Barneville, Baroness d'Alnoy, a.k.a. Countess d'Alnoy, 1650/1651–1705) with the phrase *conte de fées*. Although it is widely believed that fairy tales were originally intended to reach multigenerational audiences, over time they have come to be more and more intimately associated with children. The circle of witty ladies active in the climate of the salon culture of seventeenth-century France dubbed *Les Précieuses* is held to have played a key part in fostering that connection. Since the Brothers Grimm's publication of their works under the title of *Children's and Household Tales* (1812/ 1814/1822), the bond has grown incrementally tenacious. This is an offshoot, to a considerable extent, of the fairy tale's unmatched malleability as an enculturing and socializing tool.

Up until quite recently, it was common for educational authors to commend the fairy tale's beneficial import without pausing to consider the duskier connotations of the tradition in which it is embedded. Laura Kready's writings paradigmatically exemplify this trend by proposing that while fairy tales are able to "contain" the child's "interests," they can also be seen as an edifying "means for the expression of his instincts and for his development in purpose, in initiative, in judgment, in organization of ideas, and in the creative return possible to him." Kready would plausibly have questioned the educational worth of the fairy tale tradition as sculpted and reinterpreted by anime since she seems to view all forms other than the literary as morally dubious, wishing "to show what fairy tales must possess as classics, as literature and composition, and as short-stories; to trace their history, to classify the types, and to supply the sources of material" so as to establish the true value of the "creative return" one could realistically expect of a child. "The fairy tale," Kready blithely argues in the climactic segment of the preface to *A Study of Fairy Tales* (1916), "is also related to life standards, for it presents to the child a criticism of life. By bringing forward in high light the character of the fairy, the fairy tale furnishes a unique contribution to life. Through its repeated impression of the idea of fairy-hood it may implant in the child a desire which may fructify into that pure, generous, disinterested kindness and love of the grown-up, which aims to play fairy to another, with sincere altruism to make appear before his eyes his heart's desire, or in a twinkling to cause what hitherto seemed impossible. Fairy tales thus are harbingers of that helpfulness which would make a new earth, and as such afford a contribution to the religion of life" (Kready).

This sunny approach to the fairy tale tradition's pedagogical utility has come increasingly under attack in recent years as a result of some unsentimental anatomies of the far-reaching ideological and psychological implications carried by that discourse across numerous societies. Jack Zipes, in particular, has eloquently contended that even though fairy tales have been firmly inscribed in history as "universal, ageless, therapeutic, miraculous, and beautiful" (Zipes 1991, p. 1), they are in fact imbricated with processes of regimentation of the young according to contingent ethical and aesthetic programs. The crucial usefulness of fairy tales as acculturing weapons first asserted itself in the context of seventeenth-century France, where the traditional aristocracy and the ascending bourgeoisie alike were addictively keen on domesticating children's natural drives and on imparting the principle of self-discipline as the foundation of acceptable behavior. The murkier and rowdier aspects of traditional fairy tales have, since that epoch, been progressively excised, softened or edulcorated, and starkly polarized gender positions have accordingly been enthroned as unquestionable and immutable standards. At the same time, the degree of violence attached to the depiction of a villain's punishment has been amplified — in ways one might not automatically deem child-friendly — to cautionary ends.

Beside their dubious repercussions as far as children are specifically concerned, these ruses have had lamentable consequences in broadly philosophical terms. This is because they have tended to obfuscate the richness of fairy tales, their polyphony, their multilayered construction and — most importantly — their status as three-dimensional puzzles wherein truth and fact never easily coincide. Thus, the fairy tale tradition's enculturing agendas have served to regulate and dumb down not solely juvenile conduct but also the interpretative capacities and imaginative responses of audiences of all ages. In fact, fairy tales are uniquely resourceful vehicles — regardless of whether they literally or metaphorically feature fairies and other magical species — for plumbing actual social milieux with an astute admixture of drama and humor, for articulating personal odysseys through the uncharted labyrinths of the psyche, and for enacting adventures where inner and outer dimensions relentlessly — yet mysteriously — coalesce or clash. The profoundly cross-generational relevance of fairy tales is memorably foregrounded by Italo Calvino. The writer commends the loving cultivation of the most diminutive descriptive details evinced by traditional stories as felicitously conducive to the evocation of protean and tentacular universes through sparse rhetorical and pictorial touches. In addition, Calvino is deeply fascinated with the "economy, rhythm and hard logic with which they are told" (Calvino 1996, p. 35), placing special weight on the value of conciseness as instrumental in a supple handling of time whereby vertiginous speed and ponderous stasis alternate with seamless fluidity. On the temporal level, likewise remarkable is the potentially indefinite amplification of a tale's scope by means of internal digressions, bifurcations and ramifications.

Calvino acknowledges the usefulness of theoretical approaches that tend to emphasize the emanation of singular stories from a supposedly transhistorical deep structure. Yet, he also warns us against the latently reductionist thrust inherent in those templates. Specifically, he intimates that concentrating on the affinities exhibited by individual tales or clusters of narratives in relation to an overarching paradigm could finally be tantamount to obfuscating or even ignoring each yarn's specificity, local color and genius. It is therefore vital to appreciate, according to Calvino, that "reducing the tale to its unchanging skeleton contributes to highlight how many geographical and historical variables form the external casing of this skeleton; and establishing rigorously the narrative function, the place assumed within this scheme by specific instances of social existence, the objects of empirical experience, the implements available to a given culture, the plants and animals of a particular flora and fauna, can provide data which would otherwise elude us regarding the value which that particular culture ascribes to them" (Calvino 1988, p. 113). Relatedly, while fairy tales are eminently repetitive in the treatment of their themes and imagery, variety is no less critical a marker of their generic and formal identity. The delight fostered by heterogeneity is never swamped by the recognition of underlying uniformity. Repetition, for its part, ironically enhances the impact of difference when this can be felt to have occurred and to have punctured the veil of sameness. The tale, in this regard, is akin to "an arabesque of multicolored metamorphoses that issue from one another," as patterns do in an Oriental carpet (p. 146).

Calvino's twin concern with diversity and recurrence recalls Vladimir Propp's mapping of folk and fairy tales on the basis of a morphological schema predicated upon the occurrence, in an invariable order or sequence, of a constant and limited set of "functions"— the actions that are invested with axial significance within the story's cumulative trajectory — and "spheres of action"— character-types by means of which the functions are performed (Propp). Like Calvino, Propp is keen to foreground the importance of contingent peculiarities and divergences as far more intriguing than presumably universal similarities. Calvino, however, takes the celebration of diversity a step further by suggesting that since any one individual yarn only harbors a selection of elements drawn from a capacious reservoir of possible ingredients, its meaning is bound to depend not only on what it contains but also on the substantial portions of that supply it leaves untouched — on the pockets of absence ineluctably rupturing its narrative self-presence: "in any tale that has a meaning," the author avers, "one may recognize the first tale ever told and the last tale, beyond which the world will not let itself be narrated in a tale" (Calvino 1988, p. 126). Calvino thus reminds us with disarming honesty that the "figures of darkness" (p. 137) unremittingly coalesce with "auroral light" (p. 129). Ultimately, as noted in a study of Calvino himself, "any story *is* by virtue of what it *is not*. Any story is always on the verge of metamorphosing into another story which might have, could have, perhaps should have been told instead or, more importantly, exists but might, just as feasibly, have never existed" (Cavallaro, p. 65).

According to Joseph Campbell, fairy tales function for both boys and girls as "initiation ceremonies" or rites of passage deemed capable of "killing the infantile ego" (Campbell, p. 168). Relatedly, as L. C. Seifert advocates, both sexes are ensnared in the hegemonic imperative to secure "the harmonious existence of family and society at large" (Seifert, p. 109). More ominously still, fairy tales have been obliquely invoked to justify infantile abuse — this theme being ubiquitous to the form but more often than not tamed to be made to look like an impartial expression of necessary discipline. According to Marina Warner, this sinister trend finds a parallel in legends meant to justify the ill-treatment and victimization of the very young or even, in the most abominable scenarios, infanticide. Supernatural beings have indeed been brought into play to explain the disappearance of infants or small kids and thus ratify deaths caused by entirely human agencies as otherworldly events: "A changeling," for example, "could be discreetly made to disappear, as an evil gift of the fairies, or even of the devil; to dispose of a human child on the other hand, however unwanted or damaged at birth, lay beyond the frontiers of acceptable conduct. ... Infanticide, in cases where there was nothing untoward, could thus be concealed" (Warner 2000, p. 29).

G. K. Chesterton's evaluation of the fairy tale tradition is likewise eager to emphasize its imbrication with somber realities in a resolutely unsentimental fashion, drawing attention to the inexorably conditional and rescindable nature of human achievement and pleasure. "It is all very well to talk of the freedom of fairyland," the writer states, "but there was precious little freedom in fairyland by the best official accounts. Mr. W. B. Yeats and other sensitive modern souls, feeling that modern life is about as black a slavery as ever oppressed mankind (they are right enough there), have especially described elfland as a place of utter ease and abandonment." This utopian approach gives Chesterton reason to "doubt whether Mr. Yeats really knows the real philosophy of the fairies. ... If you really read the fairy tales, you will observe that one idea runs from one end of them to the other — the idea that peace and happiness can only exist on some condition. ... all happiness hangs on one thin veto; all positive joy depends on one negative" (Chesterton).

These darkly sobering remarks undoubtedly deserve serious consideration. Yet, the fairy tale tradition as appropriated and chiseled by contemporary anime repeatedly shows that fairy tales, notwithstanding their disciplinary and cautionary potentialities, remain capable of celebrating the young's flair for living with darkness, deriving the occasional frisson from its menaces and even taking pleasure from its mysteries. The majority of grown-ups, meanwhile, scrabble and stumble through daylight in an inane endeavor to comprehend and contain it. This is most evident where the fairy tale tradition colludes with the ludic instinct. Indeed play, in spite of its socializing role, challenges any conclusive attempt at regimentation by recourse to irony, whereby pleasure and fear are enabled to coexist dynamically. As an occupation in which practically all children engage from an early age, play combines physical activity — in itself pivotal to the development of both the self and its interactive capacities — with cognitive, emotional, imaginative and communicational impulses. These are essential in fostering not only understanding but also the desire for experiment and hence creativity. Exposure to potential sources of terror, including self-generated ones, is a key component of this process.

Warner substantiates this contention by emphasizing children's proclivity to "make fun of intimidation, and turn its threats hollow." This inclination is nourished by an ostensibly instinctive inclination "to play the bogeyman and scare themselves into fits. The pretence appears to match the observed pleasure in fright that children take: it defies fear at the very same moment as conjuring it. It exemplifies a defensive response that is frequently adopted in real experience: internalizing the aggressor in order to stave off the terror he brings" (Warner 2000, pp. 168–9). An analogous purpose is served by popular rituals with powerful symbolic connections with the fairy tale tradition likewise intended to help their performers cope with evil and fear. Occasions such as Halloween, ceremonies staged to honor patron saints in many Catholic societies, pageants, processions and carnivals all deploy exuberantly monstrous effigies, costumes and masks. According to Warner, these events have been gradually spawned by a desire to proclaim in a figuratively ritualistic fashion the human resolve to confront, survive and ultimately even laugh at danger: "The magical attempt to secure safety takes two predominant forms: either the participants impersonate the danger itself, as in the carnival masks and fancy dress of Hallow'een, and thus, cannibal-like, absorb its powers and deflect its ability to inflict harm; or they expose themselves and by surviving the ordeal, prove their invulnerability" (p. 112).

Fairy tales have been categorized in numerous ways — for instance, by recourse to morphological systems such as Propp's aforecited formalist matrix or the Aarne-Thompson taxonomy, to folkloric concepts meant to extrapolate their overarching cultural significance and to various psychoanalytical theories. Among the latter, both Freudian and Jungian perspectives have played prominent roles. Bruno Bettelheim epitomizes the Freudian approach to fairy tales, focusing on their affective and symbolic significance for the very young. He thereby proposes that those stories' darkest themes enable children to negotiate their own anxieties and fears in symbolic terms, and thus develop emotional and intellectual resources bound to assist them in their future lives as responsible adults. "Like all great art," Bettelheim maintains, "fairy tales both delight and instruct; their special genius is that they do so in terms which speak directly to children" (Bettelheim, p. 53). In the context of Jungian criticism, the writings of Marie-Louise von Franz are especially notable. "Fairy tales" are here posited as "the purest and simplest expression of collective unconscious psychic processes" (von Franz, p. 1). Pivotal to their distinctive language are the concepts of the "archetype," which designates "the structural basic disposition to produce a certain mythologem," and the "archetypal image," which refers to "the specific form in which" the archetype "takes shape" (p. 8).

Of no less considerable significance for the purpose of this book is the work of Hayao Kawai, where psychoanalytical ideas of Jungian provenance are ingeniously integrated with reflections on the distinctiveness of Japanese fairy tales by comparison with Western narratives in the same fundamental tradition. Japanese fairy tales often bewilder Western audiences, argues Kawai, due to their seemingly incomplete character and use of traditional tropes that may only make authentic sense in an autochthonous context. Among them are the quintessentially Japanese concept of *mono no aware*—the melancholy contemplation of the ephemerality of beauty, joy and life itself—and the notion of *urami*—a feeling of bitterness or regret associated with the narrative figure of the woman who disappears sorrowfully from this world in order to return with renewed powers and redeeming abilities.

Also vital to the local fairy tale tradition as theorized by Kawai is the idea of the Japanese ego as fundamentally feminine and the attendant emphasis placed on active female protagonists, which typically results in the presentation of several male personae as pointedly unheroic, if viewed through Western eyes, due to their temporary relegation to a state of inactivity and silence as the prerequisite of self-discovery and inner growth. Most critical, in Kawai's analysis, is the topos of interpenetrating worlds in fairy tales. "One of the characteristics of the Japanese people," argues the Jungian scholar, "is the absence of a clear distinction between exterior and interior world, conscious and unconscious. ... In short for [the] Japanese the wall between this world and the other world is ... a surprisingly thin one. That the membrane between inner and outer or this and that world is paper-thin like a *fusuma* (sliding room-divider) or *shoji* (a paper door-window) reflects the nature of the Japanese ego" (Kawai 1988, p. 103). This markedly antibinary outlook is mirrored by the Japanese fairy tale's assiduous engagement with fluid encounters of inner and outer realms of experience. Kawai simultaneously emphasizes the impact on this world view of the philosophy of *Hua-yen*, one of the main Buddhist schools, according to which "all things freely interpenetrate each other." This concept, known as *yüan-ch'i*, is elucidated as follows by Toshihiko Izutsu, whom Kawai cites in *Dreams, Myths and Fairy Tales in Japan*: "nothing in this world exists independently of others. Everything depends for its phenomenal existence upon everything else. All things are correlated with one another. All things mutually originate ... Thus the universe in this vista is a tightly structured nexus of multifariously and manifoldly interrelated ontological events, so that even the slightest change in the tiniest part cannot but affect all the other parts" (Kawai 1995, p. 33).

Kawai's message resonates throughout the anime here studied in various guises as their characters confront the most ultimate and undiluted alterity, embark on perilous voyages of often quasi-epic proportions, endeavor to give voice to their inchoate creative drives, or struggle for survival — as bouncily as their imaginations allow — in dystopian realms of post-apocalyptic balefulness. The dream world and the actual world, moreover, often interpenetrate fluidly. Even more important than the exploration of the oneiric dimension as such, for the actors involved, is their introduction to *another* intermediate, interstitial or liminal domain — a place of mystical obscurity that may only be sensed (and, even then, only precariously) through humble and patient openness to its elusive whispers. Once that space has been accessed and its deep darkness commodiously embraced as an awakening friend rather than a blinding adversary, the characters are in a position to interact sentiently and productively with the images they receive from the cryptic beyond. Thus, the anime could be said to summon the fairy tale tradition as a means of evoking potent metaphors for creativeness itself, dramatizing the Dark Night of the Soul, to echo St. John of the Cross, in which one must abide while waiting for passage to the prismatic world of imagination and invention.

Junichirou Tanizaki's aesthetic assessment of the role played by darkness and shadows — thematic and symbolic ingredients of the fairy tale tradition for time immemorial — are here worthy of notice as further corroboration of the specificity of Japanese attitudes to the unfathomable Other. Darkness and shadows, argues Tanizaki, are ideally equipped to accommodate a "magic" space infused with "a quality of mystery and depth superior to that of any wall painting or ornament" (Tanizaki, p. 33). It is in Japanese culture's conception of spectral creatures — namely, beings with enduring fairy tale credentials — that the "propensity to seek beauty in darkness" is most strikingly foregrounded: "Japanese ghosts," Tanizaki maintains, "have traditionally had no feet; Western ghosts have feet, but are transparent. As even this trifle suggests, pitch darkness has always occupied our fantasies, while in the West even ghosts are as clear as glass" (p. 47). The cultural context portrayed by Tanizaki exhibits an ancestral and instinctive attraction to caliginous locales, in much the same way as it views the coexistence of tenebrous otherworldliness and daylight reality as a natural inevitability and not as a hazardous disruption of sacred boundaries. The Japanese perspective on the interplay of darkness and spectrality is poetically corroborated by Tanizaki's depiction of old houses wherein the very "color" of darkness could be perceived in the "suspension of ashen particles" flooding the rooms. "It must have been simple," the writer suggests, "for specters to appear in a 'visible darkness,' where always something seemed to be flickering and shimmering, a darkness that on occasion held greater terrors than darkness out-of-doors. This was the darkness in which ghosts and monsters were active" (p. 53).

Although Kawai is undeniably correct in foregrounding the divergence of Japanese fairy tales from mainstream Western expectations, it should be noted that many valid attempts have been made to bridge the gap between Japanese and Western traditions surrounding the fairy tale. A case in point is Lafcadio Hearn, an author well-known for his collections of Japanese fairy tales and ghost stories (the aforementioned germaneness between the two forms makes itself felt again in this context). In his preface to the delightful volume *Chin Chin Kobakama*, Hearn nostalgically points out that although not very many fairies are likely to be living in Japan in the modern era, having plausibly been scared away by rampant technological progress, tales about them still exist and such an enduring legacy will bravely withstand the test of time (Hearn). Another writer renowned for her endeavor to bring together Japanese and Western outlooks through the fairy tale tradition is Yei Theodora Ozaki, the author of imaginative translations of Japanese fairy tales, adapted so as to appeal specifically to young Western audiences (Ozaki). A further fascinating encounter between Japanese and Western traditions with the fairy tale at its core consists of the illustrations produced by Warwick Goble (1862–1943) for *Green Willow and other Japanese Fairy Tales*, where artistic influences of the Meiji Period blend perfectly with the artist's post–Victorian watercolor sensibility (James). No less significant is the collusion between East and West gorgeously choreographed by the artist Yoshitaka Amano in the volume *Fairies*. Ranging from Shakespeare's Titania, Irish leprechauns and Scottish brownies to English mermaids and the Arthurian figures of Merlin and Nimue (among many other creatures), Amano's concurrently sumptuous and ethereal portraits chronicle the uncanny universal appeal of supernatural beings by bringing together and imaginatively reinterpreting a stunning variety of both indigenous and imported fabulous figures.

The interplay of anime and the fairy tale tradition reveals fantasy's power to invigorate with unparalleled vigor the fabric of both the actual and the hypothetical, braiding through its warp and woof the impish thread of the unexpected. In the process, it captures with distinctive verve Marcia Lane's beautiful description of the fairy tale as articulated in the lyrically entitled volume *Picturing the Rose*: "A fairy tale is a story — literary or folk — that has a sense of the numinous, the feeling or sensation of the supernatural or the mysterious. But, and this is crucial, it is a story that happens in the past tense, and a story that is not tied to any specifics. If it happens 'at the beginning of the world,' then it is a myth. A story that names a specific 'real' person is a legend (even if it contains a magical occurrence). A story that happens in the future is a fantasy. Fairy tales are sometimes spiritual, but never religious" (Lane, p. 5). It is at this level of the discourse that it becomes feasible to relate intimately to fantasy-imbued yarns as correlatives for the buried landscapes of the human psyche and hence as elemental energies capable of abetting our interminable pilgrimages of self-exploration and self-discovery. Opening our minds to the fairy tale's figurative veracity and affective cogency, even as we acknowledge its empirical unreality, is comparable to taking mature cognizance of the unfurling of our own life story as an ornate damask — a texture woven of inchoate dreams interlaced with layers of ostensibly impenetrable symbolism. In this perspective, the fairy tale tradition could be said to offer a scenario of sheer virtuality based on the stretching of spatial and temporal boundaries beyond the very concepts of origin and originality to approximate the dawn-like state in which anything may become possible one more time. We are thereby regaled with a metaphorical cosmology woven from the hypothetical history of a panoply of texts that have been progressively inscribed, dislocated, altered, reconceptualized and grafted on one another over many centuries or possibly even millennia.

In focusing on the subjects of alterity, voyages, creativity and dystopias over the four chapters devoted to the investigation of specific titles, this book encompasses four principal areas of analysis, to which discussions of individual stories consistently return. These are briefly outlined below.

- *Cultural identity.* The fairy tale tradition has contributed significantly over the centuries to the establishment, consolidation and maintenance of collective (and/or communal) identities in disparate cultures. This book tackles two related expressions of this phenomenon. On the one hand, it looks at the tropes and strategies through which both anime informed by the fairy tale tradition and actual fairy tales akin to them in form or imagery have fueled the mores of real-life cultural formations, thereby bolstering their identities. On the other hand, it focuses on imaginary cultures — and attendant identity constructs — indigenous to the anime themselves, and reflects on how these operate as metaphorical correlatives for real-life cultures by speculative transference.

- *Power relations.* The fairy tale tradition has been imbricated for time immemorial with the portrayal and either the critique or the celebration of particular structures and distributions of power. This topos encompasses two categories: the systems (such as class-based and wealth-based hierarchies) upon which whole societies are erected, and the apportioning of power on a generational basis by recourse to tight programs of enculturement and socialization of the young.

- *Nature and environmentalist issues.* In traditional fairy tales, nature operates as one of the richest — arguably *the* richest — repository of symbols, lending not merely a setting but also a narrative and dramatic backbone to the story and its personae. If in classic narrations, the passage through a forest of thorns often emblematizes the vicissitudes of the innocent and the vulnerable, in anime inspired by the fairy tale tradition, the natural environment insistently asserts itself as a protagonist beset by its own injuries, torments and travails as a result of human folly or exploitativeness, throwing into relief social issues of great urgency.

- *History and its retelling.* In articulating their allegorical commentaries on particular cultural realities through the lenses of various materials influenced by the fairy tale tradition, the anime here explored engage in imaginative reconceptualizations of history. In this context, history is viewed both as a mobile galaxy of lived experiences resisting official inscription and as a textually encoded discursive formation of widely accepted authority. In so doing, they invite us to reflect on the processes through which actual events come to be situated in specific ideological molds that frequently do not mirror faithfully the ordeals of real people but rather edit them (more or less arbitrarily) in the service of cultural stability.

In exploring the chosen titles with reference to the four areas of analysis outlined above, the discussion also engages with the phenomenon of transcultural interaction. As indicated, the fairy tale tradition has manifested itself practically across the entire globe in terms of recurrent, plausibly archetypal, images and themes. This realization encourages an evaluation both of that tradition per se and of the particular forms it permeates and shapes in the guise of dialogues engaging diverse societies at different points in history. It concomitantly invites us to ponder the extent to which such exchanges might be considered the outcome of a deliberate and consciously pursued effort and the degree to which they might, conversely, have accrued in a coral-reef fashion as a corollary of the repeated deployment of materials garnered from chance encounters — either among distinct cultures or else of one individual culture with a transcultural imagination.

The ever-evolving complexity and sophistication of the materials and debates surrounding the fairy tale tradition, marked by ongoing developments in its reception and theorization, have increasingly infiltrated the anime enmeshed with that discourse, thereby rendering recent manifestations of the art form particularly cogent objects of study in the present context. Such developments are open to critical exploration along both the paradigmatic and the syntagmatic axes. The paradigmatic perspective, concerned with the fairy tale tradition's material reservoir, helps us to assess the nature and magnitude of the changes mentioned above with reference to the body of texts available for inspection at any one point in time. This corpus embraces:

- the anime: appropriations of fairy tale themes, images and symbols by anime eager to reflect upon reality in an allegorical vein;
- the tales: exemplary fairy tales from different cultures exhibiting salient affinities with the anime under scrutiny;
- the theories: critical models and approaches focusing on the fairy tale tradition's ramifications and on how to read them.

The syntagmatic perspective, concerned with the fairy tale tradition's evolution over time, points to changes impacting on three levels of the discourse:

- functions: changing forms and cultural purposes of the fairy tale tradition — e.g., performative, explanatory, disciplinary;
- frames: changing critical, philosophical and social approaches to

the fairy tale tradition — e.g., educational, psychological, transgressive, cross-cultural;

- fairies: changing representations of Other personae in the fairy tale tradition — e.g., demonic, providential, cute, forbidding.

In pre-modern cultures, fairy tales would often provide the narrative and dramatic substance of public performances adaptable to the requirements of different strata of society and related aesthetic expectations, modes of delivery and stage contexts. At the same time, they could be deployed as a means of constructing figurative explanations for the workings of both the natural realm and human society. Upon serving a disciplinary purpose, fairy tales would be expected to condition their audience's affective dispositions, responses and, ultimately, entire behavior in order to consolidate the status quo.

Explorations of the fairy tale tradition conducted through diverse theoretical lenses bear evident connections with the functional modalities just described. The conception of fairy tales as educational vehicles clearly entails a belief in their potential to inculcate moral lessons capable of strengthening and perpetuating specific ideologies. The impact of those lessons can be effectively intensified by the infusion therein of cautionary messages designed to awe the reader or listener into submission in the form of both overt warnings and implicit threats. Numerous interpretations of the psychological significance of fairy tales have emerged over the past century and speaking of a single psychology-oriented approach to the fairy tale tradition would therefore be grossly inapposite. It is possible to argue, however, that most of those approaches operate on the premise that the tales are symbolic expressions of the human psyche and inner experiences and can therefore provide tantalizing insights into our actions. Increasingly, the regimenting function of fairy tales has come under scrutiny by critics eager to question the doxastic perceptions of the fairy tale tradition emplaced within many cultures to contain the stories' disparate and more challenging implications — for example, by deriding them as vapid escapism, upholding their moralistic import or relishing the formulaic definitions of infantile innocence often connected with the form by the culture industry. Moreover, in adopting this intrinsically transgressive and interrogative outlook, several authors have engaged in a sustained analysis of the processes of cultural cross-pollination through which normative strategies intended to delimit the fairy tale's influence have come into effect — and come apart. As the functions which the fairy tale tradition has been held to fulfill and the theoretical frames of reference brought to bear on its study have changed over time, so have the representations of its characters unleashed by disparate media. The broad descriptive terms employed above (demonic, providential, cute, forbidding) merely denote some of their more frequent and instantly identifiable types. The word "fairy," it must be stressed, is here used not as a literal appellation but rather as something of a code name in order to designate both cumulatively and metaphorically the multifarious figures animating the fairy tale tradition.

The analysis conducted in the main body of the book focuses on the three interrelated areas of study encompassed by the paradigmatic perspective outlined above: the anime deemed suitably illustrative of the themes and issues under scrutiny; a selection of fairy tales mapped upon analogous matrices in the articulation of particular themes, images and symbols; theorizations of the fairy tale tradition offering diverse ways of approaching, interpreting and divulging its polysemous messages. Concurrently, it investigates these interrelations in light of evolving approaches to the form's goals, perspectives and images perceivable at the syntagmatic level. The book's parameters, defining its overall scope and speculative underpinnings vis-à-vis the foregoing observations, can be schematically rendered as follows:

Thematic Foci	Areas of Analysis	Body of Materials	Evolving Factors
Alterity	Cultural identity	anime	functions
Voyages	Power relations	tales	frames
Creativity	Nature and	theories	fairies
Dystopias	environment		
	History and its		
	retelling		

This study constitutes, *in nuce*, an attempt to rehabilitate, with reference to an appropriate range of narrative and scholarly voices, the fairy tale tradition's ironical ambivalence as a flickering interplay of darkness and delight. Its central argument is that through the collusion of discordant impressions, the fairy tale tradition asserts its value as a potent metaphor for speculative possibilities that have been lamentably marginalized by profit-driven and glamour-worshipping cultures all over the world. Such options can be summed up as an openness to the unknown, the unnamable and the unrealized — a disposition without which the human imagination ineluctably fails to thrive. Indeed, that openness is the key prerequisite to the desire to ask questions and to the preparedness to tolerate the absence of conclusive answers. The generosity of spirit that allows us to encounter a fantastic tale in a playfully inquisitive vein, as minds unhampered by rationalist dicta, is akin to the frame of mind that allows an honest physicist to contemplate without shame even the apparent silliest "what if" and to reconsider his or her hypotheses whenever necessary.

CHAPTER 2

Alterity

If you want your children to be intelligent, read them fairy tales. If you want them to be more intelligent, read them more fairy tales.

— Albert Einstein

Let him know his fairy tale accurately, and have perfect joy or awe in the conception of it as if it were real; thus he will always be exercising his power of grasping realities: but a confused, careless, and discrediting tenure of the fiction will lead to as confused and careless reading of fact. Let the circumstances of both be strictly perceived, and long dwelt upon, and let the child's own mind develop fruit of thought from both. It is of the greatest importance early to secure this habit of contemplation, and therefore it is a grave error, either to multiply unnecessarily, or to illustrate with extravagant richness, the incidents presented to the imagination.

— John Ruskin

Both conventional fairy tales and their anime correlatives take full cognizance of the deeply ingrained global tendency to posit the Other as a concept or entity which, though instrumental in the definition and constitution of the Self, its roles, and its cultural context, is routinely posited as subordinate and hence stigmatized, denigrated or marginalized. More importantly, however, those texts endeavor to show, each of them in a distinctive style and tenor, that as long as the creation of identities and boundaries, both individual and national, pivots on a process of Othering — i.e., on the active exclusion of the Other — it can only lead to alienation: to the Self's estrangement in and from itself. Indeed, that move ultimately amounts to an act of self-mutilation insofar as the Self cannot truly subsist in the absence of the ostracized party. The texts in question accordingly tend to foreground, with variable degrees of emphasis, the necessity, desirability and final inevitability of embracing the Other as pivotal to the construction and cultivation of concurrently private and collectively shared configurations of personhood. The effectiveness of this strategy, it must

23

be stressed, depends vitally not only on the genuineness of the spirit and intent with which the Other is espoused but also on a mature recognition that this action should not be tantamount to either domestication or containment — which would merely constitute hypocritical variations on the themes of deliberate excision and discrimination — but rather to a modest and respectful acceptance of the Other's fundamental difference as a reality that remains forever beyond any effort at conclusive capture. It is on this basis that the Self may truly open itself to the Other and gain access to exhilarating opportunities for reflection, speculation and experiment unfettered by the ossified mores of the so-called civilized world.

In their treatment of alterity, the anime under inspection in this chapter lend themselves to interpretation in accordance with all of the principal functional modalities proposed in the previous chapter. In the cases of both *Last Exile* (TV series; dir. Koichi Chigira, 2003) and *Le Chevalier D'Eon* (TV series; dir. Kazuhiro Furuhashi, 2006-2007), the performative dimension is vibrantly communicated by a preference for fast-paced kinetic drama securing the plot's advancement through a tightly knit chain of incidents, while in the case of *Petite Cossette* (OVA series; dir. Akiyuki Shinbo, 2004), it tends to inhabit the psychological tug of war progressively engaging the two protagonists. Although explanatory agendas are not explicitly disclosed by any of the three titles, their allegorical significance as commentaries on the iniquities of personal and social formations in real life makes it possible to read their stories as figurative elucidations of actual phenomena in a displaced guise. In this respect, the anime here examined also hold disciplinary potential insofar as, in the hands of stern educators, they could well be deployed to inculcate ethical lessons concerning the perils of solipsistic self-aggrandizement predicated on a blind disregard for the Other's most fundamental rights. In allowing for such varied interpretations of their narrative/dramatic functions, the chosen shows simultaneously open themselves up to investigation with reference to a broad range of theoretical perspectives — from the educational or cautionary through the psychological (with or without archetypal leanings) to the interrogative or transgressive and the cross-cultural.

While acknowledging the anime's openness as potential objects of multifunctional analysis, their imbrication with certain salient features of Japanese aesthetics should also be recognized. The three shows indicate that a human being's encounter with alterity is bound to prove most unsettling when the nature and roots of this baffling reality are left undisclosed or, at any rate, are only partially revealed. This tendency mirrors a pivotal facet of the indigenous approach to the aesthetic appreciation of both nature and art: an almost instinctive fascination with the inconclusive, the approximate and the incomplete in preference to any vision of presumed fulfillment or plenitude, and an attendant desire to convey the richness of a sensory or mental experience through allusion and adumbration rather than by recourse to explicit statement. This proclivity, intriguingly, brings Japanese philosophy and the fairy tale tradition into intimate collusion insofar as the latter is likewise inclined to rely on hints, insinuations, whispers and mirages rather than naked presentation.

Accordingly, the Other as conceived of by the productions under scrutiny reverberates with echoes of various aesthetic concepts treasured by Japanese culture over the centuries. In its embodiment of inscrutable forces of feasibly timeless and unquantifiable magnitude, that Other recalls the principle of *yugen*, whereas its status as a relatively partial and obscured dimension brings to mind the notion of *wabi-sabi*—i.e., a taste for fragmentariness, imperfection and artless simplicity. Insofar as alterity may only be negotiated, in the final analysis, by embracing its irreducible difference or transcendence rather than through inane attempts at containment, the anime's human protagonists are often enjoined, explicitly or implicitly as the case may be, to cut themselves off from their familiar realities and empirically tested certitudes and take imaginative leaps into alternate domains. This aspect of the stories here studied mirrors closely the aesthetic concept of *kire tsuzuki*. Grounded in the lessons of Zen Buddhism, this principle captures the essence of the "cut" required of an individual that is frankly willing to contemplate the world with eyes unclouded by contingent self-interest, prejudice and dogmatism. This is an act of both courageous and playful self-severance and self-eradication from everything comfortable and everything rationally knowable. The fairy tale tradition encapsulates in its own fashion the aforementioned aesthetic tenets: within its nacreous cradle, a sublime sense of the eternal akin to *yugen* coexists with a deep respect for simple and unassuming gestures (*wabisabi*), and the necessity to relinquish one's attachment to the familiar in a mode redolent of *kire tsuzuki* is simultaneously posited as the prerequisite of discovery and enchantment.

Where the anime's portrayal of characters symbolically associated with the realm of Faërie is concerned, demonic and providential roles are accorded to various agents of transformation or epiphany, in keeping with the established and myth-encrusted proclivity to marry those roles to transcendental or even blatantly superhuman powers. At the same time, however, those characters' graphic depiction as aesthetically enticing personae veers toward the cute end of the representational spectrum, whereas their more somber connotations as the beleaguered casualties of injustice and strife point to the forbidding horizon of the fairy tale discourse. In order to grasp the exact import of this polychromatic approach to characterization, it is useful to consider the broad discursive backdrop against which the chosen shows situate themselves within the harlequin universe of Faërie lore — and, by implication, the fairy tale tradition at large — in relation to the ubiquitous phenomenon of Othering. This can help us appreciate with contextual accuracy the strategies through which the series both appropriate and redefine that tradition in accordance with specific aesthetic and ethical priorities.

Alterity, both as a state and as a process, is in one sense threaded through the fairy tale tradition as a whole insofar as the elements which this discourse accommodates are so disparate as to hold the potential for mutual Othering even as they coexist in peace. As Susannah Marriott maintains, "fairy lore" indeed comes across as "a mish-mash of beliefs, stitched into each other like patchwork, and cut and pasted into a crazy-quilt" (Marriott, p. 6). In the anime here discussed, this deep-seated perception of the ubiquity of Otherness is variedly documented through the portrayal of diverse fairy-related typologies. It is vital to bear in mind, as anticipated in the foregoing chapter, that the use made in the current context of the terms "fairy" and "fairy-related" is eminently metaphorical. It would be indeed preposterously arbitrary to describe any of the characters featuring in the anime here at stake — or in those addressed in subsequent chapters, for that matter — as literal fairies. What those characters do capture, however, is the *fairiness* of the traditional fairy and it is this very quality that enables them to fulfill particular dramatic roles and to imbue the stories they inhabit with the flavor of present-day conceptualizations of the fairy tale tradition. Fairiness alludes to the hypothetical essence of a creature, whose traditional association with folklore, magic and legend, and persistent endowment with bafflingly contradictory ethical attributes allow it to stand out as a unique incarnation of a multiperspectival metaphysical vision. Hence, the personae examined in the present context partake of fairiness to the extent that, though ostensibly human, they are steeped in supernatural mystery and myth, and typically manifest their transcendental dimensions through an admixture within one single being of clashing, discordant or even logically incompatible traits. To complete this portrayal, it is crucial to remember that such attributes would not necessarily result in the construction and animation of especially interesting personalities were it not for those characters' concurrent knack of investing their whole worlds with disquieting preternatural qualities.

One recurrent factor connecting the three productions under scrutiny deserves special attention. This pertains to the tendency to underscore a systemic discrepancy between the spiritual qualities associated with the anime's metaphorical fairies and the physical appearance of those characters. Their roles point to the possession of superhuman powers, to their embroilment in dangerous events, and to their inextricability from an aura of mischievous transgressiveness. Yet, the actual visual images through which they are depicted typically emphasize their ethereal beauty, elegance and seemingly imperturbable perfection. This is true of all three of the key heroines brought into play by the series: Alvis in *Last Exile*, Lia in *Le Chevalier D'Eon* and the eponymous lead in *Petite Cossette*. Attractive well beyond the formulaic parameters of character stereotypes and endowed, more importantly, with a beauty rendered tantalizingly alive by their intelligence and mettle, Alvis, Lia and Cossette are also enveloped in an atmosphere of unrelenting peril and foreboding that harks back to the fairy type's darker connotations. In this respect, the three anime's pivotal figures reflect a major facet of the fairy tale tradition as a whole, whereby fairy characters often embody sinister and menacing energies, abetted by morphing abilities and whimsical dispositions, belying their gracefully enticing semblance. Fairies' most tenebrous undertones are also intensified by their association with the realm of the dead, whose souls they are believed to symbolize in various traditions. This perspective is especially pertinent to *Petite Cossette* and *Le Chevalier D'Eon* due to these anime's enthroning as axial to their dramas of characters precariously poised between the world of the breathing and that of the departed with the titular heroine and Lia respectively. Moreover, the shows emphasize that in their cultures, as in the fairy tale tradition at large, beauty and benevolence never proceed unequivocally hand in hand.

Traditionally, the most dazzling underworldly creatures are often also the most dangerous, whereas proverbially unseemly beings, such as several kinds of goblins, are generous and kindly. This moral enigma is complicated by the physically hybrid nature of many fairy types: this is the very aspect of their physiognomy to which humans are most potently drawn as though in response, at a subliminal level, to those entities' ability to disrupt the anatomical rules dominant in ordinary mortal existence. The fairy-related personae presented in the three anime incarnate the spirit of hybridity in their own peculiar fashions as emblems of conflicting forces that exuberantly disrupt the everyday confines of discipline and propriety. The dichotomy evoked by the three shows' portrayal of their heroines echoes the conflicting affects elicited by the traditional image of bands of Good Folk reveling within a secluded enclosure (*rath*), amid streaming lights and spellbinding tunes. Such an image, as innumerable tales intimate, exudes dread and delight in equal measures. Their fairy figures' baleful undertones come most ominously to the fore with the anime's dramatization of the topos of possession — a theme, it should be noted, of pivotal significance to Japanese lore for time immemorial. In *Petite Cossette* and *Le Chevalier D'Eon*, the theme manifests itself quite explicitly as Cossette, on the one hand, sucks Eiri into an increasingly self-destructive whirlpool of infatuation and vindictiveness and Lia, on the other hand, progressively inundates her brother's body and soul with the fury of a tsunami. In *Last Exile*, the possession topos is less overt but nonetheless notable as a privileged dramatic trigger. This is made evident, in the early phases of the diegesis, by Claus and Lavie's decision to remain aboard the Silvana after delivering Alvis to its crew, even though this completes the mission they have been appointed to undertake, driven by an almost irrational urge to protect the girl at any price.

By radically violating the Self's boundaries, the phenomenon of possession epitomizes the fairy figure's inveterate penchant for eroding the human ability to discriminate clearly between the known and the unknown, the permissible and the illicit. Indeed, boundaries exist not merely, or univocally, to demarcate civilized and colonized territories within which humans may feel that they are in control of nature but also to remind us of the lurking presence of an Other residing *beyond* the closed and neatly mapped-out margins of society. They thus draw attention to the existence of dusky liminal domains wherein putatively irreconcilable worlds meet and interplay. In Japanese lore, notably, the topos of spirit possession is closely bound up with shamanic practices and rites. As Norma Field comments, "Shamanic figures" were traditionally renowned "for their ability to send their souls on distant missions" and over time it became common to assume that "the spirits of the living" were as free to "forsake their bodies" as the souls of the deceased. The spirit of a living person wandering around of its own accord would normally go by the designation of *ikiryou* ("living ghost"). According to Field, "the word *mononoke* (spirit possession)" thus acquired great prominence in indigenous culture (Field, pp. 51–52). Possessions are most disturbing, in several texts, when they bear witness "to a state of instability" causing "people to experience themselves as other," which also entails "heightened self-awareness" (p. 53). These conditions, simultaneously enabling and disabling, are trenchantly replicated in the predicaments endured by the male protagonists of both *Petite Cossette* and *Le Chevalier D'Eon* as the dramatic substratum of problematic power relations.

Insofar as it entails a drastic collapse of the individual Self's boundaries, the phenomenon of possession epitomizes an important aspect of Japanese lore: namely, its persistent emphasis on both spiritual and corporeal experiences based on the attenuation of personal singularity in the service of collective configurations of personhood. This attitude has contributed vitally to Japan's perception of its own cultural identity. A paradigmatic example is supplied, in this respect, by the conception of the soul fostered by early Japanese civilization. According to Ivan Morris, "the soul (*tama/tamashi*) was a communal entity, to be distinguished from the heart/mind (*kokoro*), which was the physical site of individual vitality, emotions, sense-impressions, and so forth. The *kokoro*, like other organs, died with the individual body, but the *tama* left the body to continue existing in other bodies. It is immediately apparent that the practice of ancestor worship, which is inherently communal, presupposes such a phenomenon" (Morris, p. 132).

While Cossette and Lia's credentials as metaphorical possessing demons constitute fundamental aspect of their characterization and dramatic effectiveness, it must be noted that the two characters' connection with the fairy tale tradition does not end with the possession topos. In fact, both heroines also evince, in an appropriately sublimated allegorical form, some of the traits specifically associated with fairy wives and fairy lovers. These characters feature in a variety of guises, including fairy men and women captured by their mortal counterparts and, conversely, human beings abducted by fairy folk, as well as visiting fairies fleetingly but irresistibly disrupting the human world. Cossette and Lia participate in all of these categories. They are akin to fairy ladies forced into the mortal dimension insofar as they do not naturally belong to that sphere of existence, yet have no choice but to enter and interact with it in order to obtain their revenge and reveal the truth behind their dire fates. At the same time, they also function as abductors to the extent that they draw the mortal men whose support they require in order to fulfill their goals into a baleful parallel reality governed by rules which they alone can fathom. Since neither Cossette nor Lia have the power to abide in the human world on a full-time basis, so to speak, and may only infiltrate their male helpers' spaces when congenial circumstances arise, their role is also redolent of the part played by sporadic fairy visitors in traditional narratives.

Le Chevalier D'Eon is keen to underscore the sheer intimacy of its hero's connection with his sister. This is most explicitly borne out by the episode in which D'Eon actually *becomes* Lia by donning one of her gowns, which Queen Marie of France has carefully preserved in anticipation of its strategic expediency. *Petite Cossette* analogously foregrounds the corporeal connotations of its drama by showing with a profusion of graphic details that the price which Eiri has to pay for his preternatural relationship with Cossette is his exposure to a barrage of incrementally noxious demonic attacks which result, by and large, in severe injuries. By emphasizing the eminently physical implications of the phenomenon of possession, the two anime also allude to a popular belief whereby, as Katharine Briggs points out with reference to Manx lore, "certain abnormal states" of a psychosomatic nature tend to be "regarded as the effects of intercourse with fairies and spirits" (Briggs, p. 149). In fact, there is ample evidence across diverse cultures for the tendency to blame on the Little People all manner of mental and physical disabilities and congenital disorders, as well as wasting illnesses, rheumatism, and inexplicable afflictions such as the fairy blast (or fairy stroke)—a tumorous growth or a state of paralysis held to stem from contact with a fairy.

Countless traditions have endeavored to underscore fairies' symbolic bond with one of the elements, an aspect of the natural habitat or a form of vegetation. For example, Western alchemy subdivides fairies according to their elemental affiliations, linking water with undines, fire with salamanders, earth with gnomes and air with sylphs. The anime *Aria the Animation* (TV series; 2005) and its sequels *Aria the Natural* (TV series; 2006), *Aria the Origination* (TV series; 2008) and *Aria the OVA ~Arietta~* (OVA; 2007), all of which were helmed by Junichi Sato, resort to the alchemical system in the representation of the fairy-related characters indigenous to the city of "Neo-Venezia" and to the planet "Aqua" to which it belongs. These include "Undines" in the role of gondoliers, "Salamanders" in the guise of characters responsible for monitoring the planet's climate, "Gnomes" in the capacity of regulators of Aqua's gravity and "Sylphs" as nimble airmail deliverers. An analogous matrix obtains within Eastern thought, where Golden Devas are held to embody the Sun's energy, White Devas to pervade the air, Green Devas to animate the vegetable realm, and Violet Devas to sustain the etheric essence of the whole cosmos. Other systems define fairies' variable relationships with the natural environment by differentiating between Trooping (or convivial) fairy types and Solitary ones, or between the Seelie (benevolent) and Unseelie (malign) Courts.

D. J. Conway proposes an especially interesting interpretation of fairyhood, refuting the alchemical model on the grounds that while elemental entities "can work only within the element to which they are attached," fairies are able to "work within and with all elements" (Conway, p. 2) and to "communicate with every species of creation." Accordingly, though fairies' "knowledge of magick" is so substantial as to be "nearly equal to that of dragons," it is "more nature oriented and answers to physical needs" (p. 5). This holistic apprehension of fairies' intercourse with nature is underpinned by the conviction that their "bodies are formed of the same basic materials as humans" and that therefore, "most of them look very much like us." The crucial difference between fairies and humans is that fairies, unlike common mortals, have the power to "become visible or invisible by changing the vibrational rate of their bodies" (p. 1). Relatedly, fairies can be seen to share with humans a wide range of physiological attributes and cultural tendencies: they "age, although much more slowly than humans do.... They can become ill, have difficult childbirths, become injured, or even die." On the jollier side of the equation, they are also known to be "very fond of jewelry and fine clothes, music, dancing, riding horses, weapons, exquisite banquets, hounds, and, depending on the clan, even cats" (p. 5).

Fairies are even prone to vanity for that matter. This is substantiated by the fact that they are proverbially fond of mirrors and other reflecting surfaces not only because they find them handy as transportation and teleportation channels but also, quite simply, because they derive pleasure from their specular images. The world view promoted by Conway positively opposes the stark Othering of Faërie by the human world as an irredeemably alien and latently monstrous reality. This perspective is reinforced by the assertion that in ancient times, fairies existed "in close proximity with humans" but were forced to seek refuge in their own parallel realities by human fear, suspicion and even downright persecution. Hence, they resolved to avail themselves of their bodies' distinctive physical properties and use the cloak of invisibility in order "to move back and forth between worlds in the form of highly tuned energy" — which entails a refreshingly anarchic transgression of the boundaries supposedly separating the known realm of Self from the magical mysteries of the Other. As long as fairies were recognized and valued as "a species unto themselves" (p. 2), and accordingly "treated with respect because they live by different rules" (p. 4), their Otherness was not deemed to constitute an obstacle to the possibility of fruitful interaction between fairies and humans. In fact, it could be argued that they were honored *because of* their alterity and not *in spite of* it.

In virtually all instances, the connection borne by fairies of all sorts with the concept of liminality has led to the belief that they are inclined to elect as their preferred abodes transitional locations on the edge of human civilization. Most typically, fairies are associated with forests, seashores, rivers, marshes, clouds, burial mounds, hills, mountains and underground caverns — yet, this list is by no means exhaustive since portals to fairyland may be descried even within a suburban garden as long as it is not too punctiliously manicured. As Conway emphasizes, even though fairyland is a distinct realm, it "interpenetrates our world" at all times (p. 38) and the "natural doorways" opening onto its reality, therefore, "are not on different levels." Whether or not they may be entered depends entirely on a person's disposition and frame of mind, becoming "available according to the growth in" his or her "personal life" (p. 39). Arnold van Gennep maintains that liminality carries an eminently temporal significance insofar as it typically designates a phase within a developmental process in the course of which a person encounters the transitional domain between two distinct social roles: "whoever passes from one [zone] to the other finds himself physically and magico-religiously in a special situation for a certain length of time: he wavers between two worlds" (van Gennep, p. 18).

If, as Peter Narváez proposes, the "temporal usage of liminality" is extended to "a spatial understanding of areas between known space (purity) and unknown space (danger)," it is feasible to conceive of fairy realms as locations of both bodily and spiritual suspension (Narváez, pp. 337–338). According to Diane Purkiss, fairy folk's legendary location in interstitial areas of reality emanate from a transcultural *horror vacui* whereby "Human nature seems to abhor a blank space on a map." The reason for which the lacunae in our world come to house fairies — and portions of the cosmos unoccupied by heavenly bodies come to house alien beings — is that the human mind is simply unable to tolerate empty "darkness" (Purkiss, p. 3). In addition, the fairy figure's seemingly natural connection with liminality could be said to emanate from her status as "a gatekeeper," a creature who "guards the entrance to a new realm" and is accordingly held, in many cultures, to supervise and monitor "the borders of our lives" — e.g., transitional moments such as "adolescence, sexual awakening, pregnancy and child-birth" (p. 4). The temporal meaning of liminality highlighted by van Gennep is again brought into prominence by this hypothesis.

Relatedly, the Little People are related to the borderline hours of dusk and dawn as ideal moments for their penetration of the mortal world and for humans, in turn, to take a peek into their realms. As Marriott emphasizes, in assessing fairies' relationship with time, it is also important to remember that being by and large nocturnal creatures, they tend to carry out many of their activities (obnoxious ones included) "during the hours of darkness, while mortals lie sleeping." Unsurprisingly, in the circumstances, fairies are connected in disparate cultures with troubled sleep. In German fairy lore, for instance, elves are regarded as the artificers of nightmares, as attested to by the fact that *Albtraum* (i.e., nightmare) translates literally as "elf dream," whereas in Japan, their cause is held to be *Baku*, "eater of dreams" (Marriott, p. 230). Fairyland's temporal liminality is pithily, yet lyrically, captured by Ralph of Coggeshall's twelfth-century tale *The Green Children*, where the fairies' subterranean domain is described as a land in which there is "neither sun nor moon, but a perpetual dim light, like that before dawn" (cited in Zaczek, p. 90).

Furthermore, fairies are bracketed together with specific moments in the human calendar and cosmic cycle. The summer and winter solstices, as privileged transitional points, are deemed especially amenable to world-crossing opportunities by facilitating the opening of gates between otherwise insulated dimensions and hence fostering unpredictable intersections. Alongside the solstices, and especially "23 June: Midsummer Eve" as the "most celebratory time of year for fairies and a good night for divination," other crucial dates in the fairy calendar are "30 April: May Eve," which fairies "favor ... for fighting"; "31 October: Hallowe'en; Eve of Celtic festival of Samhain," which is considered ideal for "fortune telling and divination"; "24 December: Christmas Eve," when "Norse ancestor spirits must be welcomed in the home"; "31 December: New Year's Eve," when "supernatural divination, license, and gift-giving" are honored; and other more general moments such as Fridays and nights with a full moon, when fairy powers reach their peak (Marriott, p. 141).

An example deserving particular consideration in the present context due to its utilization of settings that bear potent affinities with the historical and quasi-historical milieux of both *Petite Cossette* and *Le Chevalier D'Eon* concerns the body of legends in which mortals are spirited away in the night to stately manors where they are courteously waited upon by lovely servants garbed in exquisite clothes of brilliantly colored silk, satin or velvet and regaled with splendid refreshments, only to find, in daylight, that such venues are entirely illusory. When humans are able to perceive the reality ensconced behind the sortilege, they are likely to face a blood-curdling truth. What is more, those who partake of a fairy feast may well remain spellbound forever. It is also worth noting, in this regard, that fairies are often renowned for the radiant and even riotous beauty of their attire, where hues overtly derived from the natural realm reign supreme and an opulent feel of silken fluidity or velvet plushness is ubiquitous. Green, symbolic of fertility, red, the emblem of life itself, and white, coterminous with purity, are markedly prominent. Particularly sumptuous costumes regale the periodic Fairy Cavalcades, during which sinuous lines of riding fairies on their white steeds may be fleetingly glimpsed. Flowing gowns adorned with silver and gold patterns, satin slippers, fur-lined or thistle-lined capes, embroidered vests and doublets, leather gauntlets, multicolored breeches and feather-decked wide-brimmed hats, alongside glorious jewels of all conceivable shapes, are among the most conspicuous items one could hope to behold on such occasions.

A splendid pictorial example of an event of this kind is provided by Sir Joseph Noël Paton's "The Fairy Rade Carrying off a Changeling, Midsummer Eve" (1867). Where Paton's painting is replete with imagery inspired by Arthurian lore, Renaissance art, the Pre-Raphaelites and Classical mythology, thus evoking an overall impression of solemnity, a jocular rendition of the Fairy Cavalcade comes with "The Fairy Tree" by Richard Doyle (1824–1883). This picture evinces a playful and gently satirical take on the theme, presenting its fairies as streams of pantomime figures engaged in what looks like a wildly disjointed game of tag unfolding in disparate directions — as though the players had lost track of the distinction between the pursuer and the pursued, or even forgotten the reason for their procession altogether. Likewise humorous, though more unsettling, is the painting "A Dance Around the Moon" by Richard Doyle's younger brother, Charles Altamont Doyle (1832–1893), the father of Sherlock Holmes' creator. In this picture, the sense of directionlessness already evident in "The Fairy Tree" is accentuated to frantic extremes. The fairies, depicted as a motley assortment of acrobats, jockeys, angelic maidens, policemen, devils, hunters, lawyers and businessmen, as well popular figures from fairy tales, are caught in a shambolic chase redolent of a Dionysian rite at the heights of inebriation and frenzy. The iconically central image of the full moon neatly epitomizes the quintessence of lunacy.

As Iain Zaczek explains, "Accounts of these rades were commonplace in ballads.... Some folk claimed to have witnessed one of these events, drawn by the eerie sound of jingling bridles, clattering hooves and low chanting, though it was highly dangerous for mortals to spy on a rade" (Zaczek, p. 32). It is also worth pointing out that clothes often reflect a fairy's personality and lifestyle in much the same way as our own choice of garments can speak volumes about ourselves as humans. Thus, as Conway observes, it is common for "solitary fairies" to prefer "long robes or loose trousers and tunics, the colors of which blend in perfectly with their surroundings," to the more flamboyant apparel favored by revelers, paraders, hound and bird handlers or dancers (Conway, p. 111). However, just as the Fair Folk's grand banqueting halls, ballrooms and chambers invariably vanish in the clear light of day, so their garments' bright colors tend to fade into airy nothing as one moves closer to the wearer. (Fairy fashion is discussed in depth in Chapter 4: Creativity and also touched upon in Chapter 5: Dystopias.) *Le Chevalier D'Eon*, to dwell on a specific anime-related example, harks back to the sumptuous venues and costumes traditionally associated with fairyland with the sequences devoted to the masked ball held by the Russian Empress. In this instance, the topsy-turvy world of fairy lore, where both time and space are suspended and identities are irreverently exploded, is evoked by the very nature of the indigenous concept of "masquerade" as a festival entailing not merely the adoption of a disguise but also the practice of cross-dressing. The event, incidentally, offers D'Eon a perfect opportunity for turning up at the palace in Lia's garb and hence test the Empress' loyalties.

A mortal's confrontation with Otherness of potentially life-altering magnitude consists of the sight of a circle of dancing fairies, a visual trope that finds a direct parallel in Japanese fairy tales where humans spy upon, or inadvertenly catch a glimpse of, a bunch of reveling spirits. According to Marriott, the ring is "a means of drawing mortals into the warped time and space of fairyland.... Join the circling dancers at your peril: once entranced, few make it home. Because a ring has neither beginning nor end, it is all but impossible to break from" (Marriott, p. 240). The circle's irreducible alterity is intensified by the fact that the dance itself is not the sole enchanting aspect of its performance: the traces it leaves on the grass are also saturated with potentially pernicious magical energies. The fundamental cause of the fairies' Otherness ultimately resides with the peculiarly reflective nature of their supernatural abilities, and related penchant for awing mortals into submission and for generating dread or, at the very least, an intimidating atmosphere. Fairies' mightiest weapon consists of our own dread of what might befall us were we to disobey the creatures' requirements or frustrate their expectations. It is from our own imaginative faculties at their most baleful and unbridled that the Little People derive their enduring strength — and, to a significant extent, roguish sense of humor. The shows under inspection echo this idea by demonstrating that people are most likely to be in thrall to both authentically and speciously supernatural agencies when they allow themselves to become victims of a paralyzing fear of alterity.

While commodiously lending themselves to critical appreciation through the prismatic lenses of diverse theoretical modalities, the anime here examined as illustrative cases engage with all of the primary areas of analysis to which contemporary appropriations of the fairy tale tradition assiduously return, as defined in the opening chapter of this study. In order to advance its dramatic vision, *Last Exile* capitalizes on the alchemical fusions at work within a tripartite conception of alterity. The Other, in this series, is incarnated at once by a concept of space, by a person and by a transcendental system of knowledge. Spatial alterity is immediately announced by the anime's setting in a cosmic sprawl, endowed with flamboyantly retrofuturistc traits and deliberate technological idiosyncrasies, which comprises countless kingdoms and related factions. If this universe as a whole feels intensely heterotopic (i.e., Other in relation to our familiar sense of place), the character of Alvis personifies alterity at the level of individual subjectivity. This notion is communicated from the start by the girl's portrayal and relationship with other key characters, and further complicated by the revelation that the value she is perceived to hold in the grand scheme of things is so unique as to warrant many people's preparedness to perish for her sake.

Spatial and personal configurations of alterity coalesce as, amid a dizzying proliferation of battles, adventures and political intrigues, it is intimated that Alvis is connected with a crucial piece of esoteric knowledge, the Mysteria, and that these vestiges of a tenebrously Other episteme may themselves be the key to the ultimate heterotopia: "Exile." A starship akin to a nomadic colony used by the first space settlers, Exile is instrumental, in response to the ceremonial recital of the four Mysteria, in conveying the saga's survivors to a new and peaceful realm. The elaboration of this Other-centered drama supplies *Last Exile* with plenty of opportunities to explore the intricate issue of cultural identity by utilizing frankly fictional social formations as allegories of real human dispensations, underpinning mores and legal systems. Those formations are themselves indisseverable from political tensions issuing from a ferocious struggle for power impacting on all relationships at both the private and the public levels. In the process, the environment is portrayed as an innocent casualty of this dire state of affairs, insofar as the image of a universe torn apart by ferocious martial exploits and that of a simultaneously polluted and desecrated habitat collude to proclaim in no uncertain terms the imperative to restore the natural equilibrium as the fundamental precondition for the reestablishment of political harmony.

The figurative history — and attendant historiography — charted by *Last Exile* in the dramatization of its cultural milieu and power relations meet and merge in a distinctive mnemotechnology: a reality in which all manner of technological products and developments operate as the memory traces encoding successive stages in a culture's evolution. It is thereby suggested that technology can fruitfully cooperate with fantasy in the genesis of myths, rituals and metaphors that enable people to function vis-à-vis both their social and their natural contexts. Concurrently, the creative energies released by that partnership have the power to foster the emergence of parallel worlds. On the one hand, these are informed by rhythms akin to the laws which animate the workings of both society and nature and are therefore graspable with reference to familiar yardsticks. On the other hand, they are capable of questioning the tenability of those laws through a radical suspension of reality markers and hence blur the distinction between Self and Other with wayward exuberance. In addition, *Last Exile* holds virtually inexhaustible transcultural connections since the yarn chronicling the encounter with alterity as a formative rite of passage punctuated by pain and loss no less than by triumph constitutes a veritable lynchpin in the fairy tale tradition the world over.

In focusing on some of the series' most salient dramatic attributes, one soon realizes that *Last Exile*'s entire constellation depends to a vital extent on its structural and thematic affiliations with the fairy tale tradition. The anime pays homage to the fairy tale's proverbial tendency to draw its readers or listeners into a hypothetical reality by introducing them immediately to its principal personae, insofar as the adventure seeks to immerse the audience right from the start into Claus and Lavie's daily lives as space couriers. The fairy tale mood is maintained as we are told that despite their menial occupation, the protagonists pursue indefatigably a superior ambition embedded in legend: flying over the "Grand Stream" where their heroic fathers lost their lives. The protagonists' fathers, it must be noted, are accorded a mythical significance redolent of the stature traditionally invested on formidable fairy kings, such as Finvarra and Oberon. The real drama begins as Claus and Lavie accidentally cross paths with a dying man and his charge, Alvis, echoing the fairy tale's penchant for stories triggered by chance rather than calculation. This is corroborated throughout by the anime's passion for unpredictability.

Like the worlds of many classic fairy tales, the hourglass-shaped universe in which *Last Exile* is set, Prester, comprises numerous realms and is afflicted by seemingly endless belligerence. In the specific context of the adventure at hand, Prester is seen to be riven by a tempestuous conflict engaging Claus and Lavie's country of origin, Anatoray, and the nation of Disith. (Although this name has probably no intentional connection with the Celtic words *di* and *sith*, it is nonetheless worth pointing out that these translate as "deity" and "fairy" respectively.) At the heart of the notoriously uncrossable Grand Stream, there lies an evil wind current bridging, and yet dividing, those rival states. The Guild, an organization that wields uncontested authority over the various kingdoms thanks to its superior technology, is supposed to act as an impartial arbitrator in the war but there is reason to doubt whether its intentions are genuinely benevolent and disinterested — largely due to its somewhat obsessive concern with Alvis' destiny. Both the Grand Stream and the Guild constitute liminal reality levels and thus echo the fairy folk's legendary preference for borderline situations and indistinct localities. A further respect in which *Last Exile* brings to mind the fairy tale tradition is its ethical stance. The anime indeed mirrors the aversion to stark distributions of good and evil so often found in that body of lore. The essential nebulousness of the fairy figure as an entity supposedly capable of both spontaneous magnanimity and premeditated malice is replicated, in the series, by characters that are simultaneously prone to exude an aura of forbidding evil and able to energize the drama with spellbinding charm. A paradigmatic instance of this ambivalent personality construct is offered by the character of the Guild's leader, Maestro Delphine Eraclea: a woman whose conflicting facets recall the likewise equivocal traits of fairy queens like Titania and Onagh (Oberon's and Finvarra's respective spouses) or the sky-related fairy lady Saeve. It is also noteworthy, where characterization is concerned, that the show's actors usually stand as representatives of contrasting civilizations indigenous to its setting, which serves to highlight their allegorical and mythical significance.

Last Exile partakes most consummately of the fairy tale tradition's legacy in its exuberant approach to worldbuilding, delivering a hybrid universe in which the rules of chivalry — famously encoded in so many fairy tales' typical ambience, costumes and rituals — coexist with some bizarre retrofuturistic technology. Redolent of the type of technovisionary imagery immortalized by nineteenth-century authors such as Albert Robida (1848–1926) and Jules Verne (1828–1905), this features flying vehicles known as "vanships" that plough through the air as ships do through water and recall biplanes from the First World War, alongside visual allusions to steam-powered riverboats, submarines, Japanese dreadnoughts, cannons, muskets and, in the context of the Guild, sophisticated equipment such as lasers and holographic displays. Integrating these images into a sweeping saga of epic amplitude, *Last Exile* delivers a world that feels at once irreducibly Other and uncannily familiar. While the awe-inspiring sense of grandeur accompanying its numerous action sequences may seem to usher us into an utterly fictive domain, the evocation of both suspense and pathos by recourse to very palpable human emotions infuses the anime's universe with disarming credibility. In this regard, the series reflects the fairy tale tradition's inveterate devotion to the synthesis of reality and fantasy as one of its pivotal objectives. Though this ploy, the here-and-now can be boldly called into question and even, at least temporarily, discredited as an absolute referent. Yet, a critical focus on actual historical circumstances and events can also be maintained by deploying the fantasy component as an allegorical tool capable of providing a dispassionate commentary on the very reality it seeks to subvert. Therefore, fantasy engages in a subtle game wherein it is at liberty to play both the role of reality's wayward Other and the part of an uncompromising examiner keen on Othering reality in order to expose its hidden folds.

In the process, *Last Exile* proves most loyal to the fairy tale tradition in its unwavering commitment to one key goal: challenging its spectators' imagination by engaging both the mind and the entire sensorium in enchanted rings of synesthetic correspondences. The anime hence echoes the fairy tale tradition as a discourse whose primary purpose is precisely to awaken the imaginative faculties of generations lulled and numbed by the vapid promises of rationalism. Relatedly, *Last Exile* reminds us that the survival of the fairy tale tradition in contemporary societies is the prerequisite for the ability to imagine not just Faërie but *anything at all* if its lessons are to be grasped as metaphors for a broad world picture extending beyond the confines of literal fairy tales. In this sense, the fairy tale tradition can be viewed as a generous supplier of the strength to believe in something that irreversibly mocks any quest for rational demonstration and empirical evidence, and to feel at ease in the presence of incongruities, anomalies and outbursts of Otherness. Concomitantly, *Last Exile* shares with some of the most loved fairy tales — Charles Perrault's *Sleeping Beauty* springs to mind as a glowing case in point — the tendency to capitalize on situations and motivations which, ironically, gain credibility from their preposterousness. This is because the story does not rely on the fantasy element in a haphazard and improvized fashion — which would cause that absurdity to seem utterly arbitrary — but rather in a sustained, judiciously argued and punctiliously detailed style. This proposition is emblematically confirmed by the mythic tapestry woven around the image of Exile. The circumstances surrounding the colony's creation and the cryptic web of both facts and legends built around its destiny are consummately fantastic, resisting any effort at rationalization, let alone domestication. In other words, they are imbued with Otherness from start to finish. Nevertheless, the anime's development would ultimately be quite unthinkable in their absence and this makes them strangely real and, above all, quite convincing, in terms of the drama's own logic.

Ultimately, *Last Exile* tangentially pays homage to the fairy tale tradition by intimating that without any recourse to the invigorating powers of imagination and fantasy, the Self cannot properly develop, for it will always shy away in fear or detestation from anything it deems incompatible with cold reason as unacceptably Other. This is the curse afflicting the children of "the house of Smallweed" in Charles Dickens' *Bleak House*. Having "strengthened itself in its practical character," Chapter XXI informs us, the line "has discarded all amusements, discountenanced all storybooks, fairytales, fictions, and fables, and banished all levities whatsoever. Hence the gratifying fact that it has had no child born to it and that the complete little men and women whom it has produced have been observed to bear a likeness to old monkeys with something depressing on their minds." Dickens' message is sarcastically reinforced by an atmospheric vignette that sets the Smallweeds' ideology in a palpably realistic social context: "At the present time, in the dark little parlour certain feet below the level of the street — a grim, hard, uncouth parlour, only ornamented with the coarsest of baize table-covers, and the hardest of sheet-iron teatrays, and offering in its decorative character no bad allegorical representation of Grandfather Smallweed's mind — seated in two black horsehair porter's chairs, one on each side of the fire-place, the superannuated Mr. and Mrs. Smallweed while away the rosy hours" (Dickens).

Being partly modeled on the aesthetic of very age in which Dickens' novel is set, *Last Exile*'s ambience reverberates with vestigial echoes of that period's mores. Therefore, even though none of its characters is as overtly inimical to imaginative thinking as the dire Smallweeds are, the anime's young protagonists must nonetheless struggle to preserve that faculty in the face of despotic adults hell-bent on their regimentation into competent and hard-working but quite unadventurous subjects. Thus, the greatest victory achieved by *Last Exile*'s kids is neither military nor political in nature but actually amounts to a courageous defense of their natural proclivities: the same childlike curiosity, daring playfulness, and willingness to explore the unknown whence the fairy tale tradition derives its elan. The anime's young actors are able to retain those qualities even when the responsibilities they are enjoined to assume threaten to turn them into hardened grown-ups ill-disposed toward the fabulous. They thus remind us that suppressing the energies embedded in the fairy tale tradition is tantamount to mutilating the Self by cutting it off from any prospects of productive interaction with the polyphonic voices of alterity.

Like *Last Exile*, *Petite Cossette* endeavors to commingle alternate versions of Otherness, deploying a spatial perspective, a heroine and an underlying body of cryptic knowledge as the mainstays of its take on the concept. The OVA series also chooses, in its climactic moments, to deepen its plunge into alterity by Othering its male lead. Estrangement asserts itself as a crucial dramatic ploy from the anime's early stages, as art student Eiri Kurahashi discovers, in the antique shop where he works, an ostensibly living girl moving within a valuable piece of Venetian glassware. Having become infatuated with the creature, whose name is Cossette, Eiri learns that she was once an aristocrat's daughter and that she was confined to her current prison by her murder. This was supposedly perpetrated by the girl's betrothed, the artist Marcelo Orlando. For Cossette to achieve freedom and peace, a man who truly loves her must be prepared to accept punishment for Marcelo Orlando's crime. The cultural identities and power relations presented by *Petite Cossette* in its engagement with the topos of alterity, and specifically through its challenging deployment of defamiliarization as a means of moving between the present day and the eighteenth century, are inextricably intertwined with the telescoping of history — a move catalyzed by the portrayal of the heroine as an equivocal being trapped in history and yet, paradoxically, enabled by her very imprisonment to travel figuratively across disparate time zones. At the same time, the OVA series suggests that the criminal perversity central to its psychodrama functions not solely as a major plot trigger but also as a specular correlative for the notion of a diseased natural order. The interrelations here entailed resonate with the principles underlying the Great Chain of Being as conceived in the West in the Middle Ages and the Renaissance, as well as with the cardinal teachings of the Japanese philosophy of the Five Elements.

Petite Cossette is also woven, albeit obliquely, into a rich tapestry of transcultural interaction by virtue of its analogies with myriad tales pivoting on the image of a magical glass surface. This theme is conspicuous throughout the fairy tale tradition as a portal to other dimensions, as famously demonstrated by narratives as diverse as the Brothers Grimm's *Snow White*, Perrault's *Beauty and the Beast*, Hans Christian Andersen's *The Snow Queen* and Lewis Carroll's *Through the Looking-Glass, and What Alice Found There*. At its most inspiring, such a gateway has the power to induce humans to take cognizance of their world's ugliness and evil and, by extension, confront those unsavory aspects of themselves which they normally strive to brush aside or occlude. It is also worth noting, in this respect, that the motif of the magical glass features prominently in the Japanese tale *The Mirror of Matsuyama*, here referred to in Chapter 4, where the entity's salutary potentialities are emphasized. A motif analogous to the one employed in *Petite Cossette* to keep the narrative of Otherness disquietingly alive throughout its progression lies at the core of Stephen King's supernatural novel *Rose Madder*—an inverted fairy tale with a heady mix of romance and terror as its plot-driving fuel. The book's protagonist trades her engagement ring for a painting depicting a woman in a rose madder gown, which she chances upon in the pawn shop, and soon discovers that the artifact is endowed with preternatural qualities. Not only is it capable of expanding its representational field to reveal more of its world than originally discernible: it also offers the heroine access to its reality by making itself penetrable in much the same fashion as the looking-glass lets Carroll's Alice enter its realm. It is in that alternate dimension that King's protagonist is able both to embark on otherworldly adventures hitherto alien to even her wildest fantasies, and eventually find peace after years of physical and psychological abuse — an achievement sealed by the planting of magical seeds in a secret grove and the growth therefrom of a deadly tree to which the woman devotes ritualistic reverence for the rest of her life (King).

Petite Cossette harks back to the domain of Faërie at its most mysteriously Other at the cinematographical level, deploying unusual camera tricks — such as blurred and fluctuating perspectives, bizarre and estranging angles, swift cuts and deformed perceptions — and thus evoking an oneiric atmosphere wherein alterity and alienation become virtually coterminous with each other. The OVA series' ever-drifting vision reaches its apotheosis through an adventurous synthesis of dynamic and chromatic effects. Most memorable, in this respect, are the sequences in which Cossette appears to glide through the glass stained with iridescent tinges of which the chalice she inhabits is made and other actors are captured through the distorting lenses of intricate patterns awash in eerie shadows. These visual effects would amount to mere spectacle were it not for their power to embody a distinctive world view that posits the Other not only as the Self's omnipresent double but also — and far more disconcertingly — as the very foundation of the anime's reality. Echoing the fairy tale tradition's dedication to the integration of the fantastic and the realistic, *Petite Cossette*'s cinematography also endeavors to blend vivid and even disturbingly graphic images of nearly naturalistic density with frames rendered ethereally remote by the use of filters that emulate the grainy or faded look of old photographs. At the same time, smooth cel animation and CGI are seamlessly harmonized to abet the show's composite identity.

The mounting sense of sheer paranoia that characterizes the anime from its inceptive stages onward is largely responsible for its overall dramatic impact. Especially notable, on this point, are the scenes in which the objects surrounding the heroine appear to feel that Eiri is a reincarnation of the deranged artist reputed to have murdered Cossette in eighteenth-century France and lash out their vengeful ferocity against the present-day art student. The situation is made particularly weird by the fact that while these preternatural occurrences unfold, Eiri's friends at first seem wholly concerned with trifles and worry prosaically about the youth's physical health with no inkling of the esoteric plot in which he has been inveigled. Akiyuki Shinbo's predilection for yarns and imagery evocative of the fairy tale tradition at its darkest is confirmed by later anime helmed by the same director, and most proficiently by the saga of ruthless retribution chronicled over the three seasons of *Hell Girl* (2004–2008). In this anime, the supernatural is enthroned as both the ultimate essence of Japanese lore and an allegorical vehicle for the exploration of contemporary societies riven by injustice and malice.

One of the most original aspects of *Petite Cossette*'s artistry consists of its recurrent utilization of sketches, line drawings, rough crayon doodles and stills of the key settings filtered so as to resemble paintings in the Impressionist style. Most striking among these graphic items are the pencil portraits of the heroine lovingly executed by Eiri throughout the series, and with increasing frequency as his obsessive interest in Cossette escalates. These technical flourishes can be regarded as self-reflexive records of the evolution of the animated image over time insofar as they mirror the artwork that underpins the dynamic pictures of which the bulk of the final product consists. The figurative fairy figure here at work is an invisible artist chronicling from the shadowy space of the anime's theatrical wings the regression of the moving image to its embryonic phases, and progression thenceforth toward sophisticated levels of kinesis. Thus, although the graphic elements that explicitly call attention to the series' constructed status may seem utterly unrealistic in the mimetic sense of the term, they actually represent the vital foundation of that magical illusion of motion which animation at large seeks to evoke — a trail of translucent fairy dust sprinkled over the more palpable fabric of the predominantly realistic (or even photorealistic) scenes. Where pointedly rudimentary scrawls are given prominence, the materiality of the image is so intense as to bring to mind not only the act of drawing but also more emphatically physical practices such as carving or sculpting. This is made most evident by the moments of horror that punctuate Eiri and Cossette's affective ordeal, where an impression of sculptural solidity is frequently communicated by the use of shapes and expressions that seem to have been hewn out of wood or stone.

In this fashion, the anime elliptically alludes to the ancestral roots of the tradition to which it is indebted, since the art forms it throws into relief are implicated in the processes of storytelling and lore-making at the most primitive and archetypal level. Relatedly, the show abounds with classic — even stereotypical — imagery of the kind one would expect to encounter in a horror plot, a haunted-mansion drama or a Gothic romance. This encompasses ruins, corpses clad in the vestments of the grave, cemeteries, chains, clocks, single disembodied eyes and eyeless porcelain dolls, as well as a sprinkling of sepulchral candelabra and distorted spiral staircases. Yet, the anime's cinematographical refinement is such as to expunge the shadow of formulaicness from the drama's cumulative purview. In summoning the fairy tale tradition's atavistic underpinnings, the series captures their very essence by exploiting to full advantage its medium's unique capacity to take an audience on a surreal ride through the murkiest reaches of the psyche while delivering vibrant and stimulating entertainment. Hence, what is undoubtedly an engrossing but also, in principle, unexceptional love story transmutes into an utterly magical experience redolent of the most haunting fairy tales ever recorded in either voice or ink.

Two tropes obliquely derived from the fairy tale tradition linger in memory most tenaciously. One of these intensifies *Petite Cossette*'s ubiquitous attraction to spatial alterity with remarkable economy by portraying a liminal location of the type so often associated with the Little People. This consists of the twilight realm in which the living and the dead are allowed to coexist. The other places Marcelo Orlando's crime on a par with a mortal's arrant violation of fairy ethics. The eighteenth-century artist murders Cossette because he cannot tolerate the prospect of her growing older and thus ceasing to incarnate the ideal of pristine juvenile beauty which he so avidly captures in his innumerable paintings of the girl. Therefore, the murder could be seen as a metaphorical negation of the principle of constant and ineluctable mutation upon which the fairy tale tradition is based. Like all blind and selfish disruptions of a non-human order by a mortal, the act is destined to lead to the perpetrator's own undoing. In Faërie, no less than in Greek tragedy though with different implications and repercussions, no crime is as irrefragably unpardonable as hubris. Moreover, this strand of the narrative finds a parallel in the attitudes toward fairies evinced by numerous modern societies. On the one hand, the creatures have been assimilated to innocent and delicate children in order to tame their more disturbing connotations. On the other, they have been equated to all manner of unruly forces threatening the status quo in order to legitimize their brutal domestication. In Marcelo Orlando's logic (and, presumably, in the logic of the age he represents), Cossette is acceptable only as long as her fairy beauty is safely tied to childhood. The moment it threatens to morph into something different and unpredictable, is must be staunched by the severest of means. An adult Cossette, in this scenario, could only constitute an anomaly, an aberration, a monstrosity.

The axial relationship dramatized by *Le Chevalier D'Eon*, whence the plot receives its driving structural impetus, consists of a psychological phenomenon that could be realistically regarded as the very epitome of the collusion of Self and Other. This anime echoes both of the shows discussed in the preceding paragraphs in its distinctive articulation of a three-ply fabric of alterity, again positing a place, a person and an epistemological system as pivotal to its Othering strategies. The place is a period-drama reconstruction of eighteenth-century Europe (and especially Paris) traversed by the esoteric counterspace of subrosa organizations. The person consists of the composite being resulting from the protagonist's supernatural melding with his alter ego. The episteme lies with a dense network of intertextual allusions overlaid by emblems of timeless resonance. An especially prominent role is accorded, in this regard, to the "Royal Psalms," lines inscribed and controlled by nefarious individuals called "the Poets" to engender monstrous transformations and achieve supernatural powers. The show's most salient feature, where its treatment of history is concerned, consists of its transposition of the exploits associated with the historical personage of D'Eon de Beaumont (1728–1810), a diplomat and spy employed by Louis XV in the mid–1700s, onto the fictional plane of a dark fairy tale. Replete with meticulously executed costumes and accessories such as gorgeous ruffles and frills, this pivots on the protagonist's pursuit of a laborious quest for truth and revenge at the cost of alienating himself from the court and both its privileges and its injunctions. This finds inception with the discovery of D'Eon's beloved sister Lia, apparently dead, in a coffin afloat on the Seine. It incrementally emerges that the hapless maiden is one of the countless fatalities of a secret society's nefarious machinations, which capitalize on the generation of mercury-bloodied zombies dubbed "Gargoyles" by alchemical means.

As in *Last Exile* and *Petite Cossette*, moral and environmental defilement are seen as practically coterminous. In the articulation of its cultural identities, *Le Chevalier D'Eon* relies to maximum effect on the juxtaposition of real and imaginary societies, blending a history of occult and forbidden wisdom with the byzantine political intrigues of pre–Revolutionary France and interspersing them with excursions into the Russian Empire and Britain while also casting as major actors several historical figures. These include Maximilien Robespierre, the Duke of Orleans, Count Cagliostro, the Comte de Saint-Germain, the Marquise de Pompadour, Empress Elizaveta, Queen Mary, King George III and Lord Sandwich. Sinister hints at King Louis XV's ultimate responsibility for the drama's most nefarious complications accumulate as the adventure progresses to reach a concurrently tantalizing and satisfying acme in the very final installment. This binary reality spawns an elaborate ensemble of subject roles and positions defined by strict hierarchies and attendant class and gender relations.

On the transcultural plane, finally, the anime vaunts prestigious antecedents among all sorts of traditional tales based on the duality of the ego and its shadowy counterpart, as well as vampire narratives and ghost stories. The most overtly preternatural character in the anime's entire cast is undoubtedly Belle, the speaking skull assisting Queen Marie of France in the capacity of a loyal advisor. Belle enquires obsessively about her mother, always obtaining in response the Queen's promise that she shall eventually be reunited with the person she longs for. Despite her sinister appearance and the dialogue's hints at a baleful past, Belle comes across as eerily appealing, thus providing a further example of the inherently ambivalent nature of many fantastic entities. Another character endowed with supernatural connotations redolent of fairy lore is Lorenza, a Poet and Cagliostro's captivating mistress. In spite of her collected appearance, Lorenza is quite willing to deploy quite ruthlessly the power of the Psalms to restrain or destroy anyone she perceives as an obstacle to her quest. This often entails the employment of fierce spellbound animals. On such occasions, esoteric words can be seen scrolling over her body as incandescent ribbons, supplying one of the anime's most stunningly original visual effects.

The intricate web of mystical and magical forces in which D'Eon's quest is increasingly embroiled as the saga progresses is cumulatively indebted to the fairy tale tradition. So is the chivalric tone pervading the activities of Louis XV's secret police, of whom the hero is a key member: an organization supposed to protect the throne with the zeal and loyalty typical of idealized medieval knights in the face of all manner of threats to the regime and of the unscrupulous traitors behind them. Known as "Le Secret du Roi," the organization actually amounts to a body of spies and saboteurs enjoined to vanquish any possible proponent of revolutionary ferment all over the world, hence playing a pivotal role in the constellation of the anime's trans–European political drama. However, the Other with which the organization must contend is a more ominous antagonist than any nest of anti-establishment rebels of the kind one would expect to encounter in a narrative animated by purely political preoccupations. In fact, it resonates with the dark harmonies emanated by the fairy tale tradition in its most atavistic, unsweetened and unsanitized manifestations. The adventure's somber atmosphere is intensified at virtually every step of the action by a proliferation of ever-shifting alliances and unsettling innuendos that serve to immerse D'Eon's whole universe in a swamp of rampant ethical ambiguity. In the process, the deployment of actual historical figures such as the ones mentioned earlier never smacks of an antiquarian passion for a romanticized revisionist historiography. Nor does it merely amount to a blunt restatement of past events in anime form — let alone gratuitous name dropping — which would be just as unpalatable. In fact, it is a means of establishing an imaginative dialogue between a contemporary fictional interpretation of the vicissitudes of historical Othering and its supposedly factual sources of inspiration, bearing witness to anime's ability to embark on vibrant dialectical exchanges with the most disparate realities to deliver its own distinctive vision of history and lore alike.

Among the areas of analysis consistently addressed in this book, the concept of cultural identity is especially relevant to the issue of alterity. In exploring the relationship between the fairy tale tradition and that concept with specific reference to the field of traditional Japanese storytelling, it is worth noting that a particular cultural Gestalt is instantly communicated by indigenous narrative features even when the concept is not explicitly invoked in thematic terms. The fairy tale *The Fire-Fly's Lovers* (in Griffis), for example, exhibits a characteristically anticlimactic resolution that may appear jarringly smooth to Western eyes. While none of the common insects wooing Princess Hotaru ("Princess Firefly") is able to win her heart by bringing her the fire she requests, the Prince of Fireflies simply enters her palace with his glowing battalions and is immediately accepted. The tale clearly reflects a strictly hierarchical world view, yet it does not offer any stark moral or unequivocal apportioning of praise and blame, preferring instead to convey the philosophical inevitability of its climax. Another typical trait of Japanese fairy tales memorably conveyed by this narrative is the penchant for inconclusiveness, whereby the ending can be seen to pave the way to an undefinable number of other potential stories as the narrator speculates about a human maiden catching fireflies to watch their love life in the hope that her own suitors might dare the impossible for her sake. This story is transculturally related to Andersen's *Thumbelina* by its distinctive take on the aquatic environment and particularly on its luxuriant water lilies. Intriguingly, luminosity, opalescence and preternatural fairness (here connoting both lightness and beauty) are among the attributes most insistently associated with fairies, and especially the more eminent in their ranks. *The Child of the Thunder* (in Griffis) is also typically Japanese in its ability to emphasize the plot's supernatural dimension: its protagonist is born out of the sky during a mighty storm, makes his erstwhile destitute foster parents quite prosperous and, upon reaching manhood, morphs into a white dragon and relinquishes the human world while the old couple lives in comfort to the end of its days. In spite of its unearthly affiliations, however, the tale refrains form indulging in theological or teleological grandeur. The act of narration as a whole, relatedly, is posited as more important than the build-up to a specific climax.

An endearing preference for seamless transitions between preternatural and mundane situations, another recurrent aspect of Japan's contribution to the fairy tale tradition, is epitomized by *The Tongue-Cut Sparrow* (in

Griffis). In this story, a pet sparrow whose tongue is viciously split by his loving master's nagging wife gains the power of speech as a result of the mutilation and leaves the human household to build his own home and family. When the former owner eventually locates him, he visits his heart-warming abode and meets his charming wife and daughters, enjoying some peace at last in the absence of his tyrannical spouse. Upon leaving the avian residence, the human protagonist is asked to choose between two baskets, a light one and a heavy one, and, choosing the former out of sheer politeness, discovers that it hosts a virtually inexhaustible supply of money and gems. The obnoxious wife, unsurprisingly, sets out to obtain her own reward, convinced that the heavy basket is bound to hold an even greater treasure, but is mocked by the provision of a container housing all manner of sepulchral and abject horrors conducive to her abrupt demise. Refreshingly, her old man enjoys a peaceful and comfortable retirement. The narration's fluid shifts between magical occurrences and homely descriptions is undoubtedly one of its most lovable and culturally distinctive attributes.

The story is also notable as an instance of the indigenous passion for the sudden eruption of grotesque and monstrous forms: a proclivity that finds paradigmatic expression in the woodblock prints of Utagawa Kuniyoshi (1797–1861) and in certain set pieces typical of Kabuki theater but can actually be seen to have pervaded Japanese culture for time immemorial and to have manifested itself most persistently as a tendency to rupture any promise of harmony or equilibrium with intimations of lurking turbulence. Vengeful ghosts (*yuurei*) and giant skeletons, repulsive sea creatures and terrifying demons abound as supreme icons of the grotesque and the macabre. Simultaneously, this representational field proclaims with unflinching dedication Japanese art's ability to traverse even the most disconcerting of images with satirical or otherwise humorous touches. In *The Tongue-Cut Sparrow* as in *The Fire-Fly's Lovers*, the narrative resolutely eschews any concessions to stuffy moralism, opting for an ending rendered frankly satisfying by its unbending devotion to dramatic justice. (A transcultural link with Andersen's *The Nightingale* can here be sensed.) The Japanese fairy tale's joyful disregard for clear-cut ethical lessons is again resonantly proclaimed by *The Ape and the Crab* (in Griffis) with an ending that is content simply to laugh at evil and reward true innocence.

With *The Wonderful Tea-Kettle* (in Griffis), we are regaled with a paradigmatic instance of the Nipponic fascination with metamorphoses of all sorts in the guise of an old kettle capable of transmuting into a most resourceful badger with a flair for clever stunts and capers. No less remarkable is the story's emphasis on the cultural reality of spectacle by recourse to both stage performance and mystical ritual — an aspect of its yarn that obliquely underscores the keenness on festivals and related ceremonies ubiquitously evinced by Japanese culture since Heian times. In this instance, a transcultural connection with Andersen's oeuvre can again be noticed, the metamorphic kettle resembling the titular entity in *The Flying Trunk*. The ending of the Japanese tale is rosier, though, witnessing the old kettle's peaceful retirement in a temple where it receives regular helpings of rice and dumplings. Tales like *The Wonderful Tea-Kettle* emplace the concepts of mutation, shape-shifting and inversion as cardinal to the fairy tale tradition, and thus intimate its ideologically subversive potential for exploding the myths of cultural stability and order on which modern nation states and attendant economic formations, alongside anthropocentric and monotheistic systems of belief, have conventionally depended for the purposes of self-legitimation and self-perpetuation.

Moreover, unrelenting dynamic change is an idea accorded critical significance by the teachings and practices of Shinto, where all facets of the cosmos, inorganic matter included, are regarded as inherently animate. Simultaneously, we are reminded that the fairy tale tradition finds a close correlative in the value of playful freedom (*jijuu*) fostered by Zen Buddhism, whereby the cold rule of reason is mirthfully exploded in favor of a childlike approach to the universe in all of its manifold manifestations. It is through this ludic take on the world that the fairy tale tradition is able to engage with latent realities eluding analytical and deductive scrutiny. At its most daring, the discourse accomplishes this delicate task by supplying those realities with both stages and voices on which and through which they may perform their unique dramas by means of ingenious allusions and tropes. Like the Sibyl in Marina Warner's imaginative account of that mythical figure's fate, the elusive genie prowling reality's interstices might be conveniently silenced but "goes on speaking," insofar as it is capable of acting as "the protagonist of the multiple legends" it relentlessly "inspires" (Warner 1995, p. 11). The "proverbial wise woman narrator," likewise, could be Othered by regular society by being "placed on the outskirts of the village, on the edge of the woods" but retained her irresistible attraction as an entertainer of undiminishing "young" audiences (p. 21).

Narratives such as the ones outlined above can be said to contribute to the consolidation of a sense of cultural identity by expressing a distinctively Japanese take on the fairy tale tradition. In the West, one of the means by which that tradition's intimate involvement with the assertion of cultural identity most often manifests itself is the metamorphic power of translation: a process notoriously affected by parochial interests and discriminatory agendas. Naomi Lewis underscores this idea in relation to Andersen's story *The Princess and the Pea*: "The first English translators could not understand Andersen's humour or his subtlety," Lewis maintains. "One pea? That was absurd. Three might be more credible. The museum is ignored. [This is where the time-honored legume is said to have been placed following the events reported by Andersen's narrator.] Sadly, some of these early versions are still in use. Look out for those rogue peas" (in Andersen, p. 13). As Italo Calvino observes, linguistic problems have also marked the reception history of Perrault's *Cinderella*: "*Glass* slippers? Balzac pointed out that dancing and running and sliding off the dainty foot, glass slippers would have shattered. There must be a transcription error: *verre* must be substituted with *vair*, squirrel fur. But *la petite pantoufle de verre* recurs several times in the text, so much so that this detail is one of the fairy tale's most memorable ones, akin to an image that stirs the imagination. And why should a dancing slipper not be made of glass in a fairy tale where pumpkins turn into coaches and lizards into footmen?" (Calvino 1988, p. 149).

A stark instance of the adoption of a blinkered nationalist perspective in the handling of the fairy tale tradition by so-called purists is supplied by the *Wikipedia* in its entry for the fairy tale vis-à-vis the Brothers Grimm's selection criteria. "The first collectors to attempt to preserve not only the plot and characters of the tale," the entry explains, "but also the style in which they were told, were the Brothers Grimm, collecting German fairy tales." As it happens, the authors were not content merely to collate the materials at their disposal: in fact, they also sought to subject their selection to specific — and not especially enlightened — ideological imperatives: "The Brothers Grimm rejected several tales for their collection, though told orally to them by Germans, because the tales derived from Perrault, and they concluded they were thereby French and not German tales; an oral version of *Bluebeard* was thus rejected, and the tale of *Briar Rose*, clearly related to Perrault's *Sleeping Beauty*, was included only because Jacob Grimm convinced his brother that the figure of Brynhild proved that the sleeping princess was authentically German folklore" ("Fairy tale").

Despite the Brothers Grimm's nationalist imperatives, as Briggs argues with reference to the work of Hiroko Ikeda, "the stories burst the bounds of nationality and were eagerly welcomed all over Europe. They even modified some of the folk-tale traditions in Japan" (Briggs, p. 224; Ikeda). Thus, the original intent putatively guiding the Grimms' project has clearly not led to the consolidation of a singular and unified cultural identity. In fact, the work's reception indicates that fairy tales are essentially precious and enduring because, with their hazy origins and meandering propagation, they propose that all societies are the product of interaction and cross-pollination. Maria Tatar pursues a cognate argument by emphasizing that the Grimms' nationalist agenda did not prevent their work from being "denounced, in the aftermath of the Second World War, as a book that promoted 'bloodletting and violence' and that endorsed cruelty, violence, and atrocity, fear and hatred for the outsider, and virulent anti–Semitism." This demonstrates that the appropriation of the fairy tale tradition as a means of advancing a particular notion of cultural identity does not necessarily produce lasting results since that very identity might fall into public disgrace to be replaced by an alternative ideal. The inherent instability of the partnership between fairy tales and cultural expectations is further confirmed by the "odd twist of fate" whereby the Grimms' collection "has also become a book whose stories have been used ... to work through the horrors of the Holocaust." A notable example is the "volume of poetry entitled *Transformations* (1971)," where "the American poet Anne Sexton produced a sinister verse adaptation of 'Hansel and Gretel' that shows the parents cooking the family dog, then resolving to adopt a 'final solution,' one that leaves the children to starve in the forest." The "oven" image, moreover, is used in such a way that "most readers will unfailingly connect" it "with the crematoria of Nazi Germany" (Tatar, p. xx). These fluctuations in the Grimms' perception of their work's meaning and function and in subsequent generations' responses to its import eloquently validate Robert Darnton's contention that traditional tales shed light on specific historical moments by bearing witness to the cultural mentalities prevalent in different epochs (Darnton). Thus, universal as much of their imagery is, fairy tales should never be totally divorced from their material roots in actual human societies and attendant mores, norms and pedagogical priorities.

Returning to the context of Japanese lore, it must be noted that the fairy tale tradition's adaptability as a vehicle for the promulgation of cultural identities in the face of an undesirable Other finds paradigmatic illustrations in the tales of *Raiko and His Guards* and *Raiko Slays the Demons*, as well as *The Tide Jewels* (in Griffis). In these narratives, the fairy tale is harnessed to the epic imperative of nation-building and to the celebration of a pointedly territorial notion of heroism. The tales' respective protagonists, therefore, are incontrovertibly portrayed not simply as champions of justice and enlightenment in a general, transhistorical fashion—even though their mythological connotations lend themselves to such a reading—but also, and more specifically, as national celebrities. It should also be noted there is something markedly masculine, at times even overtly phallic, about Raiko's devastating interventions in the demon world. His resolve to protect his land at any price results in an unswerving pursuit of the one and only goal through which a hero of his ilk establishes his own raison d'être: vanquishing the Other.

However, the seemingly invincible weapons deployed by Raiko and his companions to eradicate the nonhuman brood festering in their realm's murky lacunae do not accomplish the ultimate objective without aggravation and trouble—not least, due to the enemy's infuriating knack of self-regeneration. Raiko's sword brings to mind, in transcultural terms, the key to the door of the room hiding the eponymous character's grim secret in Perrault's *Bluebeard*. While in principle it ought to constitute its owner's legitimate and inappropriable prerogative, it can in fact boomerang and indent his erstwhile absolute power. In addition, the *Raiko* tales abound with dreadful entities immortalized by Japanese lore over the centuries, one of their most baleful specimens consisting of the quintessentially hybrid figure of the *nue*, the autochthonous version of the chimera. This is a creature of ill omen putatively endowed with the head of a monkey, the body of a raccoon, the legs of a tiger, and a reptilian tail. In some legends, the *nue* even vaunts the powers of flight and transformation into a dark cloud.

Prominent throughout the Japanese fairy tale tradition are the richly diversified magical race known by the generic name of *ayakashi*, the word originally used to describe a ghost appearing at sea during a shipwreck and later employed also to designate any spirit exhibiting an unnatural tendency to abide in the human domain. Some of the most intriguing fabulous figures associated with the local fairy tale tradition belong to the broad category of the *youkai*, a large ensemble of preternatural entities that includes evil demons and ogres (*oni*), impish fox spirits (*kitsune*), alternately nurturing and soul-sucking snow women (*yuki-onna*), shape-shifters (*obake*) and *zashiki-warashi*, specters associated with clean and capacious old houses held to bless a residence with good fortune as long as they dwell within its walls but bound to cause its rapid decline as soon as they forsake it. Also typical of indigenous fairy lore are the *noppera-bou*, faceless ghouls capable of acquiring human physiognomies, and *umibouzu* (often said to emanate from drowned monks), creatures said to inhabit the depths of the ocean and to capsize the boats of all humans impertinent enough to address them directly. Finally, the traditional Japanese tale veritably seethes with *bakeneko* ("monster cats"), characteristically viewed as felines equipped with preternatural qualities that sometimes include cannibalistic and incendiary proclivities. Occasionally, the *bakeneko*'s powers overlap with those evinced by both the aforementioned *kitsune*, as well as the *tanuki* ("raccoon spirits").

Quite a different facet of the cultural identity embedded in Japanese lore is communicated by the tale of *The Grateful Crane* (in Griffis) with particular emphasis on the theme of power relations. The story's protagonist, a young man named Musai, rescues and injured crane and some years later marries a very special bride endowed with the power to spin a cloth so uniquely exquisite as to bring him great wealth. Although the only reward which the young woman asks for her lucrative efforts is the respect of privacy while she works at the wheel, one fateful night her husband gives in to curiosity and, in spying upon her, discovers that she is not a human female but a majestic white crane. Her privacy so rudely violated, the creature leaves the household, consigning Musai and his elderly mother to lifelong poverty. This story conveys a disarmingly simple but crucial lesson for all humans to treasure: the importance of leaving the supernatural alone when instructed to do so. In its articulation of fraught power relations between the human and the unearthly, demonstrating the difficulty of their achieving lasting harmonious coexistence, *The Grateful Crane* is also careful to throw into relief the natural habitat's unique qualities, embracing a wondrously holistic approach to the entire environment. Andersen's *Thumbelina*, incidentally, again springs to mind as an appropriate transcultural correlative.

It is also worth noting that in another version of *The Grateful Crane*, the bird is rescued by a childless man and his wife (in Lane; original source: Bertoli). Her masterful weaving of a precious fabric can accordingly be read, as Marcia Lane suggests, as "a story about filial devotion.... The crane/daughter pays her parents back for the gift of her life. She does it with service and she does it with the gift of her own body. So the cloth is sold to provide for the old ones. But they break the taboo, and have to release their daughter to go back to her own fate (marriage?)" (Lane, p. 76). Therefore, even though this version of the fairy tale does not overtly bring marriage into play, there are intimations that one of its main preoccupations is the promulgation of a socially sanctioned and codified understanding of gender relations.

A Chinese analog for this popular Japanese tale is supplied by the story of *The Dinner That Cooked Itself* (in Birch), where a fairy named White Wave installs herself in the abode of a parentless and virtuous youth, Tuan, in the guise of a giant snail. Assuming the form of a lovely maiden dressed in a gorgeous silk robe in his absence, she cooks him delicious meals to compensate for his lack of a human family until the day he marries. When Tuan surreptitiously watches White Wave to ascertain the origins of his splendid dinners and discovers the snail's true physiognomy, the fairy has no choice but to leave him at once, marking her abrupt departure with the magical gift of an endlessly self-refilling rice jar. It is here worth noting that in several Western traditions, fairies operate as efficient housekeepers, eager to complete unfinished domestic chores and even safeguard a household's moral standards. At times, their protective role extends to gardens and farmland.

Both *The Grateful Crane* and *The Dinner That Cooked Itself* find apposite Western counterparts in the Western tale of *The Elves and the Shoemaker*. In this story, a cobbler finds pairs of shoes he has barely begun to fashion impeccably completed on his work bench morning after morning. Such is the quality of his produce that he rapidly acquires both fame and wealth. Peeping into his workshop at night to establish the cause of his good fortune, the man discovers that the proficient artisans are elves who perform their tasks donning nothing other than their birthday suits. Taking pity on the naked creatures, the cobbler's wife sews some tiny garments to enfold appropriately the creatures' preternatural physiques. However, no sooner do they see themselves beautifully garbed than the elves reckon they no longer have any reason for tarrying in a humble cobbler's dwelling and resolve to enjoy at leisure the big wide world (Grimm 2000). Yet again, the human beneficiaries of fairies' generosity appear destined to lose the magical entities' support once they unveil their secret presence and agency.

The pivotal theme explored in *The Grateful Crane* finds intriguing variations in a cluster of Japanese tales likewise centered on supernatural liaisons. A particularly harrowing instance is provided by the tale of *The Snow Bride*. Having killed in (literally) cold blood the protagonist's traveling companion, a mysterious woman forcibly obtains from the shocked survivor the promise that he will never mention either her or her actions to anyone. The sinister lady reappears at a later stage in the hero's life as his bride without his harboring any inkling of her true identity. He discovers the unpalatable truth upon observing that the woman reminds him of a mysterious creature he once met, at which point the Snow Bride flees her family in a rage never to return, declaring that she is only willing to spare the untruthful mortal's life on account of the children she has borne him (in Ashliman 1998–2008a; original source: Hadland Davis). Both *The Grateful Crane* and *The Snow Bride* can be regarded as examples of the typology comprising fairy tales in which, as J. C. Cooper puts it, "a taboo and its contravention, such as opening a forbidden door," provide the narrative kernel around which the entire plot gains form. These tales can be traced back "to the Amor and Psyche myth" of ancient Greece (Cooper, p. 15). A related motif, incidentally, is that of the forbidden name, of which the Grimms' *Rumpelstiltskin* constitutes one of the most famous expressions.

The supernatural wives portrayed in tales such as *The Grateful Crane* and *The Snow Bride* might seem heartless in their readiness to leave their human families behind without compunction. However, it is important to realize that stories of that kind are not concerned with measuring their marvelous characters' moral worth with reference to human standards. In fact, their primary objective is to emphasize those figures' adherence to incontestably Other principles, and thus expose the risible arrogance inherent in any attempt to frame their behavior within everyday human norms. A comparable situation is presented in the Grimms' *The Robber Bridegroom*. The horror pervading the robbers' lifestyle — most palpably, in the scene where a young woman watches her fiancé and his companions as they "cut" a girl "into pieces" and a chopped-off finger bearing a "gold ring" is sent bounding in the appalled witness' very "lap" — would feasibly have a blood-curdling impact on even the most seasoned slasher aficionado were it not for the narrative's implicit emphasis on the idea that the criminals act in accordance with values ungraspable by ordinary people and yet peculiarly logical and reasonable within their contingent context (Grimm 2000, pp. 123–124).

It is quite common for Japanese tales centered on supernatural brides such as *The Grateful Crane* and *The Snow Bride* to end with those characters' departure from the mortal world. The same applies to the plots of *Willow Wife* and *The Tale of the Bamboo-Cutter*, two greatly revered Japanese narratives discussed in Chapter 5. This type of resolution articulates a distinctively Japanese concept of beauty. As Hayao Kawai explains, "in the Japanese fairy tales, the fact that beautiful women just vanish or die, leaving a deep feeling of sorrow, symbolizes completeness in the aesthetic dimension. It is the beauty of completeness." It is vital to recognize that in this context, "completeness" is by no means synonymous with "perfection" (Kawai 1995, p. 119). In fact, in the realm of Japanese aesthetics, "the state of imperfection is more beautiful than the state of perfection" (p. 120), and indigenous fairy tales, in this respect, endeavor to "tell us that the world is beautiful and that beauty is completed only if we accept the existence of death" (p. 121). After all, it is in the presence of gaps, lacunae and aporias that the imagination feels impelled to wander and create, whereas plenitude only ever turns out to be a broken promise.

In the domain of anime, an intriguing sci-fi variation on the bittersweet resolution proposed by many fairy tales pivoting on the figure of the supernatural bride, whereby the ultramundane creature ultimately has no choice but to leave the human world, is provided by *This Ugly Yet Beautiful World* (TV series; dir. Shouji Saeki, 2004). In this case, the entity in question is nothing less than a cosmic force capable of affecting the evolution of the entire universe. This formidable energy source temporarily manifests itself in the shape of two quintessentially cute characters of supernatural luminosity—Hikari ("light") and Akari ("brightness")—and therefore embodying one of the fairy folk's most legendary physiognomic properties. The ineradicable memories left in their wake by the two preternatural girls after their departure from the mortal realm is indeed figuratively comparable to a spellbinding trail of fairy dust.

It should also be noted, in this context, that the figure of the Snow Bride is a prestigious member of a an honored and transculturally renowned lineage of Winter and Christmas Fairies that strike their roots in pagan lore and have been varyingly adapted, disfigured or simply Othered by Christianity and other formalized religions. As Louise Heyden points out, "One of the major faerie queens, the Snow Queen is both faerie and sky goddess. At Winter Solstice she rides through the snowy skies, making the snow fall by shaking the pillows on her icy chariot. Her company, known as the Wild Hunt, ride through the skies until Twelfth Night, creating snowstorms in their wake" (Heyden). Japanese lore has its own memorable version of such a creature in the mythical persona of *Yuki-onna* (literally, "Snow-woman"). The *Wikipedia* entry for this figure explains that "Yuki-onna appears on snowy nights as a tall, beautiful woman with long black hair and red lips. Her inhumanly pale or even transparent skin makes her blend into the snowy landscape.... She sometimes wears a white kimono, but other legends describe her as nude, with only her face and hair standing out against the snow.... She floats across the snow, leaving no footprints (in fact, some tales say she has no feet, a feature of many Japanese ghosts), and she can transform into a cloud of mist or snow if threatened" ("Yuki-onna"). As Marriott observes, "Japan's *Yuki-Onna*, or snow maiden, may appear as a hovering mist of white vapor, in which form she penetrates the home, bringing the dangers of the wilderness into the heart of civilization. Incredibly ethereal, palely beautiful in frost-white robes (in which form she may marry mortals), she creeps through unguarded windows and doors in the form of a mist, inhaling human life-force in a reverse kiss of life, or enticing men out into her domain, the blizzard, to perish" (Marriott, p. 33). The hapless victim of the Snow Bride's hunger for human souls presented in the opening portion of the aforementioned Japanese tale clearly opts for the former of these murderous ploys.

Likewise baleful is the relationship portrayed in *The Vampire Cat*. The story's titular character is a seemingly lovely maiden addicted to preying nightly on the Prince of Hizen who, when revealed to be a soul-devouring feline, escapes to cause havoc in the entire province until she is meted out the drastic treatment deemed fitting for the most opprobrious of demons (in Ashliman 1998–2008a; original sources: Hadland Davis and Mitford). The tale is also noteworthy as a starker version of the topos dramatized in *The Grateful Crane* vis-à-vis the relationship between humanity and nature. The injunction to refrain at any price from tampering with the environment's arcane powers is here combined with the intimation that a human being may only be able to confront, understand and even challenge the unknown only as long as he or she retains total openness to nature's lessons and, by implication, to the supernatural energies coursing therein. *The Vampire Cat* epitomizes a myth punctuating literature and lore from all parts of the globe over the centuries: that of the predatory female. A haunting transcultural relation of the Japanese Vampire Cat is the creature of the mermaid portrayed in the Scottish tale where the Laird of Lorntie, as he returns from the hunt, is enticed by a woman begging him for help. While his attendant, aware of the superhuman danger besetting his master, pulls the lord away, the mermaid ferociously proceeds to give vent to her cannibalistic drives, crying that had she captured her intended victim, she would have consumed his very heart (in Chambers).

Narratives centered on the character type of the elusive female engage metaphorically — as do *Last Exile*, *Petite Cossette* and *Le Chevalier D'Eon* via the figures of Alvis, Cossette and Lia — with the question of woman's abeyant Otherness. Neither in traditional stories nor in the selected anime, however, is the Other defined exclusively with reference to gender. In fact, race also comes prominently into play. This is borne out by the presentation of characters such as the supernatural brides of ancient lore and the three series' enigmatic females as akin to changelings: namely, entities enshrined in the darker regions of the fairy tale tradition by their radical Othering. A changeling's destiny is to be uprooted more or less brutally from the reality in which it logically belongs and relocated to an alien — and very possibly inimical — alternate world. Additionally, just as changelings have often been perceived as hybrid or even monstrous products of unnatural unions, so those females come across as disturbingly aberrant and, at times, downright repulsive despite their superior physical beauty. This is a corollary of their uncertain ontological status and, by extension, their potential capacity to dismantle other accepted categories of being. Considered as a cluster of interrelated texts, both the anime discussed in this chapter as instances of the collusion of the fairy tale tradition and alterity and the traditional tales engaging with the same discursive phenomenon can therefore be interpreted as efforts to understand, and come to terms with in figurative form, a tangle of real sociopolitical issues. John Keats' poem "La Belle Dame Sans Merci" (1819) is a prime example of the interplay of the fairy tale tradition and the question of Otherness that brings both gender and race simultaneously to the fore. Indeed, the Romantic ballad's portrayal of its fairy figure as the epitome of the *femme fatale* drawing the vulnerable knight into a tragic liaison through her glamour and bewitching song is crucially dependent not solely on the deployment of sexual stereotypes but also on the intimation that the lady belongs to an alien, obscure and hence menacing race.

A few facets of the fairy tale tradition's imbrication with the specific issue of gender that are particularly pertinent to the topos of alterity deserve attention at this juncture. These are associated primarily with a galaxy of peculiar beliefs that gained prominence in eighteenth- and nineteenth-century Europe and are therefore rendered relevant to this context by their historical proximity to the worlds explicitly painted by *Petite Cossette* and *Le Chevalier D'Eon* and alluded to by means of a retrofuturistic aesthetic in *Last Exile*. As far as supernatural brides are concerned, it is vital to acknowledge that even at their tamest, such creatures were then perceived as germane to unbridled natural energies that transcended the strictures of human laws. Hence, they were inevitably held to retain subversive potentialities, and to be capable both of disrupting, albeit fleetingly, the stable societies they infiltrated and of acting as unsettling reminders of the ancestral and unfathomable universes whence they came to join the mortal domain. As symbolic avatars of these traditional beings, the female characters portrayed by both the chosen anime and their fairy tale relations point at once to two recurrent human anxieties: the fear of entrapment by a dark atavistic force mocking reason and common sense, and the fear of separation from that same force as conducive not to freedom but to the loss of one's primal roots and to ignorance. These creatures share a baleful role, in this respect: that of captor of a powerless man in both physical and spiritual terms.

Avoiding capture by a woman endowed with mystical powers may seem infinitely preferable to a fate of possession laced with obsessive desire — for truth, for love, for compassion — and with all the classic symptoms of a chronic case of repetition compulsion. However, it is through their tormented entanglement with present-day equivalents of the swan maidens of old that the captive males portrayed in the chosen anime come to experience epiphanic disclosures which would otherwise remain intractably beyond their comprehension. The price of knowledge, in these stories, is very steep indeed. In a historical perspective, it is eminently feasible that the older worlds depicted by the anime, literally or figuratively as the case may be, would have participated in mentalities comparable to those associated by Carole G. Silver with Victorian society. In this context, what rendered the supernatural bride particularly problematic was her metaphorical incarnation of female power and independence, and her failure to thrive in the human world could therefore be interpreted as evidence of her "inability to fit in a 'normal' patriarchal world" (Silver, p. 94). Furthermore, the creature was often regarded as the epitome of uncontrollable female sexuality, a drive supposedly tarred by a penchant for promiscuousness and nonreproductive intercourse. If women generally "were closer to nature," as it was commonly held, and hence "less rational and more instinctual" (p. 100), supernatural females were bound to be seen as inflated incarnations of that proclivity.

In the cases of Cossette and Lia, it must be stressed that these heroines do not only echo the typology of the supernatural bride but also exhibit some of the more disquieting traits of humans whose personalities have been irreparably distorted by exposure to Faërie and its denizens. Commenting, with reference to Victorian culture, on the fate of mortals who have been the object of fairy abductions, Silver points out that "even when rescued, a change of body or spirit usually accompanied the return to normal life by those who had been 'away.' Those who returned were often ghosts or ghostlike, in some accounts crumbling into dust, in others wasting away in sorrow for their loss of fairy bliss. In some way, they had been robbed of part of their humanity" (p. 168). As a corollary of this seachange (at times, literally marine), a human reentering the mortal realm after a temporary — yet temporally unquantifiable — absence is always in the thrall of fairy powers even while carrying out quotidian human duties. Cossette and Lia partake of this very fate in an allegorically reimagined vein, insofar as they have been snatched away from the human world by forces which, though not literally issuing from Faërie, are rife with demonic intent, and have been reinserted into their places of origin in the capacity of undead beings.

What is most troubling about these spectral "dead-alive victims," as Silver dubs creatures of that ilk, is their ill-defined, and hence potentially anarchic, social identity. "With actual death," Silver observes, "at least, came certainty; with ... apparent death came the possibility of a flawed resurrection and a resultant uncertainty about status" (p. 171). In the specific instance of *Le Chevalier D'Eon*, Faërie also provides, in the guise of the more overtly disruptive and treacherous of the series' characters, a potent analog for the societal turbulence threatening to topple France's faltering monarchy. This aspect of the anime brings to mind Silver's contention that fairies' notoriously temperamental and unpredictable conduct has often led to their association not only with "savage or barbarous peoples" but also with "the mob" (p. 150). In this regard, they have supplied legendary correlatives for the rabble presumed to be hell-bent on "invading the civilized world from the barbaric wilderness, running amuck, taking or destroying whatever was in their path" (pp. 150–151).

As Purkiss argues, in the sixteenth and seventeenth centuries, it was also common for fairies to be compared to rural people as entertaining objects of study for the refined town-dweller. Detailed descriptions of those people's tales and customs as fanciful "curiosities" issuing from a semilegendary past became a means of emphasizing "the civility of the observer" as an "urban sophisticate" able to recognize "the hilarious fancies of his forebears" for what they truly were, without according them even a modicum of credibility (Purkiss, p. 198). Fairies came to be associated most explicitly with Other races deemed automatically inferior to the white Christian colonizer in the nineteenth century. Yet, that metaphorical linkage can actually be traced back to "the Crusades era" — a moment in history coinciding with possibly the first radical destabilization of "Western Europe's cultural certainties" due to some unsettling geographical "encounters" (p. 202). Byzantium, and later Venice, were the principal cities famous for firing the Western imagination with their spectacular displays of palpably Eastern sumptuousness and glory, and thus encouraging the equation of exotic glamour to the fabulous. As Purkiss observes, Byron unambiguously "called Venice 'a fairy city of the heart'" (p. 203).

In iconographic terms, both Eastern cities and fairies are traditionally linked up with precious gems as a way of conveying in an economical but unmistakable fashion their shared connection with exotic luxury and hence, by a leap of the imagination, with the ultramundane. It is as though humans accustomed to perceiving themselves as a master race could not bear the thought of anything or anybody exceeding their presumed excellence and therefore needed to displace their wondrous rivals onto an Other, resolutely non-human, reality. In Western art, so powerful is the association between fairies and gems that it is sometimes possible to identify a comely maiden's fairyhood purely on the basis of her possession of jewel-encrusted accessories or even just a jewelry purse. A case in point is Sophie Anderson's "Thus Your Fairy's Made of Most Beautiful Things" (a.k.a. "Take the fair face of woman," 1869): it would be arduous to recognize the figure's provenance from fairy folk, and quite possible just to admire the painting as nothing other than an enticing portrait of a honey-haired and sapphire-eyed beauty, were it not for the exquisite silk purse with gold trimmings she lovingly holds in her hands.

A paradigmatic instance of fairies' Othering on religious grounds also deserves notice in the present context. This is supplied by the Scottish clergyman Rober Kirk's *The Secret Commonwealth of Elves and Fairies*, originally penned in 1691 but left unprinted until the nineteenth century. Kirk describes the Little People as unexpectedly pious by stating that he has learned much about fairy customs and lifestyle as a result of being held captive in their secret realm to officiate their mass — and hence, it is implied, fulfill a spiritual function of which fairies themselves are incapable and, no less significantly, deem themselves incapable. The captors, ironically, are presented as figuratively analogous to a colonized people held to require the colonizer's civilizing and ennobling intervention — a racial stereotype underpinning colonialism since inception. At the same time, however, Kirk draws attention to the fairies' ineradicable alterity by describing their performance of activities which they undertake in emulation of humans as marked by non-human connotations. This is borne out by the clergyman's depiction of spinning fairies: "Their women are said to Spine very fine, to Dye, to tossure, and embroider: but whither it is a manual Operation of substantial refined stuffs, with apt and solid Instruments, or only curious Cob-Webs, impalpable rainbows, and a fantastic imitation of the Actions of more terrestrial Mortals, since it transcended all the senses of the Seer to discern whither, I leave to conjecture as I found it" (Kirk, p. 73). This portrayal resolutely foregrounds not fairies' kinship with us but their alienness, not their status as humanity's potential friends but their disconcerting — and dangerous — suspension between the human and the non-human, the Self and the Other. Kirk's designation of humans as "more terrestrial Mortals," in this respect, feels simultaneously amusing and ominous. Once again, fairies are posited as hybrids, as mercurial funambulists treading a spider's tightrope between reality and fantasy and, in the specific instance provided above, between onerous craftsmanship and flamboyant magic.

Midori Snyder's observations regarding the transculturally charismatic personage of the Swan Maiden are also worthy of consideration in this context insofar as this eminently Other bride figure exhibits crucial affinities with the Japanese characters described earlier. (The character also bears vital affinities with the heroine of *The Tale of the Bamboo-Cutter*.) As Snyder maintains, in numerous narratives pivoting on that figure, a young man is driven by his infatuation with a numinous woman to perpetrate a series of misdeeds that typically "culminate in marriage and the attempted domestication of the wild, fantastical swan maiden, turned into a wife and mother." However, such a liaison is ineluctably precarious and fraught with insoluble conflicts since the two characters are bound not by mutual respect and trust but by an act of brutal prevarication: "the husband's theft of the swan maiden's feathered gown, forcing her to remain human and estranged from her own world." Hence, regardless of the wondrous lady's apparent meekness or resignation to her unanchored state, "there remains an unspoken anxiety and tension beneath the surface of her marriage.... Her feathered robe is the sign of her wild nature, of her freedom, and of her power" (Snyder).

Another fascinating variation on the theme of the supernatural bride worthy of mention in this context is Maurice Hewlett's *The Lore of Proserpine*, a pantheistic text published as a factual account of the provenance and social standing of fairy wives. By and large unseen by ordinary mortals, these beings are said to be the "spirit, essence, substance (what you will) of certain sensible things, such as trees, flowers, wind, water, hills, woods, marshes and the like" (Hewlett, p. 160). This perspective is highly pertinent to this study due to its affinity with the conception of the cosmos promulgated by Shinto — a world picture that is seldom absent from the Japanese fairy tale tradition and undoubtedly pervades the narratives cited earlier as illustrative examples of the treatment of alterity in indigenous lore.

In its handling of the topos of alterity, the Japanese fairy tale tradition often conveys a particular sense of cultural identity through its approach to the environment. This is accorded notable prominence in *Peach Darling* (in Peirce Williston), a story endeavoring to show with unobtrusive conviction the importance of opening oneself to the natural realm unfettered by any stultifying sense of hierarchy. This lesson is principally communicated by means of the story's animal characters, the dog, monkey and pheasant encountered and fed by the human hero in his travels with his sole treasure: a modest reserve of millet dumplings. These characters are absolutely instrumental in Peach Darling's triumph over evil. In the finale, the tale offers a paean to undiluted generosity as the youth declares that his companions deserve all the praise and honor showered upon him at the end of the quest. *Peach Darling* clearly exemplifies the narratological category defined by a figure which Cooper describes as the "Helpful or Grateful Animal"— a creature willing to deploy to no obvious personal advantage "its ingenuity or magic powers for the benefit of the hero or heroine — as when Puss in Boots elevates his humble master to the rank of marquis and then king, or when Cinderella's birds (or animals in some of the numerous variants) first nourish her and are then instrumental in bringing about her marriage to the Prince" (Cooper, p. 15).

Animal allies of the kind presented in *Peach Darling* are also central to the Grimms' *The Sea-Hare*. This fairy tale deploys a dramatic structure redolent of *The Fire-Fly's Lovers* in that it focuses on a proud princess who regularly inspects the world through the twelve windows of her apartment to identify the hiding-places of her suitors, having announced that "no one should ever be her husband who could not conceal himself from her so effectually, that it should be quite impossible for her to find him." Whenever a hopeful wooer fails, he is summarily executed and his head mounted on a pike for all to see, and the princess is free to cherish the thought that she "shall be free" as long as she lives. Eventually, a humble youth triumphs with the assistance of a raven and a fish, who help him hide, and a fox, who engineers his metamorphosis into a sea-hare and thus enables him to enter the royal palace unheeded. Acknowledging that the man is an adequate match for her in both intelligence and tenacity, the princess accepts him with "great respect" (Grimm 1884, pp. 321–324).

The animal kingdom likewise plays a pivotal part in *The Eighty-One*

Brothers (in Peirce Williston), another narrative revolving around the topos of the meek youth succeeding where his doughty rivals have failed. In *The Eighty-One Brothers*, a pet hare is instrumental in securing an unprivileged brother's eventual success and recognition. The situation famously dramatized in Perrault's *Cinderella* and in the Grimms' version of the tale titled *Ashenputtel* springs to mind, upon reading this tale, as relevant transcultural relations. According to Cooper, this kind of narrative exemplifies what is arguably "the best-known and most frequent of motifs" among the various recurrent ingredients exhibited by fairy tales from diverse cultures and epochs: "that of Paradise Lost and Regained" (Cooper, p. 15). Moreover, the figure of the marginalized brother allowed by destiny to triumph over his privileged siblings finds an explicit Western correlative in the Grimms' *The Three Feathers*. In tales like *The Eighty-One Brothers*, the character of the weakest of several siblings is typically enabled to triumph despite his physical or intellectual limitations in order to intimate that in the face of the unknown, strict rationalism is inadequate and what is needed instead is a generous dose of instinct and intuitive wisdom. What is most refreshing about *The Eighty-One Brothers* is that its commitment to the celebration of animal strengths never deteriorates into a cheap idealization of nature. This is attested to by the passage in which the hare openly admits to his own errors. This part of the story also points, by recourse to narrative embedding, to the vagaries besetting the historical recording of so-called facts, as the hare's reconstruction of his own adventure about an unfortunate meeting with a crocodile resulting in the loss of his fur takes the focus away from the main plot and its protagonist for a protracted period, almost inducing the reader to forget what the main story is actually about.

The idea that commerce with the otherworldly dimension embedded in nature itself can operate as a revelatory rite of passage is also pivotal to *The Old Man with a Wart* (in Peirce Williston). In this story, a man whose dance happens to please the Storm Spirits with whom he has inadvertently come into contact is relieved of the wart that has for long afflicted him, not knowing what reward is in store for him upon offering his performance. By contrast, the man who ventures into the spirit world deliberately in order to have his own wart removed but delivers a purely perfunctory and utilitarian act gains an additional wart on the hitherto unblemished side of face. The beliefs and practices associated with the specifically shamanic element of Shinto reverberates throughout the tale's ritual atmosphere. The concept of alterity is again foregrounded by the suggestion that humans should make no facile assumptions about the supernatural Other.

Dramatic emphasis is thereby laid on the wonderful sense of arbitrariness pervading Faërie's morality as an ethical system entirely *sui generis*. On the transcultural plane, affinities may be perceived between this story and both Maurice Sendak's *Where the Wild Things Are* and Perrault's *The Fairy*. The latter is a variation on the *Cinderella* mold in which a kind and downtrodden maiden is rewarded by a godmother figure for her generosity with a most unusual gift: whenever she utters a word, a precious gem, rose or pearl will issue from her mouth. When her selfish and rapacious sister undeservedly seeks to have the same gift bestowed upon her, she is cursed with a mouth destined to disgorge slimy toads or snakes with every syllable she attempts to voice (Perrault, pp. 63–68).

All three of the anime here explored evince in variable degrees a fascination with the world of the dead — and, by extension, with the provinces of the undead and the quasi-dead — that can be seen to originate in a major area of Japanese lore to which the fairy tale tradition is profoundly indebted. As Michiko Iwasaka and Barre Toelken emphasize, death could indeed be regarded as "the *principal* topic in Japanese tradition" and this is empirically confirmed by the fact that "nearly every festival, every ritual, every custom is bound up in some way with the relationship between the living and the dead, the present family and its ancestors." The pervasiveness of death-oriented customs can be partly attributed to their ability to bring into sharp focus certain cardinal principles of an eminently indigenous world picture, including "obligation, duty, debt, honor and personal responsibility" (Iwasaka and Toelken, p. 6). However, the phenomenon highlighted by Iwasaka and Toelken also reflects the Japanese attraction to shadows, duskiness or even undiluted tenebrousness: a cultural proclivity that became firmly enshrined in both practical patterns of living and the underlying collective imaginary in the Heian era (794–1185), a period almost universally associated with the apotheosis of Japan's artistic and creative vigor — though also, on the less complimentary side of the equation, with political inanity. Despite its unprecedented dedication to colorful elegance, courtly refinement and aesthetic subtlety as qualities inextricable from a person's spiritual effulgence, Heian settings and overall ambience were primarily somber and hence exposed the ultimate inextricability of radiance and darkness. Ivan Morris and William J. Puette foreground this idea with reference to the epoch's architecture and quotidian habits, while Field views the Heian period's duskiness as intertwined with a mentality wherein the unearthly is accorded a privileged role. "On bright warm days," Morris comments, "when the shutter could be removed and the blinds rolled up, the Heian house was fairly light, but as a rule the overhanging eaves and the absence of windows kept the rooms in semi-darkness. After sunset feeble oil-lamps and occasional tapers ... provided such lighting as there was.... Women in particular lived in a state of almost perpetual twilight. As if the rooms were not already dark enough, they normally immured themselves behind thick silk hangings or screens" (Morris, p. 34).

In Puette's assessment of the Heian age, it is firmly underscored that "For the denizens of the capital, the actual world of daily activities was ... largely nocturnal" and "time was solely governed by the flow of events. People slept, ate, and committed their other quotidian duties around their social activities, which more often than not were conducted at night, till just before dawn" (Puette, p. 28). Field, for her part, argues that Heian culture vaunts a "tradition rich in ghosts" whose ghoulish characters have stood out over the centuries as a wellhead of "abiding interest," so that "even now when the darkness of Heian estates, so conducive to the play of spirits, has given way to well-lit rooms," they manage to retain their hold on the communal imagination (Field, p. 45). These voices are here worth dwelling upon insofar as it is in this same epoch that Japan's unique approach to the supernatural — to possessions, demonic incarnations, hauntings and all manner of enchantments and curses — assumes an incontrovertibly recognizable cultural identity and the fairy tale tradition, appositely, develops many of its most popular yarns and tropes.

CHAPTER 3

Voyages

The fairy tale's inveterate dedication to the voyage topos is succinctly underscored by Marcia Lane in her discussion of the handling of space in traditional narratives. "In some stories," the critic suggests, "the message seems to be, 'Stay here! Here you are safe. Out there demons abound!' On the other hand some stories say, 'You must journey in order to become more than you are!' In fairy tales, the latter far outnumber the former" (Lane, p. 11). Such a preference clearly ensues from that motif's unmatched usefulness in the articulation of a person's emotional and psychological development. The obstacles encountered by the growing self in its travels are often ideated in otherworldly form. Hence, fairy-like entities tend to pervade the experience of journeying, frequently in the guise of prankish agencies keen on capturing in a web of delusions the hapless travelers that happen to venture, albeit unwittingly, into their province and thus distort their sensory perceptions or even their minds.

As Susannah Marriott explains, this motif can be detected in legion traditions all over the world, an apposite example being the "Will o' the Wisp," known as "*Lyktgubbe* in Sweden" and as "*Sand yan Y Trad* in Brittany" (Marriott, p. 34): namely, the elf fire capable of both leading travelers safely to their destinations in the dark and, more characteristically, of ensnaring them deeper and deeper into preternatural marshes. Also notable are "West Malaysia's *Orang Bunyi,* or voice people," who use peculiar sounds to entice the traveler into their traps, "Zaire's *Eloko*" with their "tinkling bells," and "Sweden's wood-caretaker Skogra" (p. 18). Fairies are also known to both disrupt and abet human travel by recourse to either baleful storms or benevolent winds. According to Marriott, "Native American Cloud People" and the "*Ventolines,* or 'little winds,'" of "Northern Spain" fall into the amicable category, while "Slavonia's *Vily,*" several "Valkyries, battle nymphs of Nordic and Teutonic lore," and Italian "*Folletti,* wind knot fairies," exemplify the pernicious typology (p. 33). Fairies are also related to air to the extent that their "breath," as D. J. Conway maintains, "gives form to every word and thought" and does not, therefore, merely amount to "the physical act of breathing" but actually consists of "the spiritual breath that is needed to manifest desires or create events" (Conway, p. 99). Moreover, when fairies share their breath with humans, they automatically partake of their essence and hence establish a special connection with them — for this reason, they select their partners very judiciously and count on those humans' willingness to reciprocate their trust with ready acceptance of the Fair Folk's existence and active involvement in the mortal world.

The fairy figures most notorious for disrupting human journeys to deleterious effect by means of unbearably melodious song and irresistible eroticism are unquestionably mermaids and sirens. Sprites of this kind appear in myriad traditions and remain to this day some of the most intriguing sources of literary, cinematic and pictorial inspiration. These creatures also remind us of the cardinal role played by music in fairy lore as a spellbinding force and a means of initiating encounters between Faërie and the human world — frequently, alas, with disastrous romantic implications. The relationship between music and fairies will be closely addressed in Chapter 4: Creativity. At this stage, it is useful to note that fairy tunes may also act as potent sources of artistic inspiration but can easily lead the artist to lunacy perdition. It is also worth bearing in mind, on this point, that when fairies and humans intermingle at a physical level, having somehow managed to overcome the obstacles inherent in the wooing phase, peculiar generic admixtures are the likely outcome — and societal ostracism is likely to be the destiny awaiting their bearers as a result of blind racial prejudice.

The figure of the mermaid is pivotal, as argued in Chapter 4, to the series *Earl and Fairy.* Within the realm of anime, it also features in *Mermaid Forest* (TV series; dir. Masaharu Okuwaki, 2003), *Zoku Natsume Yuujin-*

chou (TV series; dir. Takahiro Ohmori, 2009) and *Ponyo on the Cliff by the Sea* (movie; dir. Hayao Miyazaki, 2008). While *Mermaid Forest* offers a thoughtful exploration of the tensions besetting the encounter between incompatible species, *Zoku Natsume Yuujinchou* proposes an original interpretation of the ancient legend according to which the consumption of mermaid blood by a human confers immortality to the drinker. *Ponyo on the Cliff by the Sea*, Miyazaki's reinvention of Hans Christian Andersen's *The Little Mermaid*, concomitantly lightens the parent tale's tone by means of a child-oriented happy ending and darkens its thematic import through a grave environmentalist message of global magnitude.

Abduction is also a journey-related topos of great importance in the fairy tale tradition, insofar as more or less forceful appropriations of mortal women to deliver and breastfeed their babies or attend their christening rituals, and of human children to augment the beauty of the fairy race or provide entertainment are pivotal to the Fair Folk's very survival. Moreover, human brides on their wedding day and night are held to be especially vulnerable to fairy assaults given their unparalleled desirability as incarnations of youth, fertility and, at least ideally, comeliness. Even when their intentions are not downright flagitious, fairies tend to evince mischief-making proclivities and a knack of deploying their subversive powers (including irresistible laughter, shape-shifting and stealth) to push the threshold of mortal sanity. Thus, while not all fairies seek to use their seductive or deranging capacities to fatal ends, the potentially momentous repercussions of their interventions in the human world can never be underestimated. Nor should one ignore their proneness to unforgiving vindictiveness if ill-treated or inappropriately rewarded. It is also true, however, that weird occurrences traditionally imputed to fairy meddling in the affairs of mortals are often the result of people's own carelessness and laziness — not only in the context of travel but also within the domestic sphere. For example, while nothing is easier than accusing fairies of having purloined the things we are unable to find even after long and exasperating searches, it would be more honest, on countless occasions, to admit that it is our thoughtless disposal of objects around the house that indirectly invites the Little People to nab them to their own advantage.

Likewise, when the thirteenth fairy in the Grimms' *Briar Rose* is inadvertently left uninvited to the celebration of a princess' birth and feels so inconsolably slighted as to resolve to wreak havoc on both the royal protagonist and her whole environment, we would do well and ponder where culpability truly lies. In *Sleeping Beauty*, Charles Perrault's version of the tale, the vengeful fairy, Uglyane, is actually the eighth, seven fairies having been invited to attend the ceremony in accordance with the popular belief that "seven is a lucky number." The King and Queen's failure to invite Uglyane is made to seem most unforgivable by the narrator's disclosure that at the time, "Fairies were already growing somewhat scarce" (Perrault, p. 3), and it would have been appropriate, therefore, to include as many of their caste as possible in such an unrepeatable event. The eighth fairy's exclusion is indirectly justified by her iconographic association with the domain of witchcraft, since she is said to have left the christening "upon a broomstick" (p. 7). The uninvited fairy could also be seen to symbolize the murky side of the self which the rational — or supposedly rational — mind endeavors to anesthetize in order to proclaim its unproblematic mastery over the entire environment and the forces at work within it.

Edith Nesbit's tale *Melisande* lends a delightfully humorous twist to the classic topos, as the King and Queen refrain from inviting any of the fairies to the royal christening, and the fairies are shown to behave uncharacteristically by turning up after all and competing for election to the bad role. The very history and historiography of Faërie are potentially endangered by this transgression. As a result, the King is left with no choice but to sternly rebuke them as follows: "How can you be so unfairylike? Have none of you been to school? — have none of you studied the history of your own race? ... Listen to reason — or you'll be sorry afterwards. A fairy who breaks the tradition of fairy history goes out — you know she does — like the flame of a candle. And all traditions show that only *one* bad fairy is ever forgotten at a christening party and the good ones are always invited." The narrator draws the accident to a close with these sober and parodically elitist remarks: "Several of the better-class fairies ... murmured that there was something in what His Majesty said" (Nesbit, pp. 163–164).

Numerous fairies are doubtlessly keen on tomfoolery as an end in itself but no fewer members of their species are only too keen to reward mortals who do not shun their faculties. Their gifts might be material goods such as precious metal or gems but the greatest prize on offer is access to an alternative plane where transformative experiences akin to rites of passage or even a Dark Night of the Soul may be undergone and fresh wells of creativeness may be discovered. Children are far more likely to benefit from this gift than adults thanks to their more capacious perception of reality's confines. Seemingly small but memorable acts of kindness often glean the greatest rewards. Retaining one's honesty and equanimity in the face of potentially sinister spells is axial not only to the maintenance of one's sanity but also to the possibility of initiating a con-structive relationship with something that is in essence inscrutable and bound to remain so. A very special prize is held to be fairy ointment, whereby a human whose eyes have been affected by the potion in the course of a sojourn in fairyland remains capable of perceiving fairies in the mortal realm — a very mixed blessing indeed. Residence among fairies for a more or less protracted spell may also result, according to Conway, in the acqui-sition of "strong gifts of prophecy or healing." Although in rare cases, pre-ternatural endowments of this kind can be passed down from one generation to the next within a family over several decades, powers bestowed by the fairies do not normally "extend beyond a single person" (Conway, p. 6).

Fairies, it should never be forgotten, can also deploy their talents to assist humans in their work, and to protect the home in the capacity of guardians or housekeepers, as well as moral guides and dispensers of sweet dreams to infants in the nursery. Japanese fairy lore features an endearing version of the domestic fairy type with the figure of the *chin-chin kobakama*, an elflike creature eager to bless and watch over tidy households but quite unforgiving in the persecution of untidy housekeepers. (An easier Japanese fairy to befriend is the *kobito*, an ant-sized creature with a ten-dency to dwell in tiny holes in the proximity of mortal homes, supposedly drawn by the human victuals she is believed to cherish.) The gifts bestowed on humans by fairies are not always, therefore, concrete. They might even, in fact, come in the most elusive and intangible forms of all: language. Gifts of this kind consists of charms, incantations, proverbs, lullabies and poetry. According to Diane Purkiss, an especially intriguing instance of such a gift is the Queen Mab speech delivered by Mercutio in Shakespeare's *Romeo and Juliet.* Comparing this play with one of the Bard's most fairy-oriented worlds, *A Midsummer Night's Dream,* the critic points out that "Mab is as much Mercutio's servant as Puck is Oberon's" but whereas "Puck is the instrument Oberon uses to control the plot," Mercutio's fairy queen "is a thing of words only. Mercutio's control over Mab and her activities, his rhetorical prowess, mocks his inability to manage the plot's events," and therefore functions essentially as no more solid a reward that "a con-solatory fantasy" (Purkiss, p. 169).

Like the anime studied in Chapter 2: Alterity, the productions here covered potentially lend themselves to investigation along the lines supplied by all of the key modalities described in the book's opening segment. At the same time as they deliver visual and rhetorical constructs of transcultural resonance, the anime are also open to interpretation as culture-bound performances and as figurative explorations of specific sociohistorical circumstances. Thus, they are in a position to connect both with audiences drawn primarily to the fairy tale tradition's universal messages and with audiences inclined to engage with the medium of anime as a means of delving into distinctive cultural milieux. Moreover, the anime's ideological connotations render them valuable, at least in principle, as teaching materials imbued with educational, if not necessarily disciplinary, potentialities. As a result, diverse frames of reference can be brought to bear on these productions in the pursuit of theoretical analysis. Most vitally, their symbolic affiliations with the fairy tale tradition call attention to their standing as fecund receptacles of some age-old archetypes, thereby encouraging a sustained investigation of the stories' psychological dimension by recourse to an enduring collective reservoir of images and motifs. Virtually countless tales issuing from disparate cultures over an unquantifiably protracted period of time deal precisely with the sorts of themes, concerns and issues which we see foregrounded in the anime here under scrutiny, with the aid of the topos of the voyage as a simultaneously cohesive and catalyzing agency.

Concurrently, the anime's either explicit or allusive exposure of social and political injustice invites their reading as interrogative vehicles of great dramatic caliber. It is at this level that their yarns embark most overtly on a brave examination of the concept of cultural identity, eager to bring into focus the plight of the outsider and the disenfranchised within a tangle of power relations coursed by discrimination, dogmatism and prevarication. We are thereby enjoined to ponder the unfolding of history not merely with reference to official historiography but also — and more critically — through close attention to the pockets of society which sanctioned records so often neglect or occlude. Furthermore, in dramatizing an ongoing tension between the urban environment and the natural habitat, the chosen productions invite us to address the ineluctable involvement of nature itself in the establishment and perpetuation of particular cultural identities and corresponding structures of dominance, and in the shaping of specific instruments for the more or less arbitrary dissemination of their historical evolution. In voicing these broad cultural preoccupations, the anime studied in this chapter allusively hark back to the fabulous heritage delineated in this chapter's opening segment, thereby positing the voyage as a personal, societal and broadly historical phenomenon imbricated with metaphysical conundrums regarding the mystery of belonging. Hence, the domain of unfathomable unearthliness epitomized by Faërie works as a metaphor for the nexus of issues confronting the subject in his or her negotiations with self-anchoring to a particular cultural identity, and its underlying connections with specific power relations, historical accounts and the natural world' inexhaustible enigmas. The concept of belonging will be returned to later in this chapter. It is first necessary to emphasize that the theme of the journey takes on different guises and connotations in each of the anime productions here studied.

In *Kino's Journey* (dir. Ryuutarou Nakamura, 2003), a TV series that finds an apt transcultural correlative in Antoine De Saint-Exupery's *The Little Prince*, the protagonist journeys through a mystical realm figuratively redolent of Faërie in the sole company of the sentient and talking motorbike Hermes, visiting diverse lands and meeting a great variety of people, customs and beliefs in the process. *Kino's Journey* pays homage throughout its diegesis to the magical number featuring recurrently in the fairy tale tradition — three — to designate, among other classic tropes, the trials to be undergone by a character in the advancement of a specific quest, the prizes in store for the hero or heroine capable of overcoming a major obstacle, and the set of figures to be confronted in the search for self-fulfillment. The anime's protagonist indeed spends three days in each of the locations she discovers along the way, claiming that this amount of time is sufficient to familiarize her with the place's most salient aspects. Kino is well aware, however, that the true reason behind these brief sojourns is that she fears that were she to linger anywhere for longer, she might be tempted to settle down. The character, this suggests, is constitutionally averse to stable roots.

Her experiences, in this regard, capture the fairy tale tradition's quintessential spirit as the universe of endless flux and mutability. These attributes, it is worth recalling, are intimately linked up with the fluidity of the fairy physiognomy itself. Many attempts have been made to impart fairies with fixed traits: e.g., particular types of eyes, ears, limbs or auric shapes. Fundamentally, however, the creatures constitute pure — and hence amorphous — energy streams. As Brian Froud emphasizes, this constitution is precisely what enables the mystical process whereby, just as "out of chaos comes form" and "out of darkness comes light," so a fairy figure, as a distillation of the world's vital force, gradually "coalesces ... into pulsing, flowing light" (Froud). The fairy tale mood communicated by Kino's adventures emerges as a composite of contrasting affects, echoing the ubiquity, notable across the fairy tale tradition at large, of heady admixtures of terror and beauty, gloom and radiance, good and evil. The emotional tensions at the heart of the series echo this prismatic reality as Kino and Hermes repeatedly witness tantalizing juxtapositions of pleasure, brutality, loneliness, conviviality, illumination and nonsense at virtually every turn of the action in its dynamic and meditative moments alike. At the level of imagery, the fairy tale ambience is reinforced by the use of subtly anachronistic technologies seemingly at odds with the setting, whereby robots coexist with phonographs and bizarre aeronautical experiments. Alongside Hermes, a speaking dog and a moving land mass are also particularly memorable as quasi-magical entities.

Kino's Journey succinctly captures the fairy tale tradition's penchant for ambiguity by recourse to affective, atmospheric and symbolic contrasts. The portrayal of several of the lands visited by its protagonist as meeting points of light and darkness repeatedly foregrounds this proposition, and finds pithy formulation in the phrase chosen by the anime itself as an apt self-description: "The world is not beautiful, therefore it is." A somberly ironical parody of the Cartesian *Cogito* is thereby proposed. Tyranny, strife and the omnipresent phantom of loss are here posited as the dark facets of life without which benevolence, joy and companionship could never shine forth in all their radiant, albeit inevitably transient, glory. The motley crew met by Kino includes quite abominable creatures, such as the sadistic monarch who requires all visitors to his country to engage in violent tournaments for his entertainment, or resign themselves to the status of puppet-like slaves. Kino's own country of origin, the "Land of Adults," is reputed to thrive on a dubious ethical system whereby all children must be subjected to an operation intended to secure their transition to responsible adulthood upon reaching the age of twelve. A "perfect adult," in this world, is an individual who, having had the child within surgically removed, is willing to spend his or her entire life working away cheerfully without ever questioning the meaning of such a life, let alone whether it allows for any genuine happiness.

When the protagonist, inspired by the words of a foreign traveler to her country, asks her parents if there are any ways she might grow up without undergoing the crucial operation, the couple fiercely turn against her and the whole town, prodded by a ruthless "inspector," rapidly resolves her to slaughter Kino in public. The girl's father himself is accorded the honor to "dispose" of such "a waste of a girl" and thus make atonement for his connection with an obvious "failure." No less puzzling, in the eyes of the rigidly programmed "Adults," is the traveler's self-sacrifice, which they simply consider "against common sense," as he interposes his body between the girl and her bloodthirsty father and is fatally penetrated by his butcher's cleaver. This sinister aspect of the series echoes the fairy tale tradition's recurrent dramatization of the victimization of the young in the service of regimenting agendas. Conversely, the sequences in which the protagonist — who renames herself Kino after the visitor to whom she owes her life and freedom — escapes with Hermes and witnesses for the first time the beauty of the outside world communicate a pure sense of elation akin to the feeling which fairy tales devoted to the celebration of an unfettered imagination have a unique power to convey. The fairy tale tradition itself features several instances of brutal and selfish parents. In some versions of the *Cinderella* matrix, for example, the heroine's tormentor is her own biological mother. In other variants, Cinderella is persecuted by the father instead as the defenseless object of an obsessive incestuous infatuation.

Another country seemingly hell-bent on the erosion of imaginative faculties — and hence obliquely redolent of fairy tales disfigured so as to enforce disciplinary measures — appears to be occupied entirely by servile machinery. Likewise iniquitous is the land which prides itself on being a peaceful country while it is, in fact, surreptitiously training for war. These spaces of negativity, wherein the fairy tale tradition's darker perspectives on life and humanity find figurative articulation, coexist with positive realities at all times. Among the latter, Kino experiences the "Land of Wizards," a society whose strict agricultural priorities would seem to permit little leeway for the imagination but interstitially harbors ideals and aspirations that far exceed its official agenda — as evinced by the character of Nimya and her dream of constructing a flying machine, the ultimate emblem of freedom and vitality. Most remarkable, among the nations ostensibly subject to despotic laws and yet capable of creative transgressiveness, is the "Land of Books." In this country, an immense library, worthy of J. L. Borges' or Umberto Eco's bookish visions, is presumed to include all the volumes in the world but only allows those deemed educative and inoffensive — in other words, normative and supportive of the status quo — to be displayed, while keeping all questionable materials safely locked away. Kino discovers somewhat inadvertently that beneath the carefully monitored veneer of this library lurks an underground resistance determined to publish its own provocative books at any price. Through these characters, the anime enjoins us to contemplate a universe made entirely of both actual and hypothetical texts in which the dividing line between reality and fantasy is virtually irrelevant, and the words on the page of a book — or indeed in the dark recesses of a writer's psyche — are no less palpable than concrete objects. Any myth erected on the idea of a singular, reliable world is thus exploded, and the cosmos in its entirety configured in the hypertextual image of myriad alternate hypotheses.

Kino's Journey recalls most vividly the fairy tale tradition's distinctive atmosphere in its handling of the drama's temporal dimension. Its protagonist's voyage evidently lacks any obvious destination in the conventionally accepted sense of that term, and even its point of origin is understated insofar as the chain of events leading to the heroine's adoption of the name "Kino" and precipitous flight from her home town are only disclosed when the series is well under way. Thus, even though the individual adventures experienced by Kino and Hermes are situated within a time frame of sorts, the cumulative impression they evoke is one of timelessness. In this regard, the series parallels a major aspect of the Faërie realm. Indeed, as Katharine Briggs maintains, while there is a widespread "belief that time in Fairyland passes much more quickly than among mortals," it would be far more accurate to argue that "it can hardly be said to pass at all" and that "the inhabitants partake of the nature of immortality" (Briggs, p. 123). Conway, relatedly, argues that fairies function within "an entirely different time from that of the physical world," to the point that they could be said not to "operate within *any* conception of time, as we know it" (Conway, p. 6).

Furthermore, in *Kino's Journey* as in the sphere of Faërie, the perceived passage of time exhibits quite idiosyncratic rhythms, since a single day sometimes feels so densely packed with events as to carry the weight of an entire week or even a month, while just a few minutes of wordless reflection may seem to stretch on for hours. Given the prominence accorded to the natural environment by *Kino's Journey*'s diegesis, it is also appropriate to recall that the timelessness of Faërie is bound up in various traditions with the spiritual essence of the land. It is quite common, for example, for "agricultural fairies" to be associated with the souls of the departed. In this perspective, the cyclical patterns according to which the land undergoes periodic phases of death and rebirth could be seen as timeless processes since, even though they are situated within a chartable calendar, they transcend time by virtue of their everlasting recurrence. The spirits that "supervise the growth of seed" emblematize this phenomenon in fairy form (p. 126).

While the notion of the voyage finds overt application in *Kino's Journey*, in *The Story of Saiunkoku* (TV series; dir. Jun Shishido, 2006–2007), it acquires essentially figurative, rather than literal, formulation. The anime chronicles an extensive saga centered on the character of Shuurei Hong, the descendant of an aristocratic line relegated by adversity to a relatively humble place in the strict hierarchy of the imaginary realm of Saiunkoku. Daughter of an imperial librarian accorded reverence and prestige but scarce material remuneration, the heroine herself is employed as a teacher at a temple school and endeavors to eke out a living by also taking on occasional jobs in her free time. Shuurei's true ambition, however, is to pass the necessary tests and assume a post in government: a career option severely forbidden to a female citizen. The protagonist's lifestyle undergoes drastic reorientation as the Emperor's Grand Advisor invites Shuurei to join the imperial household for a period of six months in the capacity of consort to the new ruler, Ryuuki, in order to teach the youth the skills expected of a conscientious and insightful Emperor.

The relationship between Shuurei and Ryuuki hence becomes the drama's focal concern, laboriously developing amid innumerable courtly intrigues and machinations that require the heroine to unleash all her diplomatic talent in order to achieve a balance of private and national priorities. The topos of the journey is accordingly handled at several levels simultaneously. The descent down the rungs of Saiunkoku's stringently stratified system suffered by Shuurei's family and the girl's own personal ascent to a prestigious political position encapsulate the social dimension of the theme by focusing on hierarchical transitions that impact on the politics of class and gender alike. Both of those figurative journeys reflect long-standing facets of the fairy tale tradition insofar as the figure of the disadvantaged or even destitute hero or heroine capable of transcending his or her status, and attendant limitations, undoubtedly constitutes a mainstay of that discourse across many cultures.

As the private dimension of the drama unfolds, the heroine discovers that the man she is supposed to train, so as to stoke his hitherto tepid interest in courtly matters and get him actively involved in governance, is not the pampered and debauched youth he is reputed to be but a gentle and timid youth. At the same time, the new Emperor becomes incrementally attached to his advisor in amorous, rather than entirely political, terms. Thus, even though Shuurei pursues her aspirations with all the energy, wit and pluck one would expect of the most ambitious fairy tale protagonist, she cannot blind herself to the insistence of her pupil's advances. However, despite the emphasis placed by he plot over the anime's two seasons on the evolving love story at its core, *The Story of Saiunkoku* does not simply embrace the fairy tale tradition in order to dramatize an individual voyage of emotional fulfillment. In fact, Shuurei's tenacious dedication to her political role, which remains unabated even as she becomes the target of potentially lethal Machiavellian ploys, draws the drama into the public sphere with uncompromising lucidity. At this level, the anime can be seen to join hands with the fairy tale tradition to articulate not so much a private experience as a broadly cultural — and often serpentine — pilgrimage of strategic and intellectual growth. Relatedly, although some of the earlier episodes convey an inordinately utopian take on politics, intimating that benevolence and kindness are Saiunkoku's common denominator across all ranks and generations, as the saga advances, the darkness and intricacy of the political maneuverings and attempted assassinations which punctuate the plot become increasingly evident, while several characters turn out to harbor secret identities, connections and intentions of murky provenance.

If the romantic aspect of the anime captures the fairy tale tradition's idealistic and hopeful perspective, the drama's emphasis on the nefarious scheming by which Shuurei is persistently surrounded — as she juggles personal and collective interests of often conflicting import — trenchantly reminds us that fairyland is not an undilutedly fair and lighthearted domain. Even its reputation as an oneiric reality does not render it dreamy for it is also, in fact, unrelentingly entangled with the darkest of nightmares and the most intractable of burdens. A related variation on the topos of the voyage thrown into relief by the anime pertains to the educational value of journeying as an awakening of the intellect and the senses rather than a purely physical activity. Both Shuurei's role as a mentor and her father's commitment to his bookish profession are treated in a fashion that authentically honors the root of the word "education," and accordingly underlines its value as a "leading out" process meant to facilitate a person's speculative journey into hitherto unforeseen territory. The anime thus echoes the fairy tale tradition's own pedagogical thrust as a discourse capable of encouraging exposure and openness to a beyond that simultaneously throws into embarrassing relief our limitations as humans in startling and unsettling ways, and gestures toward unexpected opportunities for self-enhancement through an unprejudiced expansion of our habitual purview. Ultimately, this amounts to a preparedness to perceive the world around us — and *all* of it — as animate: a proclivity embedded in human existence since the dawn of time but too often allowed to lay dormant.

On the visual plane, the show's contrasting connotations are economically conveyed by its pervasive use of pink as the key color in the depiction of the characters' costumes, of palaces and chambers, and of the natural habitat itself. This hue can be automatically associated with love, innocence, softness and femininity. In this respect, it evokes the notion of Faërie as an eminently romantic world — a concept promulgated by varyingly edulcorated adaptations of originally darker and scarier fairy tales, and recently epitomized by the Disney Princess franchise, a quintessentially girly enterprise wherein pink and romantic dreaminess are treated as interchangeable ideas. This interpretation of the color so central to *The Story of Saiunkoku* tallies, to a considerable degree, with its private dimension. Nevertheless, pink is also, at a more esoteric level of symbolism enshrined in several traditions, emblematic of rebirth, and hence functions as an apposite chromatic correlative for the project of political rejuvenation to which Shuurei is devoted. In some cultures, moreover, pink is virtually indisseverable from purple, a hue whose connotations are by and large more somber and graver, and therefore partakes of symbolic connections with the images of mist and haze or even, in some instances, with death. Thus, the fairy tale tradition's duplicitous nature as a discourse implicated with life and death in identical proportions is vividly captured.

The anime's disinclination to allow its yarn to unfold univocally in the direction of a private romance so as to retain a mature focus on collective affairs is fully corroborated by its second season's open-ended finale. Even though Ryuuki loves Shuurei deeply and wishes she would never leave his side, he honors her desire to go on deploying her diplomatic and organizational skills for the general good, which inevitably entails protracted periods of absence from the court, and is willing to wait — even "forever" if necessary. By foregrounding the inconclusiveness of its sentimental strand, *The Story of Saiunkoku* obliquely intimates that a fate of comparable incompleteness is also in store for the large-scale political tasks in which the heroine is embroiled. In the anime's distinctive appropriation of the fairy tale tradition, romance and history alike are posited as instances of forever unfinished business. Their chronicling, likewise, is a process of incessant becoming.

The movie *Tokyo's Godfathers* (dir. Satoshi Kon, 2003), like *Kino's Journey*, handles the concept of the voyage in a fairly literal manner insofar as it actually charts the physical pilgrimage across the urban map of its key personae, yet also seeks to underscore its allegorical implications by prioritizing the characters' inner odysseys over mere kinesis. The anime follows the bittersweet ordeals of three Tokyo vagrants — the gruff heavy drinker Gin, the melodramatically sensitive drag queen Hana and the morose teenage runaway Miyuki — as they chance upon an infant amid the garbage and hence strive to locate the abandoned creature's parents. The three protagonists' experiences unfold in a plot that pays tribute to the fairy tale tradition with unquestionable enthusiasm, allowing maximum leeway for coincidences (both beneficial and detrimental to the quest), potentially irreversible catastrophes, revelations and epiphanic encounters. In the process, the film offers one of the most faithful transpositions of the fairy tale spirit to the anime screen ever witnessed — without, notably, being a literal adaptation of a preexisting narrative — and very possibly one of the purest distillations of that spirit in twenty-first-century cinema at large.

No less importantly, the movie captures a defining attribute of the fairy tale tradition's calendar: the almost unmatched significance it accords to Christmas Eve, which is precisely the anime's temporal setting. This particular day and especially the dark hours pressing toward the threshold of midnight have been associated, in countless cultures and for many centuries, with the mystical, the otherworldly and the very soul of the fairy tale tradition. They thus occupy a privileged place in the communal imaginary of even a country which, like Japan, only hosts a minute proportion of Christians within its population. Hence, it is most apposite as the setting for adventures in which the mundane and the drab unexpectedly collude with hopeful magic. As Marriott observes, the figure of Father Christmas and its variants, which have come to epitomize the spirit of Christmas virtually all over the world, are at root fairy characters and "proof that even the most cynical of us welcome fairies into the heart of the home at certain times of year" (Marriott, p. 142).

In *Someday's Dreamers: Summer Skies* (TV series; dir. Osamu Kobayashi, 2008), the literal and the figurative dimensions of the topos of the voyage seamlessly interlace to yield a series that partakes from start to finish of the fairy tale tradition's penchant for unique blends of realism and fantasy. On the cinematographical plane, this propensity is sustained by director Kobayashi's distinctive signature — and, most pointedly, by his tendency to combine intensely photorealistic settings with stylized character designs that highlight their origins in hand-drawn sketches and manga. Analogous aesthetic preferences can be witnessed in Kobayashi's *Paradise Kiss*, an anime examined in the context of Chapter 4. The employment of actors that lack any obviously outstanding somatic attributes enables the drama to focus on their affective and intellectual traits, and thereby bring out their individuality with equal emphasis on talents and eccentricities. At the same time, individual characteristics are dialectically juxtaposed within an interactive network of aspirations and responsibilities. The literal journey dramatized by the show pivots on Sora Suzuki's relocation to Tokyo from the rural village of Biei, Hokkaido. This is occasioned by the girl's recruitment as a trainee mage, requiring her to hone her already highly developed supernatural powers by attending specialist classes and residing with a mentor responsible for supervising her progress by accompanying her on various missions, undertaken at the behest of clients in need of magical assistance.

The metaphorical journey, unfolding in tandem with the literal one, registers Sora's development as both a magician and a regular adolescent by concentrating on her relationships with teachers and peers — and, most significantly, with fellow student Gouta Midorikawa. A rebellious youth with an unbridled passion for surfing, Gouta has been brought up in total oblivion of his magical blood, inherited from the paternal line, and deeply resents the schooling to which his fate has consigned him. When evaluated in terms of the fairy tale tradition's logic, the culmination of Sora's pilgrimage lends itself to contrasting interpretations. On the one hand, it could be said to depart with uncompromising starkness from the happy ending formula with which fairy tales have become practically coterminous in the Western entertainment industry, especially courtesy of Disney. On the other hand, it is readable as a positive celebration of the coalescence of human reality and Faërie. Sora may not fulfill her dreams in the ordinary world but is endowed by her powers — not only, it must be stressed, as a mage but also as an imaginative and generous human girl — to project a vision in which both her own and her loved ones' desires reach fruition, albeit fleetingly.

The series simultaneously colludes with the fairy tale tradition in its articulation of several of its embedded incidents as capsulated fairy tales in their own right. A case in point is the installment in which Sora and her friends assist a little girl afflicted by a Cinderella-inspired fantasy, and therefore inclined toward self-dramatization as an abused orphan in the shackles of an evil stepmother and her daughters when she is actually the hyperimaginative issue of two loving and playful parents. Also memorable, as a miniature fairy tale within the fairy tale, so to speak, is the episode where the Bureau of Magic is asked to send its current trainees to a beach on which hundreds of dolphins have run aground and face a painful death. The young magicians deploy their talents to visualize water bubbles or folds around each of the doomed creatures, and thus lift the victims off the shore's shallow waters to help them regain the open ocean. Even Gouta, who has thus far been utterly powerless to conjure up any wizardly strength, delivers a spectacular feat of magic thanks to Sora's ability to awaken his latent capacities. The entire sequence oozes with fairy tale sublimity as nature's own energies alternately challenge and support the magicians' noble efforts.

The world in which the anime is set parallels the reality traditionally ideated by fairy tales over the centuries in the delineation of a social system which, though well-disposed toward magic and its practitioners, abides by strict rules and codes of conduct. The fairy tale tradition makes it incontrovertibly clear that its realms, however fabulous they may seem, are informed by internally coherent laws and attendant sets of obligations and prohibitions. The anime's society, analogously, accommodates its mages within a rigorous structure designed to demarcate lawful and illicit uses of magical abilities, ensure the conscientious deployment of those powers in public and promote the performance of tasks likely to benefit all human petitioners. Magicians, in this perspective, are seen to play roles akin to those accorded to doctors, firefighters and social workers in the non-magical domain. In addition, *Someday's Dreamers: Summer Skies* shares with the fairy tale tradition — and indeed with substantial pockets of fairy lore generally — the tendency to foreground the importance of interaction. Fairy tale characters are typically constellated as dialectically interrelated groups, the significance of each individual persona depending vitally on its complementary or oppositional standing vis-à-vis other members of the cluster. In the series, all of the key figures appear to develop as a result of affective and mental journeys that require them to interact with others. Gouta's evolution is a primary instance of this trend since it is through his relationship with Sora, who selflessly operates as a mediator or catalyst enabling the boy to connect with his latent magical powers that he is able to overcome the impasse in which resentment and low self-esteem have hitherto kept him locked. Kuroda, one of Sora and Gouta's fellow trainees, likewise learns through interaction with his peers the humility to come to terms with the possibility of failure as an acceptable component of experience for ordinary humans and magicians alike.

The interactive dimension so persistently highlighted by *Someday's Dreamers: Summer Skies* corroborates Max Lüthi's speculations on the universally representative qualities held by many classic motifs enshrined in the fairy tale tradition. According to this illustrious scholar, "the fairy tale is not concerned with individual destinies. Nor is it the unique process of maturation that is reflected in the fairy tale. The story of Sleeping Beauty," for instance, "is more than an imaginatively stylized love story portraying the withdrawal of a girl and the breaking of the spell through the young lover. One instinctively conceives of the princess as an image for the human spirit: the story portrays the endowment, peril, paralysis, and redemption not just of one girl, but of all mankind" (Lüthi 1976, p. 24). Likewise, the anime could be said to utilize both Sora's personal rite of passage, culminating in an imaginative appropriation of an otherwise bleak destiny, and Gouta's epiphanic discovery of hitherto unsuspected powers as emblematic tropes, capable of capturing universal human experiences and spiritual strivings. In the series, as in the example provided by Lüthi with reference to traditional lore, it is possible to intuit quite spontaneously the collective significance of the characters' maturation processes even prior to methodical reflection or close analysis.

All of the anime discussed in the preceding paragraphs mirror the lore-encrusted belief systems promulgated by the fairy tale tradition in the dramatization of their respective protagonists' encounters — both intentional and accidental — with myriad characters, each of whom appears endowed with distinctive qualities and quirks. In the process, the anime bring into play an astounding variety of fairy figures from all of the general categories outlined in this book's first chapter. Both *Kino's Journey* and *Someday's Dreamers: Summer Skies* metaphorically posit the numerous personae met by their heroines in the course of their literal or psychological peregrinations as variations on the fundamental fairy type, taking care to emphasize the presence of both positive and negative traits across the fairy species as a whole and within each and every one of its members. Accordingly, the two series propose that the presence of providential tendencies in a figure's personality does not automatically preclude the simultaneous occurrence within the same character of demonic or forbidding tendencies, even though these may be cloaked by a patina of endearing cuteness.

The heroine herself in *The Story of Saiunkoku* stands out as a dynamic conflation of the four principal fairy typologies described in the opening chapter. She operates as a providential agent by contributing actively and selflessly to the shaping of an unthinkably intricate cultural milieu, while also functioning as a demonic force in both senses of the term: i.e., as a disruptive spirit whose powers verge on the diabolical and, in keeping with the meaning of the Greek root *"daemon,"* whence the word derives, as a tutelary spirit or moral guide. On the one hand, she unsettles the sociopolitical system in which she inserts herself by contravening age-old conventions that categorically exclude all members of her gender and social class from political life. On the other hand, she comes to embody that system's very soul as a motivating and inspirational energy without which neither cultural stability nor progress would be achievable. The anime's romantic dimension allows for the heroine's portrayal as handsome and cutely captivating. At the same time, however, the show's more realistic take on history deploys the character as a means of reflecting on a whole culture's unresolved tensions and shaky grasp of its goals, thus investing her with graver connotations.

The very title of *Tokyo Godfathers* gives us a pointer to the fairy typology invoked by Kon's movie. This clue is elaborated by the protagonists' assumption of the role of protective guardians and successful accomplishment of their self-appointed duty. Even though their credentials would hardly seem to qualify them for such a noble and onerous commitment, they actually pull out a stellar performance exuding compassion, humor and wisdom in equal proportions. In this respect, these personae could be said to provide contemporary variations on the time-honored figure of the fairy godmother. A relatively late development in the history of the fairy tale tradition, this character type first surfaced in the context of the French salon at the behest of ladies who, like the fairy godmother herself, were normally mature and experienced women with a vast reservoir of nous at their disposal, and were therefore in a position to offer shrewd and cogent advice — if not exactly splendid carriages and gem-encrusted ball gowns — to younger women in their company. Moreover, the figure of the fairy godmother is associated with the Celtic "Triple Matres" (goddesses associated with fertility and childbirth), who provide a cogent antecedent for Kon's own trio while augmenting the significance of the number three in the fairy tale tradition in general.

The most famous fairy godmother is undoubtedly the character immortalized by Perrault in *Cinderella*. In the Grimms' version of the story, titled *Ashenputtel*, the part of the fairy godmother is played by vindictive magical birds. The very fairiness of Kon's unorthodox fairy godmothers is so exquisitely understated throughout the movie as to bring to mind a delicious detail from Perrault's version of *Cinderella* which has often gone regrettably unheeded. This consists of the magical lady's casual and likewise unostentatious self-introduction: "'I am your *Godmother*, you must know, and in younger days your mother and I were very dear friends.' She omitted, perhaps purposely, to add that she was a fairy" (Perrault, p. 77).

Marina Warner has underscored the etymological and anthropological connection between the godmother figure and the ideas of gossip and storytelling. Taking as a point of reference the Italian words *compadre* and *comare* or *commare*, the critic observes that "originally" these designated "co-father or co-mother" but while "the masculine variant retained its meaning of godfather (Marlon Brando continued the custom in the film)," the "feminine version ... shifted to refer to a midwife." Over time, the word incurred further semantic metamorphosis and eventually became coterminous, as it indeed is in contemporary Italy, with "a gossip or crony, one of the grackle women dressed in black who can still be seen sitting out in the street passing the time of day with her friends in the traditional daily *chiacchiera* or gossip.... In French, *commère* followed the same downward path: originally a godmother, it too came to mean a gossip-monger, a telltale" (Warner 1995, p. 33). These historical observations are of great significance to the evolution of the fairy tale tradition insofar as they throw into relief the existence of an intimate connection between that discourse and the role specifically played by particular female types in its perpetuation. Women such as the *comare* are inscribed in a much broader transcultural network that can be regarded as largely responsible for the creation and dissemination of the sorts of narratives we have come to think of as fairy tales.

This web, as demonstrated by Warner with equal doses of punctiliousness and verve, can be traced back to the figure of "the prophesying enchantress" immortalized by "the tradition of the Sibyls," and pursued over history from characters such as "the jolly old beldame" and "Mother Goose," or "the archetypal crone by the hearth," to the present-day — "from the élite *salonnière* in the old régime to Angela Carter in our time" (p. xx). Italo Calvino has also emphasized the cardinal role played by women in the dissemination of fairy tales over time in the context of his discussion of the Grimms' output, observing that "the fairy tales the Grimms were writing down were those told to kids by German mamas and grandmas which they, in turn, had learnt from their own mamas and grandmas" (Calvino 1988, p. 83). The relevance of these reflections to *Tokyo Godfathers* and its adaptation of the fairy tale figure of the fairy godmother is multifaceted. Firstly, the film reactivates metaphorically the tradition centered on the *comare* and *commère* types by positing as central to the articulation of its story a group of people who, like those women, would most likely be perceived by many members of their societies as useless or parasitical. Secondly, *Tokyo Godfathers* endows its three protagonists with a special kind of eloquence: a collaborative product of the distinctive verbal proclivities each of them brings to bear on the drama and specifically on its dialogue. Just as not all of the yattering cronies in black normally evince the same degree of loquaciousness or identical narrative competences and rhetorical tropes, so the anime's main personae are defined by distinct registers and styles — with Hana as the seemingly unstoppable logomaniac, Miyuki as the laconic rebel, and Gin as the disenchanted failure who does not seem willing to trust language any more than he trusts anything human but gradually discloses a penchant for hermetically touching lyricism. Thirdly, the movie's key characters tell their story through a journey across their city, thus echoing the voyage chronicled by the cultural development of the storytelling figure, as described above.

At the same time, *Tokyo Godfathers* also foregrounds throughout its diegesis the central part played by the topos of the family — and the related issue of familial discord and neglect — within the fairy tale tradition at large. According to Maria Tatar, so prominent are "family conflicts and violence" in classic fairy tales that contemporary readers tend to respond more readily to this feature of the art form than to "enchanting rescues and romances." As a result, the critic goes on to propose, "when we read 'Rumpelstiltskin,' we are more fascinated by the grotesque gnome who dances around a fire than by the wedding of the miller's daughter to a king with an appetite for gold.... And the perfect fit between the glass slipper and Cinderella's foot is hardly as stirring as the efforts of the stepsisters to make the slipper fit by cutting off their toes and heels" (Tatar, p. xix).

The relationship between traditional storytellers and dynamism requires some attention at this juncture. It is vital to recognize, given this chapter's thematic emphasis, that neither Sibyls nor crones by the fire nor gossiping grannies would appear capable of moving — let alone voyaging — when one considers their customary confinement to very limited spaces, and attendant emphasis on sedentariness as one of their fundamental attributes. As to the places where many of the stories we still read and tell today came into being in the context of seventeenth-century France, these were known as *ruelles* (literally, "alleys"). A word used to designate the kind of venue in which aristocratic ladies would gather to swap and discuss both actual and fictitious tales, *ruelle* was originally the term adopted by the Marquise de Rambouillet (1588–1665) to define "the space between her bed and the wall" (Warner 1995, p. 50) in the chamber where she would receive her female guests and coordinate the conversation from "her show bed" (p. 49). *Ruelles*, most importantly, were venues "established by noblewomen in the image of the humbler, more chaotic gathering, the gossiping" (p. 50). Despite their markedly stationary existence, all of these storytelling women partake of the developmental trajectory charted by Warner as pivotal stages in its unfolding.

Thus, in enthroning the journey topos as axial to its diegesis, *Tokyo Godfathers* elliptically pays homage to the hidden history of the fairy tale tradition as the voyage of narration per se. The close connection between speech and fairy tales highlighted by these notions is further reinforced by the frequent deployment of spoken language as an important narrative motif to connote contrasting ethical characteristics and related abilities. This proposition is eloquently confirmed by Perrault's *The Fairy*, here discussed in Chapter 2. It is also worth noting, in this respect, that even though at the end of Perrault's *Little Red Riding Hood* the heroine is devoured by the wolf (Perrault, p. 31), whereas the Grimms allow her to survive courtesy of a hunter (Grimm 2000, pp. 118–119), both versions present the villain as smooth-tongued and seems to identify a significant proportion of the character's iniquity precisely with his refined speech. The extent to which speechlessness, conversely, is practically synonymous with total disempowerment is horrifically conveyed by the most famous Western fairy tale centered on a water creature: Andersen's *The Little Mermaid*.

Returning to the godmother figure as immortalized by the fairy tale tradition, it is vital to recognize that this character is not always a fairy dispensing special powers and gifts to a deserving but vulnerable human. In fact, there are also numerous instances of human godmothers who are more or less forcibly enlisted by fairies to participate in their baptismal ceremonies, in much the same way as human midwives are often spirited away to Faërie to deliver the Good Folk's babies. A delicious adaptation of this theme is offered by a story contained in *Round About Our Coal Fire*, where a gentlewoman sojourning with her spouse at a country inn is temporarily abducted by the local fairies to act as the godmother of a newborn fairy child and is rewarded for her services with a large diamond ring (cited in Briggs, pp. 133–134). The tale discreetly hints at the possibility that the lady's nocturnal escapade might have consisted of a far more human and carnal matter than she would have her husband believe when he inquires about the splendid jewel's provenance. The eighteenth-century narrative thus parallels *Tokyo Godfathers* in harnessing an element of fairy lore to a tastefully amusing allusion to the vagaries of human sexuality — a topic which the film itself frequently touches upon even though it only engages with it in an overt fashion in the treatment of its flamboyant transvestite.

Much of the time, the fairy and the human dimensions remain radically alien to each other and this typically results in mutual suspicion and fear. Indeed, there are abundant indications throughout the fairy tale tradition that the Fair Folk sees human beings themselves as spooky and mysterious, and that mortals and fairies alike will not hesitate to loose their hounds on members of the other race whom they happen to perceive as menacing. There are, however, occasions in which those dimensions coalesce, though only for the briefest of moments. Traditional stories featuring mortal godmothers provisionally relocated to the fairy world dramatize precisely such a fleeting encounter between two otherwise incommensurate reality levels. *Tokyo Godfathers* echoes that tradition, intimating that it is through the temporary assumption of their quasi-providential role as godparents that the three outcasts come into contact with the sphere of ordinary, well-adjusted and law-abiding citizens and indeed succeed, ironically, in reestablishing its fractured equilibrium.

Another interesting instance of the ephemeral collusion of the human and fairy domains consists of funerals. Fairies are reputed to appear at human interments and memorials as mourners inspired by genuine feelings of compassion and sorrow, and to exhibit, on such occasions, an appropriately cheerless mien and reserved conduct. An analogously respectful attitude often characterizes fairies' responses to the sight of dead animals. The painting "Who Killed Cock Robin?" by John Anster Fitzgerald (1932–1906) touchingly exemplifies this proposition. Although this artist's works frequently show fairies in the act of attacking nests or even tormenting birds with sadistic glee, pictures like "Who Killed Cock Robin?" portray fairies as kindly and caring types concerned with the welfare of all wildlife. As Iain Zaczek observes, the painting exudes "an unmistakable sense of grieving" and "the two main figures on the right," in particular, "resemble a couple comforting each other by a graveside" (Zaczek, p. 45). Other moving instances of fairies' charitable conduct toward woodland creatures are the paintings in which Fitzgerald portrays the Little People either tending to a wounded animal (such as a squirrel or a fawn) or involving a rabbit in their frolics as a guest of honor.

Although many traditions posit fairies as immortal beings, accounts of fairy funerals are frequent and transculturally prolific. These occasions provide further opportunities for transient cross-world encounters whenever ordinary mortals happen to witness their performance. While the behavior evinced by fairies in the presence of human mourning is characteristically solemn, fairy funerals themselves are often described as festive affairs. A classic account of a fairy funeral is supplied by William Blake (1757–1827), who claims to have observed such an event in his own garden and to have been enraptured by the vision of "a procession of creatures the size and colour of green and grey grasshoppers, bearing a body laid out on a rose-leaf, which they buried with songs, and then disappeared" (cited in Zaczek, p. 57). According to Zaczek, most folkloric reports presumed to depict fairy funerals share particular traits: "the human witness was drawn to the event by the sound of a muffled bell; the body was uncovered and resembled a tiny, wax doll; and the cortège passed through a sacred place, whether a pagan site, such a stone circle, or a churchyard. Sometimes the episode came with a warning. When the human peered closely he noticed that the corpse bore a miniature version of his own face" (Zakzek, p. 57).

The anime here examined present us with a stunning variety of spaces, ranging from lyrically graceful landscapes that chronicle the ever-rolling seasonal cycle with memorable iconographic incisiveness to stately venues and fetid slums, from visions of metropolitan glitz to provincial workaday settings with incontrovertibly prosaic attributes and functions. The atmosphere of spatial fecundity supplied by the shows does not emanate from their locations per se but rather from the speculative dimension wherein nature and art coalesce into unexpected metaphors: the alternately inimical and fair, yet always baffling, beyond whence the fairy spirit itself flows. The shows thus validate Yi-Fu Tuan's contention that as a "material environment" of an identifiable shape, "geographical place" is at once "natural" and "artifactual." It is especially notable, in this context, that "artworks such as a painting, photograph, poem, story, movie, dance, or musical composition," according to Tuan, "can also be a place" — a context by which humans may be "nurtured" in much the same way as they are "nurtured by the towns and cities and landscapes we live in or visit" (Tuan, p. 3). The concept of nurture is critical to the subject in hand insofar as it underscores the ceaselessly mutating role played by space in the molding of our minds and our bodies, and hence reminds us — in full consonance with the lessons inherent in the fairy tale tradition across the globe — that the "self ... is not fixed" (p. 4). At the same time, the places visited by Kino, Shuurei, Sora and the Tokyo bums proclaim their own inherent mobility by communicating a potent sense of aliveness. Such spaces have their own physiology, pulse, lifeblood, and distinctive biorhythms. They may come across as shelters, prisons or mazes, and concurrently operate as friends, enemies or mere observers but are never totally insensible of human ordeals.

It is on this philosophical plane that the anime bring into dramatic prominence the aforementioned issue of belonging. All of the chosen shows present the hypothetical spaces in which their protagonists' adventures unfold as nurturing loci in which the individual is forever susceptible to metamorphosis and dislocation. The central actors, specifically, are concurrently grounded in a particular social milieu and in a chain of relationships, both of which are kaleidoscopically varied to match the character's own fluidity and rootlessness as a creature in perpetual transit between one encounter and the next. As a corollary of this existential duality, which Tuan would describe as a "bipolar tug" (p. 7), the anime's protagonists perceive simultaneously "the call of open space" and "the call of home" (p. 8). Much as they need the concept of home as a stable point of reference, they are well aware that home is unlikely ever to provide an insulated cocoon into which they may conclusively shelter but rather the springboard to a potentially endless series of further forays into the unpredictable *elsewhere*. This tension enables the protagonists to maintain a delicate equilibrium of kinesis and stasis, calm and audacity, and incrementally acquire both consistency and resolve while preserving a salutary openness to the prospect of further development. In this regard, their experiences resonantly encapsulate Tuan's suggestion that "rootedness ... sets the self into a mold too soon," while "Mobility carried to excess ... makes it difficult, if not impossible, for a strong sense of self to jell. A self that is coherent and firm, yet capable of growth, would seem to call for an alternation of stillness and motion, stability and change" (p. 4).

In articulating their distinctive interpretations of the concept of the journey, and of related notions of space and belonging, the shows emphasize the importance of a commodious world picture as the primary precondition of constructive growth. This same message is pivotal to the fairy tale tradition itself, insofar as countless narratives seek to demonstrate that for any fruitful interaction between Faërie and the mortal world to occur, humans must be favorably disposed to the possibility of unexpected encounters capable of altering and reorientating their perspectives in potentially radical ways. The possible journey here at stake is essentially an experience of emotional and psychological metamorphosis. It is hence vital to remember, in this context, that the concept of transformation has often been described as the fairy tale's most distinctive characteristic — both as a theme able to animate its adventures by means of surprise, shock or revelation, and as a storytelling mechanism ideally suited to trigger dramatic plot developments and redefinitions.

Jack Zipes has extended the centrality of the idea of transformation from the thematic and narrative planes to the historical dimension to suggest that it is also pivotal to the development of the form and, more specifically, responsible for its endurance over the centuries. "The notion of miraculous transformation," Zipes maintains, "is key to understanding most of the traditional fairy tales that have stuck in us and with us. Just as we as a species have mutated, often in wondrous ways, so has the oral folk tale transformed itself and been transformed as literary fairy tale to assist us in coming to terms with the absurdity and banality of everyday life" (Zipes 2006, p. xii). At the same time, the processes of gradual transformation undergone by the fairy tale likewise sustain the phenomenon of "cultural transmission" (p. xiii) as theorized by Luigi Cavalli-Sforza — i.e., as "mutation, or transformation that brings about the creation of a new idea" (Cavalli-Sforza, p. 68). Zipes avers that by reflecting on the cultural developments through which the fairy tale has survived in ever-changing guises, we can actually appreciate how "the literary fairy tale has evolved from the stories of the oral tradition, piece by piece in a process of incremental adaptation," whereby "special forms of telling" have come into being "as species" (Zipes 2006, p. 3). Although it can hardly be denied that "Oral tales ... are thousands of years old and it is impossible to date and explain how they were generated," there is plenty of reliable evidence to support the contention that "they must have become vital for adapting to the environment and changes in the environment as soon as humans began to communicate through language. ... those that continued to have cultural significance were 'imitated' and passed on.... Bits and pieces, what we may call motifs, characters, topoi, plots, and images, were carried on and retold.... Gradually, as tales were used to serve specific functions in court entertainment, homes, and taverns, on public squares, fields, and work places, and during rituals such as birth, marriage, death, harvest, initiation, and so on, they were distinguished by the minds of the members of a community and given special attention" (p. 13).

According to Cristina Bacchilega, the metamorphic powers inherent in the fairy tale tradition are borne out by its astounding adaptability to shifting historical contexts. "Fairy tales," argues Bacchilega, "have a history of magic transformations. Scholars of folk narrative know this well and have increasingly been interested in following the tales' trajectories not only in so-called traditional or oral settings but also into the multimedia worlds of literature and popular culture. At the same time, literary scholarship has increasingly remarked on the fairy tale's versatility in history as a genre that has ... successfully morphed to codify social norms and to nurture the desire for change" (Bacchilega, p. 181). Relatedly, the responses of contemporary readers or viewers to present-day interpretations of the fairy tale tradition are bound to be influenced by their own affective and intellectual voyages through play, learning and life itself. The form's unabating suppleness is most sonorously proclaimed by the sheer number and variety of late twentieth-century writers who have appropriated the fairy tale in order to articulate aesthetic and ideological preoccupations of eminently contemporary relevance — with Carter, Margaret Atwood, A. S. Byatt, Robert Coover, Salman Rushdie and Jeanette Winterson among the most prominent names. These authors' sustained interest in present-day issues might seem incongruous with the fairy tale's otherworldly time-less, a dimension of its being proverbially encapsulated by the "Once upon a time" formula. Yet, since the present itself is a fluid mélange of echoes of disparate pasts and foreshadowings of hypothetical futures, it is quite appropriate for some of its major concerns to find expression through the time-defying alliance of contemporary fiction with an ancestral tradition.

Lüthi argues that it is also important to give careful consideration to the psychological import of transformation, and elucidates this point by using as an example the classic topos of the slimy frog's metamorphosis into a glorious prince. This image serves to communicate symbolically the metaphysical dictum according to which "Lower natures are to be trans-formed into higher ones." On the one hand, this process could be deemed salutary to the expansion of conscious "awareness." On the other hand, it shows that such a sublimating move "does not take place without suffering and sacrifice — and cruelty," which suggests that for consciousness to tri-umph, our "instincts — no matter how much they protect and nourish us — must not be left to themselves." In fact, "they must be enchanted or disenchanted, redeemed and purified by the power of the intellect," which effectively amounts to an act of violence (Lüthi 1976, p. 80). The cham-pions of enlightened rationalism will no doubt commend the fairy tale's ability to dramatize this cleansing process even if they deride or dismiss it in very other respect.

Lüthi, however, does not believe that readings of the form that focus exclusively on its usefulness to the advancement of the rule of reason grasp its whole meaning. What they fail to see, in particular, is the extent to which the fairy tale's portrayal of a character's confrontation with murky, inchoate and bestial forces points to the need to face and accept the dark-ness within the human soul itself, and not to the injunction to master or quash it. Lüthi elaborates this idea by invoking Novalis' fascinating take on the fairy tale's handling of metamorphosis: "'In one tale a bear is transformed into a prince the moment he is loved. Perhaps a similar transformation would occur if man began to love the evil in the world.'" Lüthi's own argument expands the horizon of Novalis' vision by proposing that "the fairy tale suggests this in images which produce a much more powerful effect on the mind and heart of its hearers than do moralistic doctrines" (p. 81).

The fairy tale's use of transformation ultimately alerts us with incontestable clarity to the existence of reality levels which we could never presume to master or even, at times, begin to comprehend. This is because the fairy tale, as J. C. Cooper emphasizes, posits "the supernatural" as its "primary" concern, whereas "Saga, and the legends derived from it, have their feet on the ground and the supernatural, if it occurs, is a secondary consideration." Thus, while in the narrative contexts of "saga and legend, Man is confronted with Nature and his own kind; in the realm of faerie he encounters supernatural forces that are always a manifestation of some power beyond the normal world and beyond his control. Even if this force is manifested through some perfectly ordinary event yet it confers the power of magic and transformation." As the unrivaled initiator of the wondrous phenomena issuing from such "magic and transformation," the otherworldly is therefore deployed to signal our insertion in a universe shaped by agencies "different from mankind, operating in a realm either above or below it" (Cooper, p. 18)—a parallel reality rendered deeply mysterious, even before any bizarre events have had a chance to take place within its hazy boundaries, precisely by the uncertainty of its spatial situation in relation to humanity. According to Cooper, a thorough assessment of the role played by the transformation topos in the fairy tale tradition should also take into consideration the influence upon the form of the discipline of "Alchemy, which arrived in Europe from the east and from the Arabic culture of the Middle Ages into Spain, leaving its imprint not only on scholarship but also on popular story. It gave the fairy tale the symbols of gold and silver, sol and luna, king and queen, and the concept of transmuting of base metal into silver and gold, representing the inner journey to find one's identity" (p. 21).

The fairy tale's self-transformative and adaptive powers are epitomized by *Little Red Riding Hood,* a story told and retold virtually ad infinitum both in times gone by and in recent decades with varying emphases and intentions and in different media and styles. Some versions of the classic story have sought to maximize its moral import, others have thrown into relief its sexual implications and others still have harnessed its message to the purpose of social satire. In the domain of anime, *Little Red Riding Hood* is employed to harrowing effect as a dramatic refrain in the movie *Jin-Roh: The Wolf Brigade* (dir. Hiroyuki Okiura, 1998). The transcultural connection is succinctly communicated by the recurrent appearance of a copy of *Rotkäppchen*, a German-language edition of the popular story, throughout the action. Faithful to Perrault's brutal ending, the film proposes an alternative perspective on *Little Red Riding Hood*, which consonant with its reliance on an alternate-history scenario in the main plot, viewed from the wolf's standpoint. Through this ploy, the movie intimates that the predatory pursuers are not free agents but mere puppets in the hands of far more sinister manipulators driven by a blind hunger for power and glory.

Perrault's *Little Red Riding Hood* was intended primarily as a cautionary tale alerting young women to the perils nested in sexual desire and was no doubt largely successful in its aim — so much so that the French expression *"elle avoit vu le loup"* (i.e., "she had seen the wolf") became synonymous with a girl's loss of her virginity. Ironically, Perrault's chief source was a rather lewd tale firmly embedded in oral tradition, *The Grandmother Story*, in which a girl is lured into her granny's bed by a lecherous werewolf and escapes thanks to her own resourcefulness and the help of local peasant women (cited in Orenstein). The Grimms strove to make the narrative more suitable for young audiences, ensuring that the protagonist never got into bed with the lupine predator and that the latter was properly dealt with by a male savior. As John K. Davis emphasizes, "it was not until the 1920s" that various versions of the original narrative that were not specifically designed for kids began to appear. These include "Charles Guyot's *The Granddaughter of Little Red Riding Hood* (1922), in which Red's granddaughter finds the now old and feeble wolf and tends to him; Milt Gross's Yiddish-American parody, *Sturry from Rad Ridink Hoot* (1926); and James Thurber's wry short tale, 'The Girl and the Wolf' (1939), wherein the wolf proves no match for a fully armed girl," and the "1920s essay on 'Little Red Cap' written by Nazi propagandist Werner von Bulow. In it the young girl represented Germania; the wolf symbolized her enemies; and the hunter became her protector or *Fuhrer*."

Also notable are Gillian Cross' *Wolf* (1990), a humorous tale in which "a wolf refuses to believe that Lucy [the protagonist] is not really Little Red Riding Hood"; Ann Jungman's *Lucy And The Big Bad Wolf* (2005), where the heroine's absentee father is cast in the role of a "lone wolf" terrorist; Manlio Argueta's *Little Red Riding Hood in the Red Light District* (1998), which is " Set during the political upheavals and civil war in the El Salvador of the 1970s" and portrays "the wolf" as "a radical political student"; Antony Schmitz' *Darkest Desire: The Wolf's Own Tale* (1998), which features the wolf as "a lonely and unhappy creature who has been ostracized by his own peers because of his insatiable fondness for eating children" and "sees a glimmer of hope" upon meeting the Grimm brothers, "who promise that they can cure him" — even though it is eminently possible that these characters may be "only using him for their own literary gains"; and Debbie Viguie's *Scarlet Moon* (2004), a story that takes place in the era of the crusades and pivots on the emotionally scarred Ruth and an irascible nobleman whom she suspects of being a werewolf (Davis).

As Tatar emphasizes with specific reference to the Grimms' version of *Little Red Riding Hood*, this fairy tale "has become, for better or worse, our canonical story, and we ceaselessly use it as a cultural reference point." At times, the narrative's resilience is nothing short of miraculous, if we consider the extent to which "we take liberties with its words" — for example, "by removing the bottle of wine in Red Riding Hood's basket for fear of condoning the use of alcohol (as was the case in two California school districts)" (Tatar, p. xvii). Given that an ancient interpretation of the tale intended as "entertainment for adults" depicts the heroine "performing striptease" (p. 199), it is somewhat logical that *Little Red Riding Hood* should have been appropriated by contemporary directors eager to "explore the erotic dimensions of the story" (p. 201). A preeminent case in point is Neil Jordan, the director of *The Company of Wolves* (1985), namely, a movie adaptation of Carter's own reimagining of the classic fairy tale.

The concept of transformation is relevant to all of the anime studied in this book but holds particular pertinence to those specifically concerned with the journey topos. This is because the explorative experiences which they dramatize by recourse to that theme are thoroughly shaped by various types of transformation. *Kino's Journey* and *Someday's Dreamers: Summer Skies* exemplify this proposition most perspicuously, focusing as they do on the gradual changes undergone by their protagonists' psyches and emotional baggages as a result of their exposure to diverse cultures, traditions, customs and attendant ethical values. This aspect of the two anime is rendered especially effective by their use of understatement, whereby Kino and Sora often appear so detached from the situations they witness as to remain uninvolved (and, in Kino's case, quite imperturbable) when, in fact, there are discreet indications that both their minds and their hearts are constantly at work and engaged with each minutia of the environment and its inhabitants.

In *Kino's Journey*, this contention is confirmed by the installment in which Kino deliberately journeys to a land reputed for its inhospitable attitude to visitors in order to experience at first hand the attitude of the local people. Surprisingly, they turn out to be most amiable and welcoming and the character of Sakura, in particular, strongly reminds the heroine of her own younger self. So deep is the its impact on Kino's ostensibly impassive personality that she is seriously tempted, possibly for the first time in her voyage, to spend more than just three days in this unexpected home. Ironically, this is the one land in which Kino *cannot* abide insofar as nature's own inflexible laws have decreed its cataclysmic erasure in the immediate aftermath of her enforced departure. All Kino can do is to go on traveling indefinitely with her late guests' souvenirs in her care and carry the land in her memory as the only human ever to have experienced its true kindness. In *Someday's Dreamers: Summer Skies*, Sora's preternaturally refined sensitivity is incrementally revealed by her knack of not only absorbing the subtlest nuances of mood issued by her habitat and its inhabitants but also leaving indelible traces on virtually anyone with whom she comes into contact, albeit fleetingly, and thereby contributing vitally to their ongoing affective metamorphoses.

The Story of Saiunkoku and *Tokyo Godfathers* also revolve around crucial moments of transformation. In the former, these coincide firstly with the heroine's metamorphosis into a privileged member of the imperial household, and secondly with her assumption of responsibilities conducive to decisions that dictate not only her personal development but also her entire country's progressive mutation. In the latter, the principle of transformation underpins a cluster of epiphanic discoveries crowning the three protagonists' urban odyssey and attendant efforts to piece together the fragmentary and sometimes deceitful clues left in their wake by the lost baby's parents. Transformation, in this instance, relies heavily on serendipity insofar as coincidences are instrumental in the characters' detection of potentially promising leads, and ability to preserve a modicum of hope in the face of what logic and reason would derisively dismiss as a totally unrealizable quest. In all four anime, the protagonists' vicissitudes operate as metaphors for the metamorphic processes affecting real-life societies through the interaction of disparate people and, relatedly, of manifold ideals, goals and world views. All of the anime here addressed are keen to emphasize the importance of the formative and transformative voyages undertaken by their protagonists over and above any possible points of arrival, deploying dramatic open-endedness as a succinct means of underscoring their philosophical message. In this respect, they mirror a vital aspect of the human experience of Faërie as depicted by Conway — namely, its significance as "an ongoing process" wherein "the journey itself becomes the destination" (Conway, p. 39).

In the contexts of Japanese literature and lore, the topos of the journey strikes its roots in familiar narrative conventions — in particular, what Haruo Shirane describes as the "exile of the young noble" formula, whereby "a young god or aristocrat undergoes a severe trial in a distant and hostile land" and, in so doing, "proves his mettle, comes of age, and acquires the power and respect necessary to become a true leader and hero" (Shirane, p. 3). This textual format occasionally assumes the guise of "the *mamoko-tan*, or the stepdaughter tale, in which a hostile stepmother favors her own children over the disadvantaged heroine." For a woman, "the trial ... usually occurs indoors," for a man "in a hostile country." Both of the formulae outlined by Shirane with specific reference to the Japanese context are so widespread and influential as to resonate with the transcultural power of "archetypal configurations" (p. 4). *The Ambitious Carp* (in Griffis) alludes to the inextricability of history from fiction and fantasy, thus implicitly calling into question the reliability of all manner of historiographical accounts, by emphasizing that the ultimate reward aspired to by a diligent pupil as a culmination of his painstaking study of history is a collection of Chinese fairy tales. At the same time, the identification of ancient China with a bountiful reserve of fantastic materials anticipates the utilization of Chinese geography and lore as the basis for the imaginary realm portrayed in *The Story of Saiunkoku*. *The Ambitious Carp* explicitly reinforces a distinctive sense of cultural identity through its enthusiastic enthronement of the Japanese value of perseverance as the culmen of virtue. This message is encapsulated in the image of the humble carp's eventual metamorphosis into a formidable white Dragon as the outcome of sheer hard work and guts.

The consolidation of a cultural quality instrumental in the forging of a specifically Japanese sense of identity is also central to *Lord Long-Legs' Procession* (in Griffis) and *Danzayémon, Chief of the Etas* (in Ashliman, D. L. 1998–2008b; original source: Mitford). The value here promulgated is the paramount importance of adopting a deferential attitude toward all sorts of materials and substances. Both tales tersely demonstrate that fairy tales do not unequivocally belong in the impalpable space of a never-never land but are actually quite capable of engaging with practical and materialistic human pursuits. In *Lord Long-Legs' Procession*, ample space is devoted to the celebration of the reality of commerce by means of a sumptuous parade. *Danzayémon, Chief of the Etas*, for its part, offers a detailed portrait of the social milieu in which it is set, dwelling on its meticulously conceived hierarchical structure and attendant roles, obligations and allegiances. (Please notes that "Etas" are tanners.) *Lord Long-Legs' Procession*, in addition, is notable as an adaptation of a theme of transcultural relevance that also finds proverbial formulation in Andersen's *The Emperor's New Clothes*. In both stories, a young and innocent character is portrayed as responsible for the exposure of the empty pomposity of power. In Andersen's story, a child unwittingly lays bare the absurd lies through which the monarch and his sycophants succeed in guaranteeing the public's passive acceptance of their physical and moral excellence. In the Japanese narrative, analogously, the adult crowd pays homage to the titular lord without even wondering where he actually is or what he truly looks like, while little Grub honestly states that he cannot see Lord Long-Legs at all — at which point his mother, Madam Butterfly, must admit that the only visible item in the tableau is in fact the palanquin.

With the tale of *The Magic Frog* (in Griffis), the concept of power relations and its role in an individual's voyage of self-discovery gains the limelight. The narrative focuses on the transmission of magical skills across space and time, intimating that this process parallels the divulgation of lore itself over disparate generations, lands and related cultures. In *The Travels of the Two Frogs* (in Griffis) the journey topos is likewise foregrounded but deployed in the service of an oblique commentary on the unreliability and arbitrariness of historiography. This story exploits to humorous effect the titular animals' anatomical peculiarities and the ways in which these affect their vision. When the two frogs look at the horizon standing on their hind legs, in a grotesque emulation of human posture, in order to see the cities which each of them intended to visit at the beginning of its voyage but is now too weary to reach, what each perceives is, in fact, an image of its place of origin, which leads both frogs to the conclusion that travel is utterly pointless and they might as well return to the familiar comforts of their respective home towns. In addition, *The Travels of the Two Frogs* also articulates an overtly environmentalist message in its opening lines, where the advent of coal smoke and of the "iron horse" is said to have scared the herons away from the fields. Both *The Stonecutter* (in Ashliman, D. L. 1998–2008b; original source: Lang 1903) and *Visu the Woodsman and the Old Priest* (in Ashliman, D. L. 1998–2008b; original source: Hadland Davis) utilize the topos of the journey in an eminently allegorical vein, positing their protagonists' experiences as symbols of the unpredictable processes through which history is made and unmade by the often uneasy interaction of real events and recorded facts. *The Stonecutter* opts for a drama of self-displacement, whereby the protagonist's increasingly preposterous fantasies of self-aggrandizement are fulfilled by an ostensibly sympathetic supernatural agency but eventually lead to his reversal to the humble state whence he started.

Visu the Woodsman and the Old Priest, for its part, capitalizes on the topos of temporal displacement, removing the protagonist to an alternate reality redolent of fairyland at its most unsettling for what appears to be a short period of time and then revealing, upon his return home, that several years have in fact elapsed since his departure and that all the people he once knew are dead and gone. Visu's ordeal vividly corroborates Japanese lore's ambiguity toward mountains. As Michiko Iwasaka and Barre Toelken observe, "in many rural parts of Japan, there are mixed feelings about the solitude of the mountains: on the one hand, isolation and distance from society foster the spiritual influences sought by the ascetic monk; on the other hand, distance from society also allows for accidents and erosion of those social obligations which characterize the group-centered Japanese way of life." It is no coincidence, in this respect, that it should be customary, in days gone by, to dispose of the corpses of "murdered persons (and especially those of stillborn, aborted, or murdered children) ... in the mountains." Moreover, "shamed unwed mothers," as well as "bandits and banished people," were known to elect secluded mountain regions as their shelters or haunts (Iwasaka and Toelken, p. 87). Visu clearly benefits from his hermitage insofar as the remote mountain region exposes him to hitherto unforeseen energies and lessons. At the same time, however, the character becomes so deeply alienated from human company and mores as to lose all sense of his duties and responsibilities as a member of the community and hence contravene a lynchpin of indigenous ethics.

Japanese lore accords an especially prominent place to journeys that chart the movement between the human dimension and the supernatural beyond. Ghost stories epitomize this trope as a major component of indigenous civilization across the centuries, both mirroring deeply embedded cultural values and contributing vitally to the processes through which those values are fashioned, preserved and divulged. For example, the numerous tales punctuating Japanese tradition in which mothers return from the word of the dead to protect their children could be seen both to reflect and to consolidate the importance of ancestor worship so central to many local customs and rituals. *The Mirror of Matsuyama*, discussed in the next chapter, is a notable instance of the appropriation of this long-standing topos by the fairy tale tradition. Other recurrent journeys bridging ordinary and ultramundane reality levels focus on the infiltration of the human world by preternatural messages — e.g., in the guise of omens, visions and prophetic dreams — and on the vicissitudes of a ghost ship and its crew. This motif is alluded to, for instance, in *Little Silver's Dream*, as argued in Chapter 5: Dystopias.

Mysterious forces capable of moving fluidly across dimensions to bind either human beings or portions of the natural environment in their spells are likewise notable as oft revisited narrative topoi. As Iwasaka and Toelken maintain, the sorts of voyage-based experiences outlined above document a cultural mentality wherein "the realms of the living and the dead inter-penetrate in a system of mutual responsibility" and "the world of the dead," accordingly, "remains 'alive'" among the living (p. 8). This ethos is elo-quently attested to by the fact that "the performative media — theatre, Kabuki, film and storytelling (such as the *kaidan banashi* [ghost or horror story] recitals) — are well stocked with stories which feature death, ghosts, *oni* [demons] and other monsters" (p. 13). Anime can no doubt be added to the list proffered by Iwasaka and Toelken, insofar as legion productions in that medium also bear witness to the popularity of the motifs pervading older performance arts.

In the titles here examined, the ongoing dialogue between the domains of the breathing and the departed constitutes a metaphysical expedition underlying the manifest and empirical journeys in which the various pro-tagonists are engaged. Echoes of the ritual practices spawned by the Japa-nese cult of the dead thereby make themselves audible in each anime's narrative fabric. In *Someday's Dreamers: Summer Skies*, this idea is tersely conveyed by the heroine's reverential attitude toward her late father's mem-ory. The deceased parent is connected, in keeping with the animistic and pantheistic propensities of Shinto, with the image of an august tree that is employed as a visual refrain for moments of heightened pathos through-out the series. Sora's perception of her father as a living force is akin to Claus and Lavie's stance toward their own heroic forebears as dramatized in *Last Exile* (please see Chapter 2): in both instances, the parental figure stands out both as a source of inspiration for the younger generations and as a deserving object of ritual veneration. In *The Story of Saiunkoku*, the centrality of ancestor worship to Japanese tradition is communicated by implication rather than by overt statement through the representation of Shuurei's entire world as a society so rigorously codified that it could not possibly fail to incorporate its own sets of death customs and devotional ceremonies.

Kino's Journey, by orchestrating its entire drama on the basis of short-lived encounters, elliptically portrays each of the lands and cultures touched by the protagonist and her prodigious motorcycle as a figurative ancestor to be treasured in memory as an animate presence despite its physical disappearance. In the closing installment, the series enthrones this message as a major motif, as Kino is entrusted with the tangible mementos of an extinct civilization and thus enjoined to act as the living testimony to its otherwise submerged history. *Tokyo Godfathers* adopts a seemingly iconoclastic stance toward the notion of ancestor worship with the sequences in which the main characters temporarily settle in a cemetery to discuss their future course of action and Gin instantly proceeds to appropriate the *sake*, left as an offering by some devout visitor, with clearly hypocritical self-reproach. As a pivotal moment in the anime's diegesis, marking its transition to the segment of the action in which improbable confluences begin to gather staggering momentum, the sequence does carry its own ceremonial logic, unorthodox though this may be.

Japan vaunts an ample body of orally disseminated legends centered on ghosts and visitations of the mundane here-and-now by the mysterious and fathomless beyond. This corpus overlaps with the fairy tale tradition in several respects: most importantly, the journeys (literal or figurative) entailed by the spiritual transactions that bring together the living and the dead bear striking similarities to the encounters between the human realm and Faërie that we find recurrently chronicled in that tradition all over the planet. A crucial place is held in both instances by the concept of "*anoyo*, 'the world over there, yonder,'" which is used to designate "the other side" (p. 15) both literally and figuratively. This may be located "far away over the sea," "past the mountains," "beyond a great river" or "underground" (p. 16). Anime has repeatedly endeavored to foreground the fluid intermingling of this world and the otherworld. At the same time, however, it has been keen to emphasize that there is one crucial respect in which the membrane separating those two realms remains inviolable: no magical agent — fairy, wizard or alchemist as the case may be — should ever presume to bring the dead back to life. This message is pithily underscored by Sora's lecturer as one of the main propedeutic principles underpinning magical studies. It also finds memorable articulation, within the medium of anime, in the TV series *Tsubasa: RESERVoir CHRoNiCLE* (2005), helmed by Koichi Mashimo, and its sequel of the same title (2006), directed by Mashimo in collaboration with Hiroshi Morioka. In these shows, any sorcerous scheme designed to resurrect the deceased is resolutely condemned as preposterously arrogant and shown, when implemented, to be inevitably conducive to calamitous disappointment. The same law applies, it is intimated, to entire communities and individual creatures. The royal priest Yukito maintains, in this regard, that it is precisely insofar as "lives that are lost cannot be returned" that "lives are precious, and living is wonderful."

A transcultural leap seems apposite in order to close this chapter with a genuinely stupendous instance of the collusion of creativity and the fairy tale tradition. Nowhere is the creative power of storytelling, and specifically of the narration of tales of the marvelous, more gloriously celebrated than in the *One Thousand and One Nights*— a.k.a. *Arabian Nights* (McCaughrean). It is also in this text that the reliability of both history and historiography receives one of its sharpest challenges. To prevent King Shahyar, who has the deplorable habit of killing a new wife every night before she can stop loving him, Shahrazad (a.k.a. Scheherazade), his new bride, saves herself by telling him nightly stories so engrossing as to compel him time and again to postpone her execution. Shahrazad's quest for survival against the mightiest odds, with her seemingly inexhaustible narratorial talent as her sole resource, constitutes a veritable voyage of the imagination across time and space. The monarch's exposure to Shahrazad's cunning ploy indubitably constitutes the most intriguing moment amid the unfolding of hallowed narratives told and retold for centuries all over the world, such as *The Tale of Ala al-Din* (a.k.a. Aladdin) *and his Wonderful Lamp*, *The Wonderful Tale of Ali Baba and the Forty Bandits* and the voyages of *Sinbad the Sailor*.

At this juncture, coinciding with the opening segment of *The Price of Cucumber*, the supreme ruler asserts that while every man's mind is a palace harboring his personal thoughts, a king's mind is an especially important type of palace insofar as it is meant to embed such an extraordinary plethora of ideas as to contain no room for stories. Not only, therefore, is Shahrazad's deception unpardonable on the grounds that it has been devised just to help her save her head. It is also made particularly reprehensible by its power to infest not just any odd brain but the brain of a supreme ruler with imaginary situations and people, and thus lead her spouse to neglect the stark realities of politics and governance with which he ought to be preoccupied instead. Hence, the journey charted by Shahrazad's luxuriant storytelling could be said to destabilize the rhythms of official history as a concatenation of putatively actual and measurable events by installing in their place an alternate history woven from the least verifiable of materials: stories. Nevertheless, the fabulistic journey is unstoppable since, even as she appears to be proffering her genuine apologies for exploiting a deceitful trick at the king's expense, Shahrazad immediately finds herself dropping hints at yet another possible story.

The ultimate voyage at stake in the collusion of anime and the fairy tale tradition is of the nature of a dialogue — or, to be more precise, of an accretional imagistic exchange triggered by anime's fascination with the fairy tale tradition as a fertile source of inspiration, on the one hand, and as a mobile discourse from which it can elicit responses on the other. Thus, anime consists not simply of a present-day "answer" to the questions posed by the fairy tale tradition but also of a series of questions which that discourse is, in turn, urged to address in its ongoing process of self-transformation. As anime is capable of mutating as a result of its encounter with the fairy tale tradition, so the latter enjoys a tantalizing opportunity for self-reinvention as a result of its imaginative appropriation by anime. The shows here examined are not motivated by a parochial interest in particular bodies of lore tied up with ethnic specificities or by the nostalgic pull of childhood readings. Rather, they are drawn to the unique logic — and attendant rhythms and patterns — with which fairy tales are recounted and divulged over time and across cultures.

The fairy tale tradition, in this regard, presents itself primarily as a palimpsest of storytelling possibilities, a dynamic constellation of endlessly recombinable and unpredictably proliferating options. As we explore the dialogical journey undertaken by anime and the fairy tale tradition as mutually committed traveling companions, we come to detect the spontaneous emergence of synergetic affinities between the fairy tale tradition per se and anime eager to harness their stories to the elaboration of thoughtful allegorical commentaries on specific cultural realities. The universe thus brought into being is an intensely polychromatic dimension wherein each story always appears to be carrying echoes of other — forgotten or hypothetical — stories on the wind blowing over its seas and planes and on the mist suffusing its crests and vales. The cumulative power held by such narratives, both potential and realized, for the keen anime artist lies in their ability to look at things with the eyes of someone who is seeing them for the first time and senses, beneath appearances, the elemental richness and elemental burden of being human.

CHAPTER 4

Creativity

This is a work of fiction. All the characters in it, human and otherwise, are imaginary, excepting only certain of the fairy folk, whom it might be unwise to offend by casting doubts on their existence. Or lack thereof.
— Neil Gaiman

You can understand and relate to most people better if you look at them — no matter how old or impressive they may be — as if they are children. For most of us never really grow up or mature all that much — we simply grow taller. O, to be sure, we laugh less and play less and wear uncomfortable disguises like adults, but beneath the costume is the child we always are, whose needs are simple, whose daily life is still best described by fairy tales.
— Leo Rosten

According to Susannah Marriott, accessing the fairy realm is a unique means of experiencing "transformation and enlightening creativity" (Marriott, p. 46). For this illumination to take place and for the human imagination to be able to process the raw materials (both mental and physical) gleaned from the encounter with Faërie, it is vital to retain a capacious disposition toward the inscrutable beyond. Numerous tales engage with a human's discovery of a magical point of entry to the fairy world — which may consist, for example, of a stone placed in the proximity of a fairy lake, as is often the case in Welsh lore, or of a primrose, as proposed by some German fairy tales. An especially electrifying instance is that of the doorway among stone graves or earthen ramparts left invitingly ajar, through which one may catch a glimpse of fairy folk attired in festive clothing and bathed by candlelight. A comparably tantalizing experience is supplied by the sight of fairies attending human funerals out of authentic sympathy and grief, a custom mentioned in the previous chapter. The members of the Good Folk participating in such occasions signal a radical departure from the ominous types known only to appear to mortals as the latter are about to draw their last breath. The banshee, a spirit of Irish origin from the world of the dead that plays a prominent part in *Earl and Fairy*, is arguably the most notorious member of this otherworldly category.

What is most critical, in this context, is the extent to which a human's exposure to unexpected creative energies — and resulting expression of imaginative powers — depends on openness to the latent ascendancy of forces that transcend, bypass or even mock both rational understanding and the strictures of classical logic. These, in turn, stand out as immensely creative agencies in their own right and hence as exemplary models for the adventurous human mind to emulate. Science author Arabella B. Buckley promulgated this idea in 1879 with unparalleled charm and intellectual vigor at once, seeking to usher young readers into the bountiful mysteries of the natural world by metaphorically referring to their animating energies as "fairies." In the first part of *The Fairy-Land of Science*, titled "How to Enter It; How to Use It; and How to Enjoy It," Buckley exhorts her audience as follows: "Hearken to the brook as it flows by, watch the flower-buds opening one by one, and then ask yourself, 'How all this is done?' Go out in the evening and see the dew gather drop by drop upon the grass, or trace the delicate hoar-frost crystals which bespangle every blade on a winter's morning. Look at the vivid flashes of lightning in a storm, and listen to the pealing thunder: and then tell me, by what machinery is all this wonderful work done? Man does none of it, neither could he stop it if he were to try; for it is all the work of those invisible forces or fairies whose acquaintance I wish you to make. Day and night, summer and winter, storm or calm, these fairies are at work, and we may hear them and know them, and make friends of them if we will" (Buckley). Thus, all manner of natural forms and phenomena are equated to magical creatures, and openness to the possibility of encounters with such entities is enthroned as the prerequisite of people's understanding of their environment. Seeing such a position advocated by a representative of the scientific sphere rather — as would be more customary and predictable — than by a visionary poet or troubadour is an undoubtedly uplifting experience for those who accept the existence of fathomless forces beyond the remit of the familiar, whether or not they choose to designate them as "fairies."

The world picture outlined above lies at the heart of the message proposed by all of the anime here under scrutiny in their distinctive articulations of creativity. In each, at least one character operates as a figurative fairy capable of ushering others into a speculative domain where fresh sources of strength may be fruitfully tapped and emotionally healing capacities may be discovered, while also offering an inspirational matrix. Furthermore, spectators themselves are introduced to a hypothetical realm coursed by vibrant creative opportunities for them to pursue throughout the viewing process. We are obliquely invited to ideate alternate realities in our own heads as we sample the anime's crossover domains — namely, to imagine dimensions unaffected by the constraints of physics and common sense alike that momentarily produce fissures in the here-and-now. Through such openings, we may sense an uncanny juxtaposition of the familiar world, inexplicably altered, and the magical world and thus realize that in order to access an alternate universe, physical travel is not always necessary. In fact, one of the most effective ways of stepping into Faërie requires hardly any motion at all since it consists of immersing oneself in the world of fairy art and allowing its sheer profusion of mesmerizing details to cast its spell upon our minds and senses.

Some anime imbricated with the fairy tale tradition consist of relatively straightforward adaptations of canonical manifestations of that discourse. *Andersen Stories* (TV series; dir. Masami Hata, 1971) and *Cinderella* (TV series; dir. Hiroshi Sasagawa, 1996) exemplify this trend. Others manipulate their source materials with varying degrees of originality and audacity. In *Puss in Boots* (movie; dir. Kimio Yabuki, 1969), Charles Perrault's parent narrative is subject to fairly radical reorientation as its original imagery is interwoven with supernatural motifs and a generous dose of ninja action directly inspired by indigenous tastes. The same tale is treated no less imaginatively in a subplot of *FLCL* (OVA series; dir. Kazuya Tsurumaki, 2000), where its employment as a play-within-a-play serves to underscore the theme of deceitfulness as one of the series' key concerns. Another tantalizing adaptation of a cherished fairy tale originally penned by Hans Christian Andersen is *The Snow Queen* (TV series; dir. Osamu Dezaki; 2005–2006), where the topoi of the magical mirror and its demonic artificer are invested with novel dramatic resonance and metaphysical import, while Gerda's odyssey is enhanced by the incorporation of both brand-new adventures and capsulated reconceptualizations of Andersen fairy tales other that *The Snow Queen* itself.

Likewise daring is the revisioning thrust evinced by some anime adaptations of more recent fiction bound up with the fairy tale tradition, such as *Howl's Moving Castle* (movie; dir. Hayao Miyazaki, 2004) and *Tales from Earthsea* (movie; dir. Goro Miyazaki, 2006). Adapted from novels by Diana Wynne Jones and Ursula Le Guin respectively, these films utilize their source materials as launch pads for the allegorical exploration of complex — and often unjust — structures of power and their impact on both communal and individual psychologies. Other anime collude with the fairy tale tradition by engaging with issues of mythological magnitude without, however, presuming to map out any grandiose cosmologies and focusing instead on the inner self. A case in point is *Fate/stay Night* (TV series; dir. Yuji Yamaguchi, 2006), where the venerable legend of the Holy Grail is harnessed to the dramatization of an elaborate tournament on the collective plane, and to a sensitive anatomy of fraught personal relationships on the private one. Another relevant example is provided by a further series likewise helmed by Yamaguchi, *Touka Gettan* (2007), where the erosion of age-old boundaries between the human and the spirit worlds gives rise to drastic temporal and spatial dislocations, while a motley crew of both ordinary mortals and deities in human form struggle to negotiate their twisted emotions. The theme of creativity is here emplaced as a crucial component of the fairy tale by means of sustained metadramatic reflections on the glory and torment of artistic creation. All of the anime cited above could be seen to partake of the fairy tale tradition's narrative formulae no less directly than the titles here examined as exemplifications of the coalescence of that discourse and the topos of creativity. Nevertheless, few contemporary dramas in animated format are as effective as the productions under inspection in this chapter in demonstrating the fairy tale tradition's existential significance.

Paradise Kiss (TV series; dir. Osamu Kobayashi, 2005) revolves around Yukari, a perfectly ordinary high-school student with no special ambitions, who begins to question the meaning of her lifestyle and quotidian routine just as a group of fashion design students who associate themselves with the label "Paradise Kiss" decide to pick her as the model to showcase their collection at the forthcoming school festival. Initially suspicious of this seemingly eccentric crew, so different from all the people she has hitherto had a chance to meet in her thoroughly programmed existence, the protagonist gradually comes to admire their enthusiastic idealism and to draw inspiration from their example to explore her own true dreams. As Yukari secretly becomes a model while battling with an overbearing mother (a paradigmatic incarnation of the *mamagon*, or mama-dragon), the anime proclaims its association with the fairy tale tradition by foregrounding a key aspect which fairy tales from all parts of the globe undeniably share: the Bildungsroman. Indeed, while *Paradise Kiss* is a stylish, imaginatively edited and impeccably paced show, the principal reason for which it finally abides in memory as a worthy contemporary reconceptu-

alization of the fairy tale form is precisely its dispassionate anatomy of the pains and pleasures of growing up. This dramatic focus is enriched by the employment of a subtly nuanced cast of characters whose members never degenerate into stereotypes even as they incarnate familiar anime categories. In this regard, the series closely parallels the fairy tale's inveterate proclivity to employ apparently formulaic personae only for the sake of pulling its dawn-sprinkled carpet from under our feet to reveal hidden vagaries and depths.

The cute bimbo Miwako, for example, does not function merely as an amusing flesh-and-blood prop in accordance with her saccharine appearance but is in fact invested with remarkable maturity, intelligence and a hidden history of emotional travail compounded with a contorted case of big-sister complex. The spiky-haired and multipierced punk Arashi flaunts a tough façade and anarchic disposition consonant with his public image but it rapidly transpires that his scorn of accepted mores is not merely a stereotypical fashion statement but rather a corollary of an honest belief in people's right to act of their own free will. Accordingly, his initial reservations regarding Yukari, whom he first perceives as a pampered goody-goody without a single ounce of independence give way to respect as the heroine shows an unexpected determination to make autonomous choices in defiance of tradition and conventional notions of propriety. Moreover, Arashi exhibits a veritably candy-hearted personality in his atti-tude toward Miyako, never allowing his fond memories of her former standing as a loyal childhood mate to be obfuscated or belittled by the girl's current role as a lover, most generous in dispensing her erotic favors.

No less multifaceted is the character of Isabella, a statuesquely hand-some crossdresser invariably attired in period costumes that exude a pal-pable sense of stage presence. Despite her theatricality, Isabella evinces an endearingly maternal temperament in her unflinching preparedness to lend Yukari a sympathetic ear in times of trouble and to regale the crew with both tummy- and heart-warming homemade meals at the end of a day's hard work. The character's most overt connection with the fairy tale tra-dition, alongside her favorite vestimentary register, is the château where she resides amid all manner of antique furniture and ornaments. Even the supporting actors by and by disclose remarkable degrees of psychological complexity — most notably in the case of the protagonist's overbearing but innerly tormented mother, a woman haunted by insecurity and a patho-logical inability to express her feelings in anything other than a monstrously distorted guise. Another character worthy of consideration, in this context, is Yukari's classmate Hiroyuki, a youth tormented by an agonizing sense of inadequacy despite his top marks and candidly good looks, not least due to a fraught past relationship with Miyako and Arashi — a bond redolent of the doomed love triangle often encountered in traditional narrative and lore.

George, the male lead, is arguably the most ambiguous of the show's characters, as he initially comes across as a promiscuous and carefree libertine but is incrementally shown to be actually conscientious, insightful and caring. Furthermore, George comes across as a memorable present-day adaptation of the mischievous, yet inherently benevolent, fairy type of old, especially in his treatment of Yukari. The route he takes to court the girl, both as an ideal model and as a possible girlfriend, is so circuitous and equivocal — and his laconic insistence so haunting — as to cast doubts on the honesty of his intentions, and make us wonder whether he might simply be playing an elvish game at Yukari's — and, by implication, the audience's — own expense. At times, George even brings to mind the demonic lovers and suitors immortalized by tales such as Perrault's *Beauty and the Beast* and *Bluebeard* and the Grimms' *Rumpelstiltskin*: illustrious specimens of a narratological category which J. C. Cooper rather amusingly describes as "the Loathly Mate" (Cooper, p. 16).

Bruno Bettelheim, in his discussion of what he describes as the "Animal-Groom Cycle of Fairy Tales" (Bettelheim, pp. 282–310), points out that a crucial distinction obtains between *Beauty and the Beast* and *Bluebeard* insofar as the former foregrounds the values of "gentleness and loving devotion," whereas the latter "has nothing whatsoever to do with love" since "Bluebeard, bent on having his will and possessing his partner, cannot love anybody, but neither can anyone love him" (p. 303). George's conduct frequently exudes precisely the sorts of positive affects which Bettelheim associates with *Beauty and the Beast*, playing the role of the seemingly threatening but actually affectionate lover. Yet, his creative impulse is so all-consuming and, at times, intransigent as to recall *Bluebeard*'s destructive impulses. This is especially notable when George succumbs to utter solipsism and his attitude toward Yukari grows so possessive as to suggest that he is driven by a perverse urge to engulf her entire being into his artwork: to regard her, in other words, as the breathing equivalent of a lush fabric or a rare gem. The anime also shares specifically with *Bluebeard* the image of the secret room — in George's case, thankfully, this does not consist of a blood-soaked chamber of horrors of the kind depicted in the French tale (Perrault, p. 43) but of the cabinet storing all of his favorite creations which he leaves behind at the end as a farewell present for Yukari.

Another narrative likewise concerned with forbidden chambers springs to mind in this context: the Japanese fairy tale known as *The Bush Warblers' Home*. In this story, a young stonecutter chances upon a magnificent house deep in a forest, where he meets a beautiful woman who invites him to stay there during her imminent absence, instructing him to refrain from exploring the dwelling beyond that point. The youth promises to respect the lady's will but, as one might expect, soon breaks the promise and "goes into one room after another in the house, seeing that they contain many treasures," at one point inadvertently dropping "three small eggs" he has picked up from a nest (in Kawai 1995, p. 105; original source: Seki). The tale does not deliver a happy ending in the Western sense of the phrase since it actually closes with the lady's declaration that the stonecutter's trespass has caused the death of her three daughters, followed by her metamorphosis into a bush warbler and abrupt departure. However, none of the palpable horror evoked by *Bluebeard* infiltrates the Japanese tale. The gender inversion entailed by the portrayals of the transgressor as male and of the prohibitor as female, allied to the idea that the protagonist's infraction discloses not gore but beauty, imparts *The Bush Warblers' Home* with a distinctively Japanese mood. In both fairy tales and legends, the figure of the prohibitor could be seen to embody a culture's informing value. When ordinary human beings are forced to acknowledge the prohibitor's formidable powers at their own cost, they are thereby brought face to face with that value and its ultimate authority. According to Hayao Kawai, the prohibitor in Japan's traditional narratives is normally female because the "principle" of femininity (as conceived of in a Jungian perspective) "is dominant in their culture" (Kawai 1995, p. 114).

Within the emotional carousel inspiringly dramatized by *Paradise Kiss*, the heroine herself is explicitly compared to Cinderella, her midnight equivalent consisting of the start of lessons at cram school. When George and his mates throw an impromptu party to celebrate Yukari's decision to be their model, and the girl gets inebriated on champagne to the point that she passes out, her own psyche gives in to that quintessential fairy tale fantasy — at this point, she is indeed visited by a dream in which she and George feature in roles that are unquestionably based on Perrault's *Cinderella*'s climactic moments. It is also noteworthy that Yukari is provisionally renamed by Miwako "Caroline" at the time of their first meeting and thereafter retains this alternate denomination among her new colleagues. In the fairy tale tradition, as will be shown in greater detail in the next chapter, it is commonly held that fairies' names are secret and their discovery is tantamount to a heinous crime among the Fair Folk — hence, humanity's adoption of all manner of aliases and stage names for the creatures. In being invested with a pseudonym that comes to be adopted in preference to her actual name, Yukari is elliptically equated, within the series' fairy tale logic, to a fairy of sorts. As the heroine begins to suspect that she might be trying to run away from the actual world in pursuing a career in the modeling world, and that the fashion industry might be a much harsher reality than her fantasies have given her to believe, the show evokes two conflicting interpretations of the fairy tale as an illusory escape from reality, on the one hand, and a metaphorical exposure of life's least savory dimension on the other.

On the iconographic plane, *Paradise Kiss* echoes the fairy tale tradition most economically, and yet strikingly, with its recurrent use of the image of the butterfly: a motif, as indicated in some depth in Chapter 5: Dystopias, of pivotal significance to fairy lore in countless cultures. In the anime, the image features in a range of disparate situations: for example, in the pattern on the walls of the murky staircase leading to the team's makeshift atelier, the rare specimens inhabiting the glass-mounted display cases in George's apartment, one of the several cartoon-style figures recurrently superimposed on photorealistic backgrounds of the city in the pre-credit sequences and, of course, the show's own logo. In addition, a white butterfly fleetingly rests on Yukari's empty desk on the very first day of her absence from school following her decision to drop out in order to pursue a modeling vocation. A climactically positioned installment is actually titled "Butterfly," in homage to the exquisitely intricate ring crafted by George expressly for Yukari: a poignantly fitting symbol of their volatile emotional liaison.

In its allegorical treatment of artistic and artisanal production, *Paradise Kiss* echoes an important aspect of Japan's fairy tale tradition: its commitment to the celebration of the ethos of *kazari* as aesthetic pleasure associated specifically with ornamentation. The birds meant to adorn future specimens of lacquerware in *The Gift of Old Lacquer* and the bunnies almost inadvertently fashioned by the playing kids in *The First Rabbits*, just two mention two of the indigenous tales discussed later in this chapter, are presented not simply as living entities but also as pleasingly organized decorative forms capable of eliciting feelings of both visual and tactile delight. It is vital to emphasize, in this respect, that Japan's distinctive arts and crafts do not conceive of decoration as a supplementary and ultimately dispensable addendum to a privileged shape or subject matter but rather as an axial component of the overall product contributing vitally to its aesthetic identity. *Paradise Kiss* promulgates this view by emplacing a wide range of ornamental patterns as graphic entities endowed with a discernible and pulsating life of their own. These visual elements, moreover, may function as catalysts for a fruitful interplay of form and matter, abstraction and embodiment, rhythm and substance. This is effectively borne out by the sequence dramatizing the abortive shopping trip devoted to the purchase of fabric for Yukari's festival dress. Failing to find a single pattern that pleases his aesthetic sense, George resolves to draw an appropriate decorative design reflecting his own taste, and further intensifies the motif's artistic caliber by deciding that it shall be embroidered with antique beads rather than simply dyed. George adopts a likewise perfectionistic approach in the design of the accessories meant to accompany Yukari's robe, insisting on having "real" white roses painted blue by hand instead of using pre-dyed "fake" flowers. Since there is precious little time left before the show by the time George comes up with this flash of inspiration, Arashi unceremoniously brands the task "last-minute Alice-in-Wonderland shit," thus supplying a gentle hint at the fairy tale tradition for the audience to ponder.

A further allusion to that same discourse comes with George's assertion that the substance employed to color the roses is nothing other than his own blood (a story which only Miyako, as one might expect, readily believes): this detail that could be read as another elliptical reference to *Bluebeard*. George's decision to battle on with his idealistic plan at any price hardly comes as a surprise when one takes into consideration the character's deeply ingrained belief that "there isn't a single thing that's impossible when it comes to the world of art." Therefore, even though to Arashi's pragmatic eyes George often seems to be posing as a "stupid prince," the artist himself steadfastly avers that a true designer is a "magical weaver of dreams." As Marina Warner emphasizes, the fairy tale tradition at large is virtually inseparable from fabric-related tropes, such as "Spinning a tale" and "weaving a plot," which indicates that "the structure of fairy stories, with their repetitions, reprises, elaboration and minutiae, replicates ... the making of textiles from the wool or the flax to the finished bolt of cloth" (Warner 1995, p. 23). While George's designs are so fabulous as to preclude any chance of his ever succeeding as a creator of clothes wearable in the actual world by even the most eccentric of fashion junkies, he remains loyal to his vision and does achieve recognition, eventually, in the domain of theatrical costume (with the stagy Isabella at his side, quite fittingly, in the capacity of pattern maker). This is the artistic realm offering the closest equivalent to Faërie one could hope to find in the real world.

Concomitantly, the anime is keen to draw attention, with variable degrees of explicitness and symbolism, to the design principles that underpin not solely the ambit of fashion but also the arts of interior design, packaging, wrapping, tying, tucking, folding, gardening and cuisine as equally informed by the principle of *kazari*. In the process, it intimates that no decorative item is ever too humble or trivial for the genuinely dedicated artisan or artist and that each and every fragment of the creative experience ultimately deserves respect and admiration. In this regard, the series is explicitly indebted to a virtually timeless lynchpin of the indigenous approach to design: the notion that "small is beautiful" and that no effort should therefore be spared in the execution of even the minutest of items to the highest of standards. The anime's approach to fashion design honors this value by combining gracefulness (*reiyou* or *yuu*) and flamboyance (*hade*), understated good taste (*jimi*) and innocent charm (*karumi*). The protagonist lends herself ideally to the modeling role to which the fashion students have elected her, despite her initial reservations on the matter, precisely because both her physical appearance and her inner disposition encapsulate those qualities with disarming spontaneity.

Paradise Kiss does not only reveal its indebtedness to indigenous aesthetics in its dedication to the meticulous execution of all manner of patterns, textures and fabrics. In fact, its approach to fashion design also echoes that tradition insofar as it is generously imbued with a profound sense of reverence for the actual materials deployed by designers — a feeling often conducive to the desire to communicate the specifically tactile properties of the materials and thus emphasize the ultimate roots of all art and design in the natural realm of nature. The employment of colors and substances instantly reminiscent of both the elements and diverse organic forms eloquently attests to this proclivity. In the show, George's decision to have his pattern embroidered on the fabric for Yukari's dress could be seen to emanate precisely from a desire to augment the fabric's — and hence the garment's — physical presence. On myriad occasions, *Paradise Kiss* communicates its dedication to the corporeal dimension by corroborating Sarah Lonsdale's proposition that in the specific context of Japanese fashion, Japan's "reverence of materials" is tangibly demonstrated by its "selection, treatment and manipulation of fabric." These practices endeavor to synthesize "functionality with beauty," secure that "textiles ... are highly tactile in nature" and are hence likely to prove "just as exquisite to the touch as they are to the eye" (Lonsdale, p. 36). Most crucially, the approach to sartorial productivity championed by *Paradise Kiss* emphasizes that all creative engagements hold artistic value. Fashion design itself is no less noble an art than painting or sculpture. Accordingly, its more explicitly practical aspects — such as cutting, sewing and embroidering — are considered no less imaginative than the processes of conceptualization and visualization for which George is primarily responsible.

La Corda d'Oro — Primo Passo (TV series; dir. Koujin Ochi, 2005–2006) revolves around Kahoko Hino, a student at Seiso Academy whose ordinary life abruptly comes to an end upon meeting a mischievous fairy named Lili, who adopts from the start the Latin self-designation *fata* and thus instantly calls attention to his fatalistic role. Lili, whom no-one other than Kahoko appears able to perceive, chooses to reward the girl with a magical violin and a place in the prestigious annual musical contest to which so many of the girl's peers vainly aspire. Although Kahoko is at first reluctant to yield to Lili's intentions, she ends up accepting the gift and soon discovers, while practicing her pieces, that as long as she is familiar with the basic tune and puts her whole soul into the performance, she can play practically anything at all. This miracle, it transpires, is made possible by the special connection which the instrument affords between the performer and Lili himself, as long as he or she is tuned into the same wavelength as the *fata*. Lili is said to have constructed the violin singlehandedly by magical means after years of indefatigable research.

La Corda d'Oro is categorizable as a romance, a school drama or an inverted harem comedy. Nevertheless, it stands out primarily as a contemporary fairy tale about the importance of the past and its undying legacy. This proposition gains increasing validity as its melody-laced adventures unfold. We thus discover that the school was founded by a man reputed to have saved a small otherworldly creature and to have been blessed for his kindness. In addition, a past romance between two rival violinists brought together by a fairy circulates among the student population as a favorite rumor. This idea is revamped in the additional episodes aired as a summer special, *La Corda d'Oro — Secondo Passo* (dir. Ochi, 2009), where the former competitors in the musical contest are required to convene at a training camp during the summer break and one of Kahoko's closest friends waxes lyrical about the possibility of a "Summer Violin Romance" bound to mark "the start of a new legend." The girl's reference to "midsummer" as the perfect time for such an amorous development to occur implicitly invokes the drama's connection with fairy folk, midsummer being a pivotal moment in the species' calendar. Through its focus on the past, the anime could be said to offer a lore-encrusted and hence potentially transgressive alternative to mainstream conceptions of history and to the strategies of historiographical regimentation on which they routinely depend for their perpetuation. The idea of history recorded by the show has the mysterious substantiality — perceptible yet elusive — of fairy dust: the incontrovertible assertion of either its reality or its fictitiousness is bound to be a lie.

The experiential curve traced by Kahoko's vicissitudes resembles the trajectory followed by many fairy tale protagonists in the pursuit of self-understanding, autonomy and creative freedom. At the same time, the formative role played by music in Kahoko's life parallels the likewise shaping function served by fairy tales in a child's development as described by Bettelheim. "Fairy tales," argues the illustrious scholar and psychoanalyst, "unlike any other form of literature, direct the child to discover his identity and calling, and they also suggest what experiences are needed to develop his character further. Fairy tales intimate that a rewarding, good life is within one's reach despite adversity — but only if one does not shy away from the hazardous struggles without which one can never achieve true identity" (Bettelheim, p. 24). Also relevant to Kahoko's experiences is Bettelheim's assessment of the particular type of developmental process which the tale of *Sleeping Beauty* famously epitomizes. "In major life changes such as adolescence," Bettelheim maintains, "for successful growth opportunities both active and quiescent periods are needed. The turning inward, which in outer appearance looks like passivity (or sleeping one's life away), happens when internal mental processes of such importance go on within the person that he has no energy for outwardly directed action" (p. 225).

In Perrault's version of the tale, the importance of the phase of inactivity as key to any prospect of further growth is emphasized by the veritably endemic dimensions of the slumber in which the entire castle and the woods surrounding it are rapidly engulfed. The description, replete with minute details and humorous innuendoes, is one of the most memorable in Perrault's entire opus. In the Grimms' own adaptation, *Briar Rose*, the atmosphere of hushed stillness is more economically depicted, yet rendered equally effective by carefully chosen descriptive touches, such as the image of "the fire flickering on the hearth" growing "still" as the "meat" itself stops "crackling" (Grimm 2000, p. 33). Kahoko's oscillation between moments of heightened spiritedness and moments of melancholy

reflection as equally vital parts of her psychological maturation fully corroborates Bettelheim's contention. When three chords of her magical
instrument snap, the girl decides to give up playing for good and devotes
uncharacteristically protracted periods to morose introspection. Kahoko's
inactivity at this juncture is a crucial precondition of her later ability to
recover her customary energy and enthusiasm, rediscover her love of music
as the inexperienced player of a non-magical instrument and — no less
importantly — forge richer interpersonal connections.

La Corda d'Oro immediately announces its fairy tale affiliations with
the once-upon-a-time tone of its preamble. The action itself goes on to
consolidate the mood set by the anime's inceptive sequence by capitalizing
on a widespread motif which Katharine Briggs describes as "the fairy
dependence." This designates a narrative trend wherein fairies "are not
generally conceived of as existing in an independent and self-contained
state, but have great concern with mortal things." Thus, "however much
they resent human spying or human interference," they rely on mortals
quite persistently insofar as "human help is necessary to many of their
activities, and they greatly desire to influence human destiny" (Briggs, p.
113). This proposition is eloquently validated by the drama articulated in
La Corda d'Oro through its original reinvention of the fairy tale tradition.
The fata Lili is indeed presented as a creature who, despite his blatant
unearthliness, depends vitally on Kahoko's acceptance of his magical gift.
This is because without the active cooperation of the one student able to
perceive and communicate with him, Lili would be utterly powerless to
realize his vision: spreading music and heightening people's sensitivity to
that art's unique qualities. The fata's reliance on Kahoko is touchingly
conveyed by the discrepancy between his expectations regarding the girl's
response to the present, dramatized though flashbacks to Lili's fantasies
about Kahoko's undiluted enthusiasm in the face of such an unexpected
blessing, and the unsavory reality he must confront when Kahoko actually
rejects him. When the protagonist eventually accepts the preternatural violin and enters the musical world against the odds, Lili's agenda at least
wins its chance of fulfillment.

Nevertheless, the series is principally concerned with highlighting not
the dependence of the fairy upon his human associate, which would turn
Kahoko into something of a passive tool and Lili into a mere parasite, as
the value of interaction between the supernatural and the mortal realms.
It is in this interaction, we are continually reminded, that true creativity
lies. Accordingly, La Corda d'Oro does not seek to celebrate the sense of

absolute power which fairies may enjoy by controlling humans or to expose their inadequacy in the absence of human allies. Rather, it is interested in exploring the processes through which fairies and humans alike evolve as creative agents within a dialectical relationship — and not solely by magical means but also, and no less vitally, through courage, resilience and perseverance. The anime's finale as dramatized in the first season enthrones this message by foregrounding Kahoko's determination to learn how to play proficiently without recourse to supernatural aid, and by maximizing instead the import of the lessons she has learned along the way concerning the matchless value of genuine and tested friendship. Lili himself is shown to derive pleasure not only from the fulfillment of his personal vision but also from his heartfelt appreciation of the generosity and resourcefulness channeled by Kahoko into the venture. In some respects, Lili echoes the figures cited by Briggs in support of her argument regarding fairy dependence — e.g., Irish fairies reputed to "need a human to give them strength for their battles and games" or the specters in the *Odyssey* that must "drink blood to give them strength to answer" the hero's "questions" (p. 114). At the same time, however, the show's take on the fairy tale tradition indicates that fairies who, like Lili, are motivated by essentially altruistic objectives are in a position to abet their human helpers' own quest for self-discovery and self-realization.

La Corda d'Oro validates with disarming candor and tenacity at once Maria Tatar's contention that "Fairy tales are up close and personal, mixing fact with fantasy to tell us about our deepest anxieties and desires. They offer roadmaps pointing the way to romance and riches, power and privilege, and most importantly to a way out of the woods" (Tatar, p. xiv). In so doing, they provide a unique lens through which we may dispassionately assess our growth over time by pondering "what was once at stake in our life decisions and what is at stake today" (p. xix). The anime repeatedly underscores this point by proposing that honest development is only possible when we compare ourselves today with ourselves yesterday — and not with other people. At the same time, the show is keen to emphasize that no achievement is ever conclusive, no route out of trouble immune to infiltration by misleading detours. Fairies and magic may occasionally abet our efforts, in a metaphorical or literal fashion depending on our attitude to their existence. However, no achievement is possible without our own steadfast commitment to the task in hand. The character of Tsukimori makes this incontrovertibly clear, when his student colleague Tsuchiura opines that Kahoko "is a Cinderella whose magic wore off," by stating that the girl's own "persistence" is "real" and this is the only thing, ultimately, that truly matters.

Undeniably, the anime depicts Kahoko as a present-day version of the fairy tale type epitomized by the eponymous heroines of Perrault's *Donkeyskin* and *Cinderella*—i.e., the kindly and honest girls whose virtues are occluded by the humble appearances they are forced to adopt. Kahoko claims that her music is "fake" and her talent "deceitful," and that she simply has no "right" to play. Nonetheless, it becomes increasingly clear, as both regular and music students express genuine grief at her decision to give up the violin, that Lili's magical instrument enables Kahoko not to adopt a façade but rather to give her personality full expression — to maximize parts of her being that have not previously found any outlets. Kahoko's willingness to let her real self shine forth by playing the violin is the anime's equivalent of Donkeyskin and Cinderella shedding their imposed masks. While emphasizing its protagonist's creative achievements, the series closely mirrors the fairy tale tradition in its eschewal of neat answers in favor of circuitous explorations of human emotions that renew at each turn the necessity to go on asking questions as the precondition of genuine inventiveness. In the anime, as in the fairy tale tradition, there are no routes offering an unproblematic "straight ahead." Thus, Kahoko must learn through her own independent efforts the true significance of creativity and the magnitude of the sacrifices, humiliations and setbacks littering the path to fulfillment. Neither Lili nor any other preternatural being could ever guarantee her unrescindable success were she not willing to confront an introspective journey of unforeseeable and perturbing complexity. The Good Folk, it is thereby intimated, can only abet mortal ventures as long as humans are prepared to embark on a dynamic dialogue with the dusky beyond that is genuinely free of prejudices, of anthropocentric yearnings for mastery and, above all, of insular fear.

It is in its utilization of music, finally, that the anime lends fairy lore the most imaginative twist. In countless legends and anecdotes, fairies are said to resort to spellbinding melodies as a means of drawing humans into their domains, often with profoundly disturbing consequences. Music, therefore, is traditionally posited as a weapon through which the Little People assert their irresistible magnetism. *La Corda d'Oro*, by contrast, deploys music as an instrument capable of facilitating the collusion of otherwise incompatible reality levels — and hence as the very epitome of creative interplay. Importantly, music operates as such a bridge by bringing together not only Faërie and the mortal sphere but also the two starkly divided student categories accommodated by Seiso Academy.

Whereas *La Corda d'Oro* draws an explicit bond between music and the fairy tale tradition via the character of Lili the *fata* and his prodigious violin, the anime series *Nodame Cantabile* (dir. Ken'ichi Kasai, 2007) and its sequels, *Nodame Cantabile: Paris* (dir. Chiaki Kon, 2008) and *Nodame Cantabile: Finale* (dir. Chiaki Kon, 2010), infuse its music-dominated story with fairy tale elements in an oblique fashion. In so doing, it brings out the form's more exuberant and carnivalesque proclivities by recourse to comedy, while simultaneously engaging in the thorough exploration of a transformative process of self-discovery and maturation. The anime revolves around Megumi Noda, a.k.a. "Nodame," as she insists on being called: an exceptionally gifted second-year piano student at Momogaoka College of Music. The show's zany dimension comes immediately to the fore with its heroine's characterization as a sloppy, lazy and gluttonous girl who will use any excuse to play by ear rather than according to proper notation. Central to the action is Nodame's romantic attraction to the megatalented third-year student Shinichi Chiaki. A conceited polyglot born into a musical family, the youth is equally accomplished at the piano and the violin but dreams of becoming a conductor and trains himself accordingly while majoring in the piano. At the same time, he is persecuted by a preposterously acute fear of flying that makes him the butt of several visual jokes but incrementally gathers psychological depth as the phobia's root in a traumatic childhood experience is unearthed. Concomitantly, Nodame's aversion to strict musical training is gradually revealed to originate in her juvenile subjection to an abusive piano instructor.

Although Shinichi is slow to acknowledge Nodame's true worth, the two characters tortuously establish a mutually enriching relationship through which they learn some invaluable lessons about themselves and about their peers, tutors and sponsors. Shinichi, urged by Nodame to lead a student orchestra, is able to transcend the cage of his solipsistic arrogance by coming to appreciate other people's talents and ambitions and to respect both their merits and their foibles. Nodame, for her part, learns from Shinichi how to face her fears and take risks in her musical development. In this anime, as in practically all of the titles examined in this chapter, the coming-of-age component of the fairy tale tradition is enthroned as pivotal to the entire drama. *Nodame Cantabile* may not feature literal fairies but there can be little doubt that the aura of enchantment and wonder exuded by its protagonists' creative quests places it firmly within a fairy tale mentality. Relatedly, it is through a quintessentially fairytalish property, charm, that the anime succeeds in holding together its romance, its comedic ingredients and its more somber messages with magisterial dexterity. In this context, "charm" alludes at once to a particular kind of aesthetic and tonal appeal and to a spellbinding force able to capture and retain the viewer's attention from beginning to end. *Nodame Cantabile* also echoes two distinctive preferences evinced by Japanese fairy tales: that is, a predilection for non-linear narration allowing for a spontaneous accumulation of events and incremental disclosure of character traits, and the detailed representation of quotidian activities of the most mundane kind imaginable (such as cooking, eating, sleeping, bathing) alongside epiphanic moments with no concern for rigid hierarchical considerations. A visual atmosphere redolent of the fairy tale tradition at its most mellow is concurrently communicated by the watercolor style adopted by the animation, most strikingly in the execution of both natural and urban settings.

The fairy tale tradition makes a cameo appearance in the show when Shinichi, as a privileged youth who has never had to endure a single moment of financial hardship in his entire life, is taunted by Nodame with the question of whether he knows what poverty is, and immediately proceeds to entertain a mental image of the hapless protagonist of Andersen's *The Little Match Girl* as she nears death. The brief scene flashing through Shinichi's mind at this juncture in the form of faded anime footage is rendered in a style so deliberately stereotypical as to verge on parody, suggesting that for the young man, the fairy tale tradition functions as a repository of archetypal formulae to be invoked in the face of the unknown as the provider of pat readymade answers. In the course of the same segment of the drama, we also find an indirect allusion to the preference for tales of the supernatural based on malefic spells, well-ingrained in indigenous lore, with the trope of the "cursed violin" supposed to have caused a prosperous businessman's economic ruin.

Nodame herself plays a fairy-like role throughout, reflecting the Little People's proverbial ambiguity. Therefore, whereas she is compared to an "imp" while behaving in a mischievous or scheming fashion, she is also portrayed as a benevolent agent, capable of acting as a catalyst among discordant forces and thus bringing together disparate people or even leading antagonistic parties to reconciliation. The girl's capacity to reawaken the imaginative side of Shinichi's family, repressed in the name of financial success and philistine common sense, bears witness to this power with great dramatic verve. In addition, one of the key judges evaluating the participants' performance in a competition joined by Nodame in the anime's climactic episodes exhibits a marked penchant for fairy tale imagery. At one point, he overtly compares the heroine to an "*onibi* [demon fire] trying to bewitch travelers." Intriguingly, this assessment is proffered in the course of Nodame's performance of Franz Liszt's Transcendental Etude No. 5 in B-flat *Feux Follets* (i.e., Will o' the Wisp). Later in the contest, another performer is compared to "a little demon wandering the streets late at night, when people seldom walk," reminiscent of "the phantom Scarbo"—the judge's assistant is quick to point out, at this juncture, that Scarbo is actually supposed to be "a fairy." The piece being performed is indeed Maurice Ravel's *Gaspard de la Nuit*, Third Movement, "Scarbo," where this creature is posited as something of a spectral goblin. Nodame herself has a tendency to visualize the pieces she plays throughout the series in terms of fairy tale scenarios replete with fantasy figures and enchanted locales and punctuated by appearances of the characters from her favorite anime and multimedia franchise, *Puri-Gorota*. Despite Nodame's flamboyant imagination and preference for childlike pursuits, the girl's approach to the fairy tale tradition never revels in romanticized cuteness. In fact, some of the most memorable scenes she envisions in this vein feature doomed characters and tragic endings. This proposition is starkly confirmed by Nodame's visual interpretation of the "pitiful end" endured by the titular clown puppet Petrouchka from Igor Stravinsky's ballet, which she perceives as analogous to her own failure when a spiteful rival (the "Scarbo" player himself) taunts her with crippling memories of her childhood afflictions.

However, it is not so much through its hints at actual fairy tales and legends as through its sensitive articulation of a genuinely uplifting rite of passage that *Nodame Cantabile* mirrors the fairy tale tradition's intrinsic ethos. This is particularly true of the installments in which the erstwhile snooty Shinichi learns to interact with people who, though far less talented than him, have the power to teach him the unsurpassed value of collaborative effort and selfless creativity. In this respect, the youth learns more from the idiosyncratic members of "Orchestra S" than he could ever hope to learn either from the highfliers of "Orchestra A" or indeed from any great maestro of international repute. At the same time, *Nodame Cantabile* frequently evinces the fairy tale tradition's proverbial taste for unpredictability. This is typically borne out by the events surrounding Shinichi's earnest attempt to create a proper orchestra consisting of top-notch students with good chances of becoming professionals after graduation, and facing the prospect of a public début in a vast and esteemed hall. Aware that several members of his orchestra are also scheduled to take part in a prestigious contest, and worried that their anxiety — compounded, in a few cases, with the experience of first love — might adversely affect their performance, the budding conductor resolves to suspend all rehearsals until the aftermath of the competition so as to alleviate the pressure. Things take an unexpected turn as two of the most promising musicians perform abysmally in the contest due to their affective vicissitudes and attendant contretemps, and hence become determined to leave their mark by pulling off an impressive performance at the upcoming concert — which fortuitously militates in favor of Shinichi's own vision. In this portion of the drama, as in the fairy tale tradition at large, chance, accident and contingency are far more powerful forces in determining a situation's outcome than any degree of rational planning and cold calculation.

In enthroning music as a pivotal component of their thematic and technical makeup, *La Corda d'Oro* and *Nodame Cantabile* echo a long-standing alliance between music and fairies. This is widely typified by the prominence of song, melody and dance in legion accounts of the fairy folk's rituals and customs. Fairies may be glimpsed as they flit through twilight skies while playing harps or jingling bells, or as they dance in rings on shores and over mossy glens with a full moon shining upon them. Moreover, while they are reputed to be able both to mind-read and to speak all human languages (current and extinct ones alike), fairies are no less renowned for their knack of forging exquisite instruments out of flowers and leaves, such as snowdrop lutes and bluebell trumpets, and — most intriguingly — for their ability to teach birds how to sing and use magical strains of music to draw woodland creatures to their side. The painting "The Fairy Musicians" (a.k.a. "The Concert") by John Anster Fitzgerald (1832–1906) captures this particular belief with mesmerizing charm. While Fitzgerald's image is magical in a quintessential sense, exuding charm, numinosity and wonder in equal measures, and has the power to transport the viewer to an alternate reality at a mere glance, Richard Doyle (1824–1883) offers a humorous variation on the subject with "Rehearsal in Elfland: Musical Elf Teaching the Young Birds to Sing." Its caricatured birds come across as clumsy performers, either puzzled by their mentor's instructions or else powerless to reproduce the desired notes and more likely, in fact, to squeak or squawk most awkwardly. Intriguingly, the elf is visually reminiscent of both Hinoko and Nodame, particularly by virtue of its hairstyle and impish expression.

According to Iain Zaczek, "In all the early reports of fairy activities, one of the most consistent elements was the emphasis on music. It played an important part both in their revels and in their solemn processions. The music itself varied considerably to suit these different occasions. Sometimes it was wild and frenetic, ideal for dancing. At other times it resembled a low chanting, echoing the fairies' ambiguous association with the spiritual world." The common belief that fairy music is hazardous to human ears due to its beguiling powers "did not deter musicians from trying to learn its secrets. Many bagpipe and fiddle tunes are said to be based on the plaintive melodies heard by rural folk, when eavesdropping at fairy gatherings" (Zaczek, p. 57). The kinship of fairies and music is further attested to by the proclivity evinced in various cultures to enshrine the fairy tale tradition in the musical domain. Nineteenth-century Europe provides a paradigmatic instance of this trend. In this context, a substantial volume of classical pieces inspired by fairies and fairy lore rapidly blossomed, often fueled by the Romantic passion for supernatural themes and pantheistic idealization of nature. Fairies were also frequently regarded as Euterpe's progeny and hence deemed capable of acting as inspiring muses for the zealous composer. Not seldom, these muses would find visible materialization in the graceful ballerinas peopling the contemporary stage.

As Christopher Wood maintains, numerous "composers" of this period found inspiration in the world of Faërie, "from Weber to Gilbert and Sullivan," and its denizens rapidly infiltrated "opera as well as ballet." "Weber was the first," Wood avers, "to turn 'A Midsummer Night's Dream' into an opera, which he entitled 'Oberon, or the Elf-King's Oath' (1826).... Inspired both by the play and by Weber's 'Oberon,' Mendelssohn composed his 'A Midsummer Night's Dream Overture' to write a scherzo on the theme of Shakespeare's Queen Mab speech in 'Romeo and Juliet'" (Wood, p. 58). This is clearly not the place to enumerate all — or even a substantial proportion — of the fairy-related musical works created in the nineteenth century. What must be stressed, however, is that even when the public's interest in fairy music began to flag in the early twentieth century, as shown by the limited success enjoyed by "Gilbert's ... operetta entitled 'Fallen Fairies, or the Wicked World,'" the genre retained its appeal in many quarters. Thus, "Dvořák's 'Rusalka' of 1901, which tells the story of a handsome prince who falls in love with a wood nymph, was a success, and has remained a popular opera ever since." This would appear to indicate that even though the fairy tale tradition mutates over time, it never becomes conclusively obsolete. According to Wood, "fairies are one of those recurring themes that every age has to reinterpret for itself" (p. 60). Briggs corroborates this proposition with specific reference to "English fairy beliefs, which from Chaucer's time onwards," she argues, "have been supposed to belong to the last generation and to be lost to the present one. The strange thing is that rare, tenuous and fragile as it is, the tradition is still there, and lingers on from generation to generation substantially unchanged. Every now and then poets and writers draw on the tradition, and make out of it something suitable to the spirit of their age" (Briggs, p. 3).

La Corda d'Oro and *Nodame Cantabile*'s appropriation of the fairy tale tradition via music does not connect them solely with Victorian culture. In fact, it draws attention to the intimate bond tying the visual realm — here epitomized by the medium of anime itself— and music over an extensive historical span. The series indeed reminds us assiduously that musical and visual sensibilities have colluded in multifarious ways throughout human civilization. Their studious rendition of monuments and edifices, which reaches its apotheosis with the statue of Lili enthroned in Seiso Academy's forecourt and the academic compound as a whole in *La Corda d'Oro* and diverse concert halls in *Nodame Cantabile*, underscore throughout the shows that their aesthetic merit is somewhat inextricable from the flow of melodies coursing and invigorating their whole texture in the guise of life-sustaining lymph. Concomitantly, the anime's graphic compositions meet and merge with the musical compositions constantly performed within the series' worlds, while the notes and harmonies issuing from the music coalesce with the notes and harmonies of the anime's color schemes. As the shows' polysemic language adventurously reaches toward musical visuality and visual musicality at once, their enchantingly varied soundtracks come to be saturated with pictorial qualities that allow the spectator to visualize their power and rhythm.

La Corda d'Oro interleaves the contemporary reality of Japanese academic life with ancient legend. *Paradise Kiss* and *Nodame Cantabile* likewise focus on a present-day cultural situation, yet hark back to a time-honored perspective on artistic production infused with allusions to fairy tales. Electing a past epoch as its setting, *Earl and Fairy* (TV series; dir. Kouichirou Sohtome, 2008) ushers us into one of the most problematic periods and places as far as the fairy tale tradition is concerned: Victorian Britain. Proverbially obsessed with the hegemonic promulgation of the cult of science as the ultimate arbiter in the order of things, this milieu is nonetheless renowned for its passion for fantasy-laden titillation and preternatural encounters. The anime's protagonist, the "fairy doctor" Lydia Carlton, is caught right in the middle of this double-bind mentality. Blessed with the rare power to see and interact with fairies, which she has inherited from her late mother, the heroine must contend with the dicta of a society that bluntly refuses to believe in the existence of those creatures. Even though Lydia's honest, resourceful and highly resilient disposition nourishes her determination to go on communing with the realm of Faërie in the face of both skepticism and derision, and hence prevents her from surrendering to despondent disenchantment in the way less mettlesome fairy doctors have done, her services are seldom sought out. It is hardly surprising, in the circumstances, that she should be regularly strapped for cash and resigned to a fundamentally uneventful provincial existence in suburban Edinburgh. Her only steady companion is the liquor-loving fairy cat Nico, a shrewd shape-shifter endowed not merely with the faculty of speech — which might be expected on generic grounds — but also with a penchant for elaborate rhetoric and witticisms. Moreover, Lydia's everyday life is unremittingly energized by a natural environment that seems purposely designed to accommodate Cicely Mary Barker's delicious Flower Fairies amid impeccably rendered vegetation. Barker's art, as Kimie Imura points out, is indeed a major influence behind many of Japan's contemporary depictions of fairies (in Amano, p. 78).

Akin to psychic detectives or even the nomadic medicine sellers of times gone by, fairy doctors operate as "liaisons between humans and faeries." One of their principal objectives is to safeguard the supernatural entities' welfare in a world so blind to their existence as to be often likely to harm them, albeit unwittingly. Should a fairy accidentally spill into the human domain, for example, a practitioner like Lydia has the power to help her return to her natural home by creating magical paths pointing in the right direction. The heroine's sedate and modest routine is abruptly brought to an end by the advent of Edgar Ashenbert. Stating that he is the rightful heir of the leader of the Fairy Nation, Blue Knight Earl (a.k.a. the Earl of Ibrazel), and that this entitles him to the possession of a magical heirloom known as the "Noble Sword of the Merrow," Edgar seeks Lydia's assistance in the retrieval of his inheritance, supposedly absconded three centuries earlier, in order to "assert his royal claim." An inherently schizoid figure, Edgar comes across as devious, conceited and narcissistic in the extreme, yet also charismatic, gallant and highly polished. This fascinating juxtaposition of contrasting traits makes it arduous for Lydia to resist the young man's advances, which grow in both frequency and intensity as the story progresses. However, what ultimately draws the fairy doctor to her employer is not so much the arsenal of mannerisms and rhetorical flourishes peppering his wooing style as her deep-seated feeling — sustained by the kind of sixth sense which only proficient fairy doctors are held to possess — that Edgar is intrinsically honest.

It is also noteworthy that despite his reputation as an irresistible Casanova and socialite, Edgar harbors a dark past of dispossession, humiliation and abuse. Born in an aristocratic family, the young man is said to have been deprived of his status when his father, accused of treason, resolved to slaughter his entire line with the sole exception of Edgar and commit suicide. In the wake of these horrific events, the boy endured slavery and torture, and although he is now free at long last, he still carries the "mark of a slave" branded on his tongue by his tormentor during his captivity. Furthermore, Edgar is unrelentingly hounded down by the sinister character of Gotham, a psychiatrist eager to utilize his intended prey's brain as a fitting object of study in his perverse research into criminal psychology. Thus, Edgar's fairy tale credentials as a roguish variation on the formula of the Knight in Shining Armor are persistently counterbalanced by a murky legacy redolent of the fairy tale tradition's duskier horizons. The young man's closest fictional relative, in this regard, is *Jane Eyre's* Edward Rochester.

Earl and Fairy abounds with more or less explicit allusions to famous members of the Fair Folk, including the fairy queens Titania and Gwendolen, alongside references to objects and emblems typically connected with the fairy tale tradition — jewels, amulets, weapons, heirlooms and costumes among them. At one point, Nico sports a costume, supposedly given to him by the Earl as a special present, that places him overtly in the role of an anime reincarnation of the titular hero from Perrault's *Puss in Boots*. Most importantly, the anime accommodates a veritable panoply of preternatural beings, depicting representative specimens of each category it brings into play as thoroughly individuated creatures through the ingenious amalgamation of established motifs and details of the show's own creative conception. Alongside the aforementioned banshee, the fairy types featuring as either physical presences or verbal references in the series include pixies (Celtic fairies), spunkies (a.k.a. will-o'-the-wisps); phoukas (shape-shifters often materializing as wild horses), coblynau (mining gnomes), hobgoblins (prankish tricksters like Shakespeare's Puck), leprechauns (naughty fairies in the form of old men garbed in green), chulichauns (alcohol-loving spirits), and several members of the Unseelie (i.e., unholy) Court. Among the most intriguing fairy characters are the anime's brownies, fairies well-versed in the undertaking of household chores that have served as the model for Girl Guides aged between seven and ten.

Likewise worthy of attention are selkies (or silkies): namely, sea fairies endowed with seals' coats which they can wear as a form of camouflage in the proximity of mortals and shed to revel on sandy shores on moonlit nights. As the tale of *The Mer-Wife* shows with memorable pathos and an upliftingly joyful ending, should a selkie's marine dress be lost or stolen, the creature would be condemned to a fate of poverty and squalor in a permanent human form (in Gibbings). This narrative, well-known in the context of Scottish mythology and lore, finds a direct Japanese correlative in the fairy tale *The Tale of the Bamboo-Cutter*, where a practically identical drama is proposed with the difference that the role played by the selkie's pelt in *The Mer-Wife* is here assigned to a celestial maiden's feathery gown. This story and related variations on the same theme in Nipponic lore is addressed in Chapter 5. The classic selkie is honored by *Earl and Fairy* through the enigmatic character of Raven's sister, Ermine: a human girl said to have become a metamorphic fairy upon her death and to be bound to the story's archenemy, the "Prince of Misfortune," by the villain's unlawful possession of her magical pelt.

One of the most interesting characters presented in *Earl and Fairy* is undoubtedly Kelpie, a handsome, prepotent and yet deeply sensitive young man hell-bent on making Lydia his wife at any price. Kelpie's true form, as it happens, is that of a formidable black-maned water horse. In Scottish mythology, kelpies are indeed magical steeds notorious for leading their human riders to enchanted houses beneath the roaring waves whence the hapless mortals are unlikely ever to return. The kelpie's victims are said to stick to the fairy stallion's slick body as if magnetized past any hope of self-severance from it. The anime's character may well wish to have the same conclusively proprietorial impact on Lydia but the fairy doctor's intellectual acuity, lucidity and independence of spirit preclude any such outcome. Another notable fairy character featured in *Earl and Fairy* in a prominent position is Raven, Edgar's magical assistant. Saved and sheltered by his master when everyone else seemed to want his destruction, and despise his presumed lack of humanity, Raven is undeniably implacable when it comes to protecting Edgar from his enemies and would not hesitate to kill in cold blood and by the most gruesome of means were he to sense the slightest threat to his benefactor. Incrementally humanized by Lydia's presence, and hence enabled to adopt attitudes that transcend his erstwhile robotic loyalty, Raven stands out as a paradigmatic incarnation of the fairy folk's conflation of contrasting tendencies and meanings, and thus tersely reminds us of the fallaciousness of all monolithic cultural perceptions of those creatures.

The anime does not fail, in its enthusiastically commodious inclusion of disparate fairy types, to dwell on the unique fascination held by merfolk. This species populates the show's entire yarn with variable degrees of emphasis and explicitness — the term "merrow" associated with the magical object pivotal to the adventure being indeed synonymous with merfolk. In *Earl and Fairy*, merfolk features both in the guise of the classic mermaid as a gold-haired beauty capable of drawing mortals to dismal ends and in the more original form of the human-fish hybrid typified by the character of Tomkins, Edgar's amiable butler. This persona's piscine connection is denoted merely by vague hints in his facial attributes and by the fin on his back: a feature that remains unseen by the audience of which he is immensely proud. While mermaids have been persistently associated with the perils of a human's bewitchment by a preternatural seductress, it should be remembered that those sea creatures are by no means invulnerable and that in making contact with the world of mortals, they do so at their own — potentially fatal — risk. This is attested to by Andersen's *The Little Mermaid*, where the sheer horror enveloping the hybrid's grief and pain are conveyed with almost unbearable intensity. Nevertheless, it can hardly be disputed that in sea lore at large, mortals caught in the underwater realm usually fail to flourish, whereas marine fairies displaced onto the human world are able to survive quite happily or even prosper.

The anime's wide-ranging take on fairy folk is further complemented by tasteful allusions to the pictorial vogue of the period in which the drama is set. These are most imaginatively effected by recourse to frames devoted to fairy paintings executed by the aspiring artist Paul Ferman, which evince some distinctive traits of Victorian art focused on the Little People, their environments and lifestyles, and their dramatic or lyrical incarnations (e.g., in Shakespeare's *A Midsummer Night's Dream*).

As anticipated, *Earl and Fairy* also makes original use of the traditional figure of the banshee in the presentation of the fairy member of the Ashenbert family who hosts, sealed within her very soul, its entire collective memory. While this character's portrayal is consonant with ancient lore in emphasizing her penchant for prophesying imminent death, it nonetheless evinces some inspired touches of anime genius in throwing into relief the banshee's infinite kindness and self-sacrificial heroism. The figure is indeed instrumental in abetting Edgar's claim to his title, and thereby securing the defeat of the false Blue Knight Earl who poses as her legitimate master and holds her captive, at the cost of her own survival in mortal form. The same banshee, notably, has predicted Edgar's death — a fate the hero is prepared for and faces with somewhat uncharacteristic courage in the knowledge that the ultimate responsibility entailed by his name is not so much the ownership of the Sword itself as the defeat of the "Prince of Misfortune" — a goal yet to be accomplished as the series draws to a temporarily happy close, which leaves the adventure refreshingly open-ended and amenable to revisitation.

The multifarious fairy types invoked by *Earl and Fairy* frequently bring to mind Yoshitaka Amano's own classification of diverse supernatural characters in the splendid artbook *Fairies*, a cross-cultural work of unique caliber also mentioned in this book's opening chapter. Amano devotes a substantial portion of the volume to his interpretation of characters from *A Midsummer Night's Dream*, subsequently supplying both pictorial and verbal portraits of the following figures:

- Leprechaun
- Clurican
- Boggart
- Ellylon
- Knockers
- Seelie Court
- Pixies
- Brownies
- Habetrot
- Foul Weather
- Hedley Kow
- Goblins
- Ainsel
- Puca
- Changelings
- Trpws
- Robin Goodfellow
- Swan Maidens
- Etaín
- Triamour
- Merlin and Nimue
- Mermaid
- Gwragged Annwn

Just as *Earl and Fairy* harnesses a quintessentially Japanese medium to an adventurous fictionalized depiction of a particular component of Western culture, so Amano enlists his graphic, chromatic and poetic sensibility to engineer an alchemical coalescence of Eastern and Western lore. Many fairy categories of the kind portrayed in *Earl and Fairy* and Amano's artbook alike are proverbially two-faced. Elves, for instance, may abet mortal craftsmen such as cobblers or dressmakers but also love devising elaborate birthmarks for the as yet unborn. Boggarts may inhabit a human household without causing any trouble but are also notorious for disturbing bed covers and curtains, close doors and rearrange pots and pans at their will. Kobold are even more explicitly helpful as members of the household but are easily piqued and prone to vindictiveness if they are not punctually provided with sweet milk. Nisse and Trasgues are likewise short-tempered and will rapidly shift from a mood of domestic cooperativeness to one of vengeful indignation whenever they feel slighted.

As Imura intimates in the inspiring essay placed at the end of the art-book, it is important to realize that the part played by fairies in both traditional and contemporary Japanese culture is in itself intrinsically ambiguous. On the one hand, fairies might not seem to feature as such in Japan's visual arts "until the 1980s," when indigenous "artists began to produce their own drawings and models of fairies" (in Amano, p. 78). On the other hand, "a being that resembles a fairy" known as "sennyo" features "in Japanese literature in the *Genko Shakusho* in 1322," while entities such as "Tenjou (Buddhist or Taoist angel-fairies)" (p. 76), "kappa (water imps)," "amanjaku (river demons)," "yama otoko (mountain giants)" and "yama-uba (mountain crones)," though not literally classifiable as fairies in the Western sense of the term, indubitably evince strong similarities with them. In any case, as emphasized at several points throughout this study, there is no unequivocal definition of the fairy figure — let alone the essence of fairyhood — in any known Western civilization and assuming to find a singular direct equivalent for a being that is largely undefined even *within* a culture *outside* that culture's compass would be simply absurd. What is vital to acknowledge in the present context is that shows that deal either overtly (like *Earl and Fairy* and *La Corda d'Oro*) or else metaphorically (like *Paradise Kiss*, *Honey and Clover* and *Nodame Cantabile*) not simply with fairies but with the fairy tale tradition at large can be seen precisely as attempts to work productively with the fairy figure's culturally ambiguous status. This tendency is attributable to two interrelated factors. At one level, they venture into Western traditions by deploying characters and situations we can recognize as familiar, while at another level, they remain resolutely Nipponic in relying upon the aesthetic and technical qualities of an art form — anime itself — that is saturated with indigenous values and is appreciated as such all over the world even by those who seek to emulate it adaptively to satisfy the expectations of societies other than Japan.

The TV series *Honey and Clover* (2005) shares its director with *Nodame Cantabile* but while the later anime affords Kasai copious opportunities for zestful comedy and occasional forays into farce and satire, *Honey and Clover* evinces a cumulatively broodier atmosphere. The concomitantly creative and emotional evolution chronicled by *Honey and Clover* is akin to Hans and Gretel's forced excursion into the wilderness,

Sleeping Beauty's quiescent transition to maturity, the Fire-Fly's Lovers' pursuit of cherished treasures, the Japanese frogs' exploration of unknown lands. In short, it is a developmental experience infused through and through with fairy tale topoi of great significance. The knots and brambles of the anime's figurative wood are its characters' churning emotions, its silent chambers, those of young minds in search of dreams; its precious rewards, their chances of fulfillment; it exotic territories, those of their unforeseeable futures. The series revolves around three art students living in the same derelict apartment block and attending the same college — Yuuta Takemoto, Shinobu Morita and Takumi Mayama. These characters' routine is disrupted by the appearance on the scene of first-year student Hagumi Hanamoto, with whom Yuuta and Shinobu, in particular, become instantly infatuated. Whereas the latter intimidates Hagumi with his overly explicit professions of interest and obsessive urge to photograph her or otherwise treat her physique as an endless source of creative inspiration, Yuuta keeps quiet about his feelings and strives instead to befriend her. Initially shy and reclusive, the girl by and by opens up to her new acquaintances, revealing hitherto submerged facets of her personality. This love triangle is complemented by a second variation on the same theme. This pivots on Takumi, the popular pottery master Ayumi Yamada, and Rika Harada, an older woman who runs an inventive architecture studio. While Ayumi is besotted with Takumi and thus disregards the attentions showered upon her by several young men, Takumi himself is in love with Rika.

These emotional vicissitudes would no doubt seem trite and formulaic were it not for the anime's intelligently sustained effort to instill them with rare psychological credibility and thereby articulate a realistic language of feeling. The anime's realism, in turn, would not reach us as effectively as it does were it not for its fusion with an ambience tangentially derived from the fairy tale tradition at its most dreamlike and surreal. This is most poignantly evoked by character presentation, and especially by the use of soft outlines and mellow colors to mute the actors' rawest emotions through subtle expressions. The anime's depictions of various facets of both the built environment and the natural world are modulated so as to supply a keen match for these physiognomic features. As each pivotal persona enjoys a moment in the spotlight, the show's mood transits fluently between energetic action and angst-ridden contemplation, comedy and pathos. What we are never allowed to ignore, even at the heights of glee, is the drama's propensity to ponder the darkness that besieges at all times the seemingly safe daylight of mundane concerns and preoccupations. This is the very darkness to which the fairy tale tradition consistently returns in order to symbolize, as Diane Purkiss puts it, the "dissolution of identity." The principal reasons for which "we fear the dark," the critic contends, are that "we cannot see in it" and, at the same time, "cannot be seen in it, cannot be known, recognized." Darkness is a borderline area between life and death, presence and absence. The metaphorical assimilation of darkness to the evaporation of selfhood reaches a forbidding culmination with the equation of darkness to "unlife" (Purkiss, p. 15) — to "the darkness of death" itself, where our existence might be "forgotten" altogether, and identity might be irretrievably "lost in the sense of never having been known" (p. 22).

This is the fate which Sora in *Someday's Dreamers: Summer Skies* dreads most, over and above the corporeal reality of death as such — which is why she longs for Gouta to remember her even after, in some hypothetical future, he has got married and become a father. It is also why, when she uses her magic to revive a woman who has been locked in a coma for a long time and discovers that upon awakening, the patient preserves no memories of her previous life, Sora feels utterly devastated. (The anime as a whole is here discussed in Chapter 3: Voyages.) *Honey and Clover* itself colors its drama's perception of darkness with distinctive nuances by maximizing the disquieting connotations of the phenomenon of marginality traditionally associated with Faërie and its inhabitants through its emphasis on the vicissitudes of adolescence and early adulthood as quintessentially liminal stages in human development (and indeed in the growth of many domestic animals), thus offering a generational equivalent for the liminality of fairyland itself. Few anime with a college romance at their core have been able to make use of their characters' adolescent status so poignantly. The darkness dramatized by *Honey and Clover* lies with the tangle of emotions which its character chemistry assiduously foregrounds: an amalgam of insecurity, weakness, irrational anxiety, a lacerating longing for indistinct goals, the fear of rejection and abandonment, twilight loneliness. This affective topos remains axial throughout, finding further elaboration and provisional closure in the sequel *Honey and Clover II* (TV series; dir. Tatsuyuki Nagai, 2006).

Hagumi herself abides in anime memory as a unique incarnation of the fairy figure's proverbial ambiguity. Neatly described by Takumi as a "tiny person" upon her first onscreen appearance, the girl is thus immediately associated by her size with fairy physiognomy. Although Hagumi is already eighteen at the beginning of the series, she looks like a child and her somatic infantilism is an undeniably integral component of her overall cuteness — a quality fueled by her golden locks and sapphire irises, which are instantly reminiscent of many a portrayals of the fairy figure in paintings of all ages and especially of the Victorian period. However, just as fairies' supposedly diminutive size often coexists with formidable powers suggestive of far more imposing presences, so Hagumi's doll-like appearance is starkly contradicted by her creative output, where gently molded forms and mellow hues coexist at all times with forbidding figures distinguished by titanic dimensions and grim expressions. Furthermore, Hagumi is explicitly compared to both "Sleeping Beauty" and to an "elf." She is akin to Sleeping Beauty insofar as she is still emotionally inexperienced and has not yet learned to grasp the real meaning of her feelings — and especially of being in love — but more like an elf when it comes to her mature apprehension of life, as borne out by her belief that Shinobu must be free to pursue his goals unimpeded even if this inevitably entails his absence and hence her pain. An additional connection between Hagumi and the fairy tale tradition is supplied by her portrayal as a *Korobokkuru* in one of the countless photographs of the girl taken by Shinobu and deployed online with lucrative intent. The image presents Hagumi as a gnome-like entity accompanied by the caption "Finally Discovered." *Korobokkuru* are a semi-legendary race of lilliputian beings in Ainu folklore and share numerous characteristics with Western fairies, including an equivocal admixture of benevolence and malice. The butterbur leaf in the shade of which Hagumi's figure stands is meant to corroborate the picture's credibility since *Korobokkuru* are commonly believed to live in pits roofed with such leaves.

All of *Honey and Clover's* principal characters harbor distinctive creative visions traversed by oblique connections with the fairy tale tradition. For example, Ayumi's devotion to the spirit of the earth whence her brilliant pottery arises brings to mind the intimate bond uniting fairies' activities and the natural domain as recorded by fairy lore over the centuries. Yuuta's creativity also harks back to that tradition insofar as the youth is said to have discovered his vocation as a prospective architect out of an instinctive inclination to make things with his hands — this proclivity echoes the artisanal competence often ascribed by fairy lore to all manner of elves, dwarfs and goblins. Shinobu's approach to creative production deserves special attention in the present context. The eclectic artist's vision is characterized by persistent efforts to marry art and business, and thus reminds us that the ideal of creativity as a metaphysical and utterly non-materialistic pursuit bears scarce resemblance to the reality of cultural consumption. The fairy tale tradition itself has been long imbricated with the actual world of commerce insofar as its pivotal actors have been at the nub of a veritable *fairy industry* for centuries. The connection between fairies and business is famously allegorized in Christina Rossetti's poem "Goblin Market" (1862), a work often seen to uphold Victorian mores regarding female sexuality and women's social standing through its emphasis on the pernicious effects of the enticing fruits sold by goblin merchants at dusk.

A more recent and blatant instance of the confluence of Faërie and commerce indubitably consists of the multi-billion Disney franchise centered on the character of Tinker Bell from *Peter Pan*, originally adapted by Disney into an animated movie in 1953. Moreover, as Zaczek maintains, "Like Tinker Bell herself, the fairy phenomenon has never quite disappeared. There are proprietary brands of soap and washing-up liquid named after a fairy — a reminder that good fairies liked to lend a hand with the housework.... More recently, the Dark Lords of Sith in the *Star Wars* films were inspired by a Celtic fairy (a *sith*)" (Zaczek, p. 9). A further instance of the productive partnership between fairies and commerce is the myth of the Tooth Fairy. Though ancient, this has gained unprecedented popularity in the aftermath of the Second World War, spawning a miniature culture industry of its own. According to Peter Narváez, this sudden rise to fame of an otherwise relatively marginal fantasy is a corollary of "postwar affluence" (Narváez, p. 413) and bears witness to an important economic development. The ritual underpinning Tooth Fairy mythology is an overt case of "open market exchange" since its implied message is "'produce and sell.'" While "non-exchange economies" would typically commend the value encapsulated by the imperative to "'produce and hoard,'" the "more fluid economies" on which the contemporary vision of the Tooth Fairy thrives foster a "marketplace logic," and the old practice of "barter" gives way to "cash payment" (p. 416).

The concept of cuteness, encapsulated by the Japanese term "*kawaii,*" has doubtlessly supported the alliance of art and business. Axial not only to *Honey and Clover*'s portrayal of Hagumi but also to Japan's contemporary representations of fairies at large, the ethos of *kawaii* has influenced deeply innumerable aspects of Japan's culture industry for several decades. The article "Japan smitten by love of cute" supplies a characteristically Janus-faced portrait of *kawaii*, arguing that "Cute is cool in Japan. Look anywhere and everywhere: Cartoon figures dangle from mobile phones, waitresses bow in frilly maid outfits, bows adorn bags, even police departments boast cuddly mascots.... Japanese have come up with nuances of cute and use phrases such as 'erotic-cute' and 'grotesque-cute' in conversation.... Sceptics

... say Japan's pursuit of cute is a sign of an infantile mentality and worry that Japanese culture — historically praised for exquisite understatement as sparse rock gardens and woodblock prints — may be headed toward doom." Less censorious cultural analysts such as Tomoyuki Sugiyama, by contrast, propose that "cute is rooted in Japan's harmony-loving culture." Moreover, current vogues associated with the *kawaii* explosion, such as collecting figurines and other diminutive ornaments as mementoes, "can be traced back 400 years to the Edo Period, when tiny carved 'netsuke' charms were wildly popular" ("Japan smitten by love of cute").

In *Honey and Clover*, a comparatively peripheral but unmissable graphic detail linked with both the fairy tale tradition and the ethos of *kawaii* consists of the portrayal of the pet poodle Midori befriended by Hagumi. The girl unproblematically perceives the dog as "cute" but Midori's first appearance is actually quite intimidating — her bare-fanged and lupine muzzle, incongruously crowned by an elaborate coiffure reminiscent of a mound of whipped cream, indeed brings to mind the classic image of the wolf in disguise from *Little Red Riding Hood*, particularly in Gustave Doré's iconic depiction of that figure. *Kawaii*'s consumerist dimension could hardly go unheeded. In fact, as Purkiss maintains with reference to contemporary culture in general, cuteness stimulates cupidity by appealing to the most viscerally possessive human drives. "Fairy cuteness," specifically, is said to galvanize "a profound maternal desire to nurture, a maternal longing, a desire to rescue the cute object and put it within a family context." This entails that consumers driven by the vapid glamour of cuteness will instinctively "long to own what is cute, to take it home." Such a propensity is likely to be felt most intensely when the cute entity is perceived "as forlorn, lacking something, somehow sad, needy. As the RSPCA can tell you, such longings are short-lived; once the cute object has been taken home, adopted, it is forgotten; the drama is about acquisition, not about care. In fact, it is about shopping" (Purkiss, p. 256).

Nevertheless, as Diana Lee emphasizes, the cult of cuteness could also be seen to derive from a culturally embedded "need to be liked" and "accepted in society." Alternately, it could be regarded as a carnivalesque means of evading the responsibilities and duties associated with an "austere life in work, family and social responsibility," and thus defying "traditional values of Japanese lifestyle." In addition, *kawaii* is entangled with indigenous philosophy, reflecting an essentially Buddhist perspective in its proclivity to embrace the principles of "weakness" and "inability" as qualities in their own right (Lee). It is also possible, in this respect, to view *kawaii*'s emphasis on the beauty of childlike simplicity and playful freedom as specifically akin to the world picture promoted by Zen. In the spirit of *kawaii*, as in Zen, those values go hand in hand with a resolutely non-teleological approach to the world. Applied to the realm of creativity, this entails that artifacts can be allowed simply to *be themselves* instead of being required to obtain justification for their existence in something other than themselves, such as a compendium of ethical precepts or an artistic canon. Though inevitably inscribed in a culturally shared sign system, those works nonetheless ask to be enjoyed as transitory presences that do not need to be sublimated into exalted abstractions.

In his discussion of the relationship between fairies and transitional localities, here examined in Chapter 2: Alterity, Narváez sketches out a cosmic topography designed to throw into relief Faërie's borderline standing vis-à-vis celestial and infernal domains, on the one hand, and familiar and threatening situations on the other. An abridged version of the suggested map is shown below:

Heaven

...

	Purity	Middle Earth	Danger
(Known Space)		...	(Unknown Space)
		Hell	

Fairies, according to the scholar, inhabit marginal areas both "on earth's horizontal surface" and in the "vertical space" of the cosmos at large (Narváez, p. 338). What is here proposed is that an analogous positioning pertains to humans temporarily situated in fairyland's liminal realms and that *Honey and Clover*'s characters, specifically, are comparable to people in that very state as portrayed in the fairy tale tradition. Both transient sojourners in the fairies' borderline worlds (in the roles of visitors or captives as the case may be) and the anime's key figures indeed experience similar moments of suspension in a "Middle Earth" type of territory placed between alternate reality levels wherein conventional notions of good and evil, cleanliness and defilement, dread and beauty are not merely irrelevant but grossly risible criteria.

The topographical categories charted in Narváez' diagram find allegorical formulation in *Honey and Clover* as dialectically interrelated components of the main personae's developmental curves. Thus, "purity" is interpreted as the ability to fit in with prescribed codes of conduct meant to guarantee an individual's functioning as a well-adjusted member of society, whereas "danger" stands for attempts at self-discovery that entail adventurous or even iconoclastic creative gestures. Relatedly, "heaven" is symbolized by the ensemble of ideological requirements that seek to enforce docile conformity, while "hell" encompasses the welter of inchoate affects which the actors struggle to negotiate in their own terms for the sake of creative honesty. The object of this creativity is not solely the medium with which each young artist experiments in the quest for self-expression but also — and far more crucially — the evolving (and involving) Self. Pivotal to *Honey and Clover*'s take on creativity is the drama's finespun hymn to the need to leave one's past behind in order to move on — to consign it respectfully to a metaphorical grave, so to speak — yet also honor its legacy as a mentor of unrivaled influence. Without a willingness to mourn the past, the individual is bound to fall into the trap of incapacitating melancholia. Without a humble recognition of the past's lessons, however, its formative import would rapidly evaporate.

The culture portrayed by *Earl and Fairy* evinces an eminently split identity: the inevitable corollary of the uneasy coexistence within its fabric of a secular and utilitarian mentality, and a fascination with a secret world of strange delights and terrors. Each facet of this schizoid formation hosts its own power structures and attendant attitudes to history, while also featuring a distinctive habitat. *La Corda d'Oro* is characterized by an analogously divided cultural identity, typified by the rigid division that obtains within the academy's power dynamics between musical and non-musical student cohorts. So stark is this distinction as to find visible manifestation in the use of separate uniforms for each of the artistically divergent groupings. This visual disparity imparts what should logically constitute a single environment with the appearance of an equivocal ecosystem wherein two incompatible natural orders clash and blend by turns. The academic environment portrayed by *Nodame Cantabile* is likewise divided, albeit less graphically. In this context, the rift is between students who cultivate technical excellence as their exclusive priority and students who prefer to trust personal inspiration instead. Officially, the latter are supposed to be regarded as problematic and errant cases, and even singled out for separate tuition as though their conduct verged on sheer delinquency. Yet, a tutor successful in tackling such types and fostering their progress exhibits a refreshingly relaxed approach to the entire issue, and is quick to appreciate that the conservatory's more orthodox members stand to learn from their apparently anarchic peers. *Honey and Clover* dramatizes a related tension, polarizing academic requirements and individual vision as frequently incompatible levels of creativity. The most inspired teachers are those who are able to recognize a student's talent, or even pure genius, regardless of his or her punctuality in submitting assignments or punctiliousness in adhering to ossified technical precepts. *Paradise Kiss* could also be approached as a dramatization of the precarious cohabitation of contrasting cultural identities and cognate power relations. In this instance, we witness a double tension whereby pragmatic conformism comes into collision with arty eccentricity, on the one hand, while the microcosm of family dynamics tussles with the macrocosm of the fashion system on the other. The histories carried by each of these dimensions concurrently evoke an underlying sense of conflict between the putative authority of official accounts and the ever-fluctuating reality of lived experience.

As latter-day variations on the traditional fairy tale, the shows addressed in this chapter veer toward that form's disciplinary function to the extent that they could be interpreted as dispassionate warnings against the dangers implicit in the blind pursuit of self-fulfillment and vulnerability to pernicious influences, eager to commend the unsurpassable nobility of disinterested and altruistic behavior. Given the relatively scarce popularity enjoyed nowadays by the disciplinary function due to its excessively programmatic approach, the anime's performative dimension is more likely to be elected as a desirable object of study in contemporary critical circles. At the same time, however, their explanatory significance should not be ignored, insofar as the stories they dramatize can abet our understanding of specific societies in relation to their temporal location and, relatedly, to corresponding cultural identities, power structures and attitudes to history and its recording. In lending themselves to interpretation through the lenses provided by different functions, the shows concomitantly engage with multifarious configurations of the fairy figure.

Paradise Kiss, Honey and Clover and *La Corda d'Oro* tend to impart their fairy-related characters with unmistakable traits by recourse to a distinctive graphic style and approach to character design. This infuses familiar anime physiognomies with pointedly elvish, sylphid or goblinesque connotations in order to highlight salient traits of a particular actor's personality in a succinct fashion. In *Earl and Fairy*, as shown earlier, a veritable gallery of fairy types is brought into play with concurrently instructive and entertaining implications for the audience. *Nodame Cantabile* partakes of the stylistic proclivities evinced by *Paradise Kiss, Honey and Clover* and *La Corda d'Oro* in its approach to characterization, while sharing with *Earl and Fairy* a fascination with its personae's multiaccentual connotations as present-day variations on classic fairy figures. Both the actual fairy types and the figuratively fairy-like human characters here involved are depicted as a broad and varied species and in ways that suggest that their creators are trying to see the world from a fairy perspective rather than anthropocentrically. Hence, the characters' portrayals, though often coursed by gentle and sentimental tones, also harbor darker elements, blending the sweet with the grotesque and the charitable with the demonic.

When it comes to the assessment of appropriate critical models for interpreting the anime's relation to the fairy tale tradition, perspectives inspired by psychoanalysis are indubitably relevant. This is because all of the shows under investigation consistently underscore the themes of self-discovery and self-development: namely, recurrent concerns of fairy tales themselves for time immemorial. As Marcia Lane stresses, in this regard, "the great and abiding strength of fairy tales is that they mirror our own growth, rites of passage. Losses, gains, and eventual ascension to adulthood.... Fairy tales place our inner struggles right up there with the conflict to be worthy of and inherit a throne. Our hopes and aspirations and dreams take on a grander metaphor" (Lane, p. 34). In so doing, they assiduously intimate that "wisdom comes at a price" (p. 33), for no achievement is possible without exposure to unpredictable dangers and the specter of defeat. Relatedly, the anime's Bildungsroman ordeals echo Max Lüthi's assertion that a fairy tale's "tension," its "inner dynamism, depends very little on the question What's going to happen?" and pivots instead on the "pattern of internal experience" it triggers in the reader or listener (Lüthi 1984, p. 73). The actual events dramatized in the series here examined play a relatively marginal part in their overall dramatic structure compared to the affects which their characters and situations are capable not only of evoking but also of constellating into complex psychological responses and personal states of mind in their viewers. Simultaneously, they invite us to ponder their potentially transgressive import by questioning the societal norms constraining an individual's personal evolution across the majority (or indeed the entirety) of human cultures. More vitally still, they acerbically expose the hypocrisy underlying the rules deployed by human societies to sanction incontrovertibly what may or may not be deemed real within a given cultural dispensation and what price a person must pay for shunning their authority. Hence, several of the anime's protagonists must endure humiliations that stem directly from their suspension of official versions of truth.

Apparel has played an important part in the fairy tale tradition, infus-

ing its texture with symbolism and magic from Cinderella's Prince–winning gown and glass slipper to the Bamboo Princess' feathered raiment, from the selkies' disposable sea pelts to the Emperor's non-existent new finery, from the wolf's granny costume to the wild swans' thistle vests, from Hop-o'-My-Thumb's seven-league boots to the frenzy-inducing red shoes, from Donkeyskin's humble hide to *yuki-onna's* frosty mantle, from the pompous mole's black velvet coat in *Thumbelina* to the soldier's invisibility cloak in *The Twelve Dancing Princesses.* The list of examples could no doubt stretch much further, with countless more instances of extraordinary garments and accessories joining its ranks. Furthermore, garments function as versatile tools in the practice of "Sympathetic Magic" as defined by Sir James George Frazer in *The Golden Bough* (1913–1920). One of the key principles by which this type of magic abides is that "things which have once been in contact with each other continue to act on each other at a distance after the physical contact has been severed." This tenet is known as "the Law of Contact or Contagion" and from it the practitioner "infers that whatever he does to a material object will affect equally the person with whom the object was once in contact, whether it formed part of his body or not.... Charms based on the Law of Contact or Contagion may be called Contagious Magic" (Frazer).

Most relevant to the present discussion is the comparable eminence of sartorial and vestimentary codes within the overall semiosis of the anime studied in this book. In some of the shows, the interest in clothing is a direct corollary of the story's generic classification as a costume drama. *Le Chevalier D'Eon, Petite Cassette, The Story of Saiunkoku* and *Basilisk* belong to this category and it could hardly be disputed that their preference for meticulously rendered dress grounded in thorough research into the vogues of specific epochs and cultures is anything short of gargantuan. In anime with sci-fi affiliations—i.e., *Last Exile, Ergo Proxy* and *Wolf's Rain*—fashion becomes an effective vehicle for the evocation of a speculative society's characteristic ambience, contributing no less significantly than architecture and machinery to the cumulative task of worldbuilding. *Tokyo Godfathers, Kino's Journey* and *Someday's Dreamers: Summer Skies* use clothing primarily as a personality marker, deliberately relying on unchanging or only minimally varied attire to indicate an actor's virtual inseparability from a certain outfit, and therefore from the emblematic meanings which this is designed to convey.

It is in the cluster of anime studied in this chapter that the different functions served by clothes in the other shows come together—with an emphasis on the historical dimension in *Earl and Fairy*, on the relationship between costume and performance in *La Corda d'Oro* and *Nodame Cantabile*, and on the intricate mechanisms of the fashion industry in *Paradise Kiss*. *Honey and Clover* also foregrounds, albeit in a more incidental mode, the creative side of fashion design through a focus on Hagumi's studious execution of wondrously refined doll outfits. Given all of the anime's marked entanglement with the sartorial domain, as well as the explicit importance accorded to apparel specifically in *Paradise Kiss*, it seems desirable to discuss the relationship between Faërie and fashion in this particular context.

As intimated in Chapter 2, numerous folklorists — and fairy enthusiasts generally — have underlined the Good Folk's fascination with clothing. Fanciful hues and dainty cuts, peaked caps and velvet breeches, leaf-shaped turned-up slippers and stylish gauntlets, alongside a profusion of shiny buttons and buckles, ribbons and girdles, are frequently cited as characteristic traits of fairies' apparel. Yet, it is not unusual for gray or dark coloring to be mentioned as more typical of *real* fairy fashion and for those jollier descriptions to be dismissed as fantasies spawned by illustrated children's literature. In the realm of painting, the most memorable fairy clothes are the multi-textured and variedly opalescent, translucent or iridescent costumes, replete with spectrally wispy fabrics and bizarre headgear, donned by Fitzgerald's exquisitely weird fairies. Faërie and fashion come gloriously together in one of the most original and beautiful contributions to fairy literature ever conceived, *Fairie-ality: The Fashion Collection from the House of Ellwand*. The winner of numerous awards, including the Stora Enso Design and Production Award, the British Book Awards and the American Library Association Best Book for Young Adults, this volume captures the ironical humor intrinsic in the fairy tale tradition by presenting itself in a style and register that emulate minutely the typical tenor of fashion books — and classier fashion magazines — produced for regular human readers.

Thus, we are ushered into *Fairie-ality*'s parallel world with these words: "The Season approaches, and it gives us the greatest pleasure to present the new spring line from the renowned House of Ellwand. Addressing all your requirements, from impeccably tailored flywear for urban and field outings to elegant ballgowns and eveningwear — not to mention the freshest visions in unmentionables — the celebrated *couturier* conjures fabrics from fantasy and dresses from dreams." The atelier itself is given a distinct location within "the ancient bluebell groves of West Sussex." Its reliability is concomitantly emphasized by both the latitude of its creative scope — which enables it to cater even "for the unwinged" by means of "a line of flight hats" providing "maximum lift" — and the thoroughness with which "orders" are "handled" at the domestic and global levels alike. The House of Ellwand's credentials are also well-established and anyone who has had dealings with them before will be well aware of their "flexibility" and "imaginative openness to the payment process" (Bird, Downton and Ellwand, pp. 6–7). Each event warranting the purchase and public display of the atelier's fashionable designs is introduced by a carefully crafted invitation or an atmospheric piece of writing intended to immerse us not only in its contingent mood but also in the long-standing element of fairy lore whence it draws inspiration. Relatedly, myriad items contribute to the evocation of the House of Ellwand's magnificent collection as an original interpretation not solely of the fashion world per se but also of the entire domain of Faërie, its customs, rituals and Gestalt.

Therefore, while the eye is regaled with images of garments and accessories so gorgeously crafted down to the minutest detail as to come across as artworks worthy of exhibition in their own right, we are also afforded valuable insights into fairy lore at large. For instance, the section devoted to "May Day" contains enlightening information about plant and flower symbolism crucial to any adequate understanding of the fairy tale tradition, culminating with a pair of dancing costumes of astounding appeal, where "lily" and "rose" petals meet "bougainvillea," "Mexican bird of paradise," "daisies" and "Queen Anne's lace" in a truly magical visual cocktail (p. 35). If May Day and roses, given pride of place in these garments, are a classic fairy match, there are other both public and private occasions inviting an exuberant display of less well-known floral symbolism. A "comet-counting party," for example, offers a perfect opportunity for the donning of a "Stargazer Spinning Dress" whose skirt bathes the senses in "a carnival of stargazer lilies" (pp. 36–37), while "Late afternoon concertos on the Green" unleash a plethora of pansy-based clothes (including the flamboyant "Arabesque Jacket" and the discreetly elegant "Pastoral Jacket") as ideal vestimentary matches for some *"alfresco"* entertainment (pp. 50–51).

The volume is also keen to emphasize that Faërie's denizens harbor a hearty appetite not only for formal situations such as royal parties and cultural events but also for impromptu fun, and will use any excuse to "run off to play" (p. 55) — without, however, forgetting to devote some time to the selection of appropriate outfits. A fairy's opportunities for fun and play are both frequent and diverse, with "sunset picnics" and "firefly hunting," as well as "moonbeam swims" and "nonstop parties," "afternoon outings at the falls" and "long woodland walks," ranking high on the list. The collection reaches its visual and conceptual apotheosis with the "Faerie [*sic*] Tale Wedding" to which the book devotes its final section: a splendid array of costumes that thoughtfully endeavor to capture the distinctive personalities of the intended wearers — from the "Mother of the Bride," through the combination of "drama and whimsy" (p. 99) proverbially associated with the type, to the "Groom," whose blend of somber elegance and playful self-confidence is emblematized by the interweaving of feathers from birds endowed with contrasting symbolic connotations. An especially enticing garment is the gown designed for the "Lily Bridesmaid," whose "celadon green" is said to have been "spirited straight from a sprite's underwater palace" (p. 103). The undisputed jewel, however, is the Bride's own dress, where the most exquisite of materials and the most unpredictable of combinations join forces to deliver an artwork of memorable caliber. As the "lily petal bodice with lily straps and rabbit's foot clover" meets the "heather flower and snail shell" forming the dainty waistband, to crown a "skirt and train of calla lily, goose feather, and skeleton leaf" (p. 110), the sum total of all the lines of poetry traditionally cited to exemplify at once fairyland's radiance and its mystery seem to merge in enchanted suffusion.

The sustained cultivation of both impeccable craftsmanship and a quasi-documentary mode redolent of a fashion log enables the House of Ellwand's fairy universe to gain credibility, ironically, from the sheer fabulousness of its creations and its milieu alike. We soon forget that artifacts such as the "Fern Frond Miter" and the "Sycamore Sorcerer" from the "Flight of Fancy" hat collection (pp. 28–29), the "Streamlined Mule" vaunting an "Upper of rose petals with cow parsley seed trim" and a "birch bark sole" (p. 25), the "bridal caplet" of "diaphanous skeleton leaves" (p. 109), the "Hydrangea Hip-Huggers" (p. 83) or the "Buttercup Beach Suit" (p. 95) would be most unlikely to feature in the so-called real world. Hence, we rapidly become absorbed in the spirit and idiosyncratic logic of the alternate reality in which they belong and which they contribute, in turn, to construct and uphold. Concurrently, we are invited to feel, by the gentlest and suavest of voices, that Faërie does not simply exist in a transcendental above or an infernal below but actually permeates the world's entire fabric — Faërie breathes, laughs, cries and sings *all around us and all the time.* There is a chance that even inveterate non-believers and disbelievers with a passion for fashion design, or indeed design generally, would not fail to relish the sheer beauty and photographic opulence of the book's plates.

Conjuring up a variety of sartorial situations, each of which is distinguished by a particular atmosphere, chromatic range and set of formal properties, *Fairie-ality* indubitably constitutes an ideal match for the anime studied in this chapter. It shares with *Paradise Kiss* a palpable dedication to the decorative component of design, whereby this is allowed to assert itself as an integral aspect of the creative act. If ornamentation is a supplement, in this context, it is such in the terms defined by Jacques Derrida in *Of Grammatology* in his evaluation of the logic of supplementarity — i.e., as a vitally sustaining force rather than a mere addendum to a privileged concept or object (Derrida). Like *La Corda d'Oro* and *Nodame Cantabile*, *Fairie-ality* underscores the significance of clothes as character definers, while also taking care to dwell on the sense of occasion with which the wearing of certain garments is associated by either tradition or personal taste. At the same time, the book's take on fashion parallels *Earl and Fairy*'s punctilious rendition of period costumes to the extent that it aims to communicate a sense of the inscription of fairy apparel within a distinct temporal dimension — though this is quite unaffected by human history and abides, in fact, by the rhythms and cycles of nature. *Fairie-ality* also bears some interesting points of contact with the approach to clothing evinced by *Honey and Clover*— notably, in its juxtaposition of practicality and charm, functionalism and cuteness. The anime's fascination with ethnic clothing, demonstrated by the presents brought home by Nodame's guardian from his travels, also finds a correlative in the volume's evocation of the culturally specific character of fairy apparel. *Fairie-ality* also echoes *Honey and Clover*'s atmosphere through its "Artist's Smock" (p. 66), a garment consisting of "calla lily petals" with "buttons ... made of honesty seeds" for the rare fairy type one only encounters "every aeon or so ... who doesn't give a fig for today's sense of fashion" (p. 67).

Just as the anime here studied assiduously situate clothes in the context of broader cultural environments, so David Ellwand, the artist behind *Fairie-ality*'s stunning photography, endeavors to extend his purview of the Faërie domain beyond clothing by means of a sister volume entitled *Fairie-ality Style: A Sourcebook of Inspirations from Nature* intended to translate the beauty of the natural environment into the language of interior design though a keen focus on the inexhaustible magic of color. Ellwand's artistry throws into relief the alchemical flair with which leaves and stones, shells and petals, driftwood and feathers — among myriad organic materials gleaned from all of the habitat's primal elements — collude and collide to produce the subtlest and most unexpected of shades. These provide the creative basis for a profusion of items of interior design, including furniture and textiles, and matching items of exquisite apparel. While this book is no less of an experiment in fantasy art than the original *Fairie-ality*, it also works as a practical tool for artists and designers eager to explore the dreamworld of chroma through their own creations. Color is a sign system underlying both the visual arts and music — as shown by their shared use of terms such as tones, harmonies, gradations and scales — and therefore constitutes an especially apposite match for the creative ventures pursued by all of the anime chosen to illustrate the particular topos under consideration in this chapter.

As Ellwand emphasizes in his introduction to the book, human beings have been "producing art with the very essence of the land" for time immemorial. When one considers the centrality of the natural world to fairy lore, persistently confirmed by legion accounts of the genesis and practice of fairy customs, rituals and artifacts in the earth, air and sea, it could be argued that this tradition epitomizes in a figuratively distilled guise a proclivity embedded in the human species itself, and specifically in its forays into artistic production. Fairy lore has possibly come into being, as a universally resonant discourse, out of a desire to embody the essence of human creativity in a comprehensive metaphorical structure of semiosis and symbolism. Ellwand posits "impermanence" as an especially intriguing facet of "natural design" — the "dandelion clock chair that lasts only for one breath of wind" succinctly encapsulates this quality. Evanescence is, of course, a central feature of Faërie's endlessly mutating reality: hence, an instant correlation between nature-based art and fairies can be perceived. Yet, transience is also intrinsic to human existence — "our past is dust," Ellwand reminds us, "and our future is dirt" (Ellwand). Therefore, fairy lore could again be seen to provide a refined metaphorical template for human life at its most elemental, and for the creative urge at its most innate. In short, human creativity draws from nature's inexhaustible reservoir, and fairy lore serves to underline the atavistic connection between art and nature. At the same time, art rooted in nature is eminently ephemeral, as human life itself is, and fairy lore again operates as a highlighter of this essential condition through its own distinctive world picture.

In the domain of indigenous lore, the theme of creativity is often employed as a means of highlighting a quintessentially Japanese aesthetic preference for the seamless coalescence of nature and art that a finds memorable expression in countless manifestations of indigenous architecture, from grand palaces to humble urban dwellings. The tale known in the West as *The Power of Love* (in Griffis) upholds this predilection by celebrating the image of a landscaped garden surrounding a teahouse as a gem of nature and art at one and the same time. This facet of the story is pivotal to its emplacement of a distinctive sense of cultural identity. In addition, the story harks back to Japanese lore by deploying the portentous figure of the vengeful woman, or *hannya*—namely, one of its most fearful demons. The tale's supernatural strain is infused with a characteristic passion for grotesque distortion and exaggeration, as the erstwhile gentle maiden responsible for managing the teahouse is seen to morph into a hideous monster, to wind her sinewy coils around the large temple bell in which her victim has vainly sought refuge and to turn the bell, the man and her own body into one melting mass that only leaves white ashes in its wake. This image reflects a profound fascination with the collapse of bodily boundaries, which makes it redolent of shamanic Shinto and hence also central to a specific configuration of cultural identity. The contrast between the atmosphere of peace and balance conveyed by the graceful collusion of nature and architecture foregrounded in the tale's opening segment clashes violently with the representation of the disappointed girl's vengeful fury. This aspect of the story, axial to the overall drama, echoes Japanese art's preference for styles capable of communicating a dialectical tension between harmonious and tempestuous energies and, by extension, of commenting elliptically on the ineluctable coexistence of serenity and turmoil within both contingent human societies and the ongoing flow of history.

In the domain of the Japanese fairy tale tradition, a memorable celebration of creativity is supplied by *The Gift of Old Lacquer* (in Griffis), where a beautiful white bird embodying the spirit of the lacquer tree teaches a farmer the art of turning its sap into a precious varnish. Although the substance is highly poisonous and the processing method recommended by the bird is both strenuous and time-consuming, the preternatural creature assiduously sustains its pupil and his own apprentices, praising them for their loyalty and perseverance through recurring dreams. The artist eventually accomplishes splendid results but never forgets the spirit responsible for his success and rewards it in accordance with the creature's own desire: to ensure that the snowy heron and the silk-white cranes shall always be treated gently by the Japanese people and allowed to appear on all manner of lacquerware as faithful companions of the mountains, trees and rice-fields. The heron and the crane indeed hold a crucially significant place in indigenous art as symbolic bridges between nature and art. Focusing on the delicate power dynamics defining the tree spirit's relationship with its mortal student, the tale delivers an imaginative interpretation of the historiographic task through its fabulistic, yet meticulous, allegory of the birth of an art pivotal to Japanese culture at large. The story's take on history points to a desire to honor tradition not simply out of antiquarian respect but also, and more importantly, to examine and savor its relevance to the here-and-now.

The specific art to which the narrative is devoted also deserves some consideration. Lacquerware relies on the native *urushi* ("lacquer tree") and is no less complex and laborious a technique in reality than it is in the ancient tale. As John Reeve elucidates, the production of lacquer "began in prehistory as a way of waterproofing wooden objects such as bowls and protecting fragile objects like combs." However, these practical concerns were soon supplanted by aesthetic objectives as it became manifest that the practice lent itself to the creation of utterly unique sensory effects. For example, "by applying many layers" of resinous *urushi* juice (usually colored black or red), "it is possible to cut through them to create sculptural effects." Furthermore, the use of "gold foil or gold dust (*makie*, 'sprinkled pictures') and mother-of-pear" could lead to a glorious impression of multidimensionality (Reeve, p. 54). Intriguingly, Junichirou Tanizaki brings lacquerware into play in an evaluation of the Japanese preference for darkness and shadows that beautifully matches the pervasively murky atmosphere of old tales keen to capture the most elusory facets of existence. Tanizaki suggests that light cannot be grasped independently of darkness: ironical though this may sound, radiance does not dissolve darkness but is, in fact, illuminated by it. This is attested to, in the context of Japanese art, by the treatment of substances whose intrinsic qualities and distinctive charm can only be adequately recognized with the assistance of darkness. "Lacquerware decorated in gold," for example, "should be left in the dark" or allowed to be merely caressed by "a faint light." It is by seeming to glide discreetly in the shadows that the material is able to summon a "dream world built by that strange light of candle and lamp, that wavering light bearing the pulse of the night" and magically laying "a pattern on the surface of the night itself" (Tanizaki, p. 24).

Lord Bag of Rice (in Peirce Williston) conveys a specific notion of cultural identity by emphasizing that the glories of nature and art combined far exceed martial prowess. The prizes gained by the hero at the end of his quest are indeed a roll of silk capable of acquiring any hue he fancies and a bag of rice that never diminishes and he can share with others in times of need. As suggested elsewhere in this study, a firm belief in the intrinsic nobility of even the most mundane of materials and substances constitutes a pivotal facet of indigenous civilization. This stance, moreover, has fostered a deeply ingrained perception of artistic production itself as a primarily physical pursuit, and has therefore contributed vitally to the evolution of a specifically Japanese approach to creativity. The tale of *The First Rabbits* (in Peirce Williston) adopts a comparably refreshing perspective on the topos of creativity. Underpinned by the lessons of Shinto, this delivers a sublime interpretation of the natural realm as a boundless reality witnessing the unrelenting and seamless commingling of disparate cosmic forces. In its celebration of the principle of creativity, the story is eager to demonstrate that sublimity and so-called maturity are not necessarily coterminous: the momentous energies animating the universe are indeed left in the hands of little kids at play and not harnessed to the agendas of stern and white-bearded celestial autocrats.

Both *Lord Bag of Rice* and *The First Rabbits* foreground the Japanese belief, underscored in relation to *Paradise Kiss*, in the eminently material character of all artistic practices and resulting artifacts, underpinned by a disregard for neat distinctions between artistic and artisanal activities of the kind commonly treasured in the West. In other words, as indicated earlier in relation to *Paradise Kiss*, any productive activity can be considered an art and all arts, in turn, constitute fundamentally corporeal realities inextricable from the materials on which they depend. It is also worth noting that the fairy tale's rabbits appear to foreshadow the snow bunnies traditionally fashioned by Japanese children in frigid climes. The snow bunny features in the capacity of a quasi-talismanic object in numerous anime — for example, *Gilgamesh* (TV series; dir. Masahiko Murata, 2003–2004) and *Kanon* (TV series; dir. Tatsuya Ishihara, 2006–2007). The snowman sculpted by Nono in *Gunbuster 2* (OVA series; dir. Kazuya Tsurumaki, 2004–2006) out of a sci-fi version of otherworldly snow also springs to mind as an apt visual correlative.

Echoing Perrault's *Snow White*—and hence the Grimms' *Snowdrop*— at the transcultural level, the tale of *The Mirror of Matsuyama* reflects on the theme of creativity with a specific emphasis on the issue of power relations. In the process, it throws into relief the creative power of love as a supremely empowering and energizing force, capable of subverting oppressive family structures and of healing seemingly irreparable intergenerational fractures. The magical mirror in which the heroine can go on beholding her mother's lovely visage long after the woman's untimely death ultimately enables the girl to tame even a quintessentially spiteful evil stepmother (in Ashliman, D. L. 1998–2008b; original source: Hadland Davis). The special significance held by the mirror in the fairy tale tradition is lyrically captured by Alexandr Solzhenitsyn's "Nobel Lecture in Literature 1970" with these words: "Some things lead beyond words. Art inflames even a frozen, darkened soul to a high spiritual experience. Through art we are sometimes visited — dimly, briefly — by revelations such as cannot be produced by rational thinking. Like that little looking-glass from the fairy-tales: look into it and you will see — not yourself— but for one second, the Inaccessible, whither no man can ride, no man fly. And only the soul gives a groan..." (Solzhenitsyn). The distinctive sensibility evinced by *The Mirror of Matsuyama* is shaped by an eminently feminine voice and this serves to distinguish it radically from *Snow White*. Indeed, while in most versions of the Western fairy tale the father plays a peripheral part, there can be little doubt that the heroine's world is fundamentally male-dominated, and that a father figure (if not a literal father) therefore operates as the invisible fulcrum — or absent center — around which that society revolves. As Sandra M. Gilbert and Susan Gubar argue, "this surely is the voice of the looking-glass, the patriarchal voice of judgment that rules the Queen's — and every woman's — self-evaluation" (Gilbert and Gubar, p. 38). In *The Mirror of Matsuyama*, conversely, the mirror's voice is female through and through, and it promulgates moral values for which the protagonist's society may have little time and respect but which nonetheless have the power to function as enduringly sustaining life forces for the individual. When the father does come into play, his role is not that of a tyrannical patriarch hell-bent on imposing his authority on either the heroine or her precious mirror but rather that of a sensitive soul willing to admit to his shortcomings and to rectify his behavior.

The ghostly mother returning from the grave by otherworldly means to comfort her destitute child in *The Mirror of Matsuyama* is portrayed as undilutedly angelic. This character type finds a darkly ironical counterpart in Angela Carter's *Ashputtle*, the twentieth-century author's adaptation of *Cinderella/Ashenputtel*. Carter's *Ashputtle* harks back to variants of the well-known plot in which the dead mother goes on supporting the heroine by means of magical gifts or a helpful animals such as a bird or a cow — i.e., symbols of freedom and fertility or maternal nourishment respectively. Accordingly, the deceased mother reappears in the guise of various animals and, though keen on assisting her daughter, she adopts an utterly unsentimental stance. When , for example, she returns as a cat and loses all her claws as she endeavors to disentangle the child's knotty hair, she draws the meeting to a close with a disarmingly unceremonious remark: "Comb your own hair, next time.... You've taken my strength away. I can't do it again" (Carter 2006, p. 395). Whereas the mother figure presented in the Japanese fairy tale is endowed with powers so great as to affect creatively not only her little girl but also, by implication, her former husband and his new wife, Carter's mother cannot accomplish any task, whatever her animal avatar, without wearing herself out altogether. She seems, not surprisingly, quite relieved when her daughter finally frees herself from the evil stepmother's shackles, and feels entitled to "go to sleep" for good (p. 396).

In emphasizing the darkness underlying the *Cinderella/Ashenputtel* yarn, Carter is closer to the Grimms' version than to Perrault's. The German tale indeed ends on a sinister note as the heroine, who is not as forgiving as Perrault's own protagonist, invites her sisters to her wedding, where doves proceed to peck out their eyes (Grimm 2000, p. 196). Carter's retelling of the story pays homage to one of the most ancient strands of the fairy tale tradition which could be said to emanate quite directly from animistic and pantheistic beliefs. This consists of the narrative propensity, discussed by Lüthi in his own evaluation of *Cinderella*, to utilize the figure of "the helping animal — usually a little cow or goat" as "a metamorphic form of the deceased mother" seeking to supply her "tormented girl with food and clothing." Such a character, like the "deceased in the fairy tale" generally, "are not ghostly ... but enter into the play of forces; the realm of plants, animals, and the deceased embodied in the hazel tree, the doves, and the mother render their friendly assistance to helpless man in the Cinderella fairy tale" (Lüthi 1976, p. 61). Furthermore, the figure of the "helping animal in the fairy tale can embody unconscious forces within us" and can therefore symbolize "our feelings, bound to nature and not yet distorted by the intellect," as autonomous forces that have the power to "nourish and guide us" (p. 80).

CHAPTER 5

Dystopias

I believe in everything until it's disproved. So I believe in fairies, the myths, dragons. It all exists, even if it's in your mind. Who's to say that dreams and nightmares aren't as real as the here and now?

— John Lennon

We call them faerie. We don't believe in them. Our loss.

— Charles de Lint

The tenth-century fairy tale *Taketori Monogatari* or *The Tale of the Bamboo-Cutter* (in Peirce Williston) — a.k.a. *Kaguya Hime* or *The Tale of Princess Kaguya* — is indubitably one of the most cherished gems in the bountiful casket of Japanese lore and has enjoyed such a venerable history of adaptations, relocations and transmutations over the centuries as to constitute an ample and free-standing chapter in the history of autochthonous literature as a whole. The august narrative actually bears eloquent witness to the impetus of transcultural interaction as a force operating not only across geographically discrete lands and countries but also between different stages — and hence social formations — in the evolution of a single location. The story deserves special consideration in the present context as an inspired interpretation of the theme of dystopia. *The Tale of the Bamboo-Cutter* certainly appropriates the concept not to portray a bleak or post-apocalyptic world stripped of hopes and ideals but rather to explore its import as a warping or disfiguring of the very notion of space, *topos*, and, by implication, of notions of origin and rootedness conventionally associated with one's place in the world. A connection may here be observed between this preoccupation and one of the central philosophical concerns examined in Chapter 3: Voyages. The tale in its entirety, regardless of its contingent orchestration, indeed pivots on its protagonist's dislocation onto a reality which, even though it accords the character special value and respect, is quite simply bound to signify a monstrous aberration of

153

the place and space where she truly belongs. The anime addressed in this chapter share with *The Tale of the Bamboo-Cutter* precisely this trenchant sense of displacement.

In elaborating its distinctive take on dystopia, the fairy tale engages with all of the key areas of analysis discussed throughout this study, bringing into play notions of cultural identity (especially through the relationship between the heroine and the Mikado); power relations (by pitting two separate categories of being starkly against each other); natural and environmental phenomena (as tersely encapsulated by the circumstances of the protagonist's appearance in the human world and departure therefrom); historical recording (by weaving together the human and the non-human in the guise of a narrative double helix of inseparable chronicles). Moreover, intriguing affinities with both Hans Christian Andersen's *Thumbelina* and the *Swan Lake* drama in its various expressions place the narrative at a nexus of vibrant cross-cultural exchanges. In most of its versions, the tale exudes a potent sense of *mono no aware*—the quintessentially Japanese aesthetic principle describing the unsurpassed beauty, in both nature and art, of the fleeting and the evanescent. (This concept will be revisited in some detail later in this discussion.) This mood is axial to the heroine's ordeal as an entity whose ineradicable displacement renders her presence on Earth an inexorably transient experience. At the same time, the story's universe resonates with a mature apprehension of reality as a process of interminable becoming whose very existence is inextricable from the Buddhist principle of impermanence (*mujou*).

According to H. Richard Okada, an early version of the tale features in the first great collection of Japanese poetry, the *Man'youshuu* (a.k.a. *Collection of Ten Thousand Leaves*, ca. 759). In this version, an old bamboo-cutter chances upon a gaggle of gorgeous celestial nymphs and, besotted with their matchless charm, cannot refrain from gazing at them in a somewhat indecorous fashion. To beg forgiveness of the heavenly beauties, the man offers them a poem as recompense for his indiscretion. The tale is here evidently used as a pretext for the poetry, which is the work's overall priority (Okada, pp. 42–43). A later version from the *Fudoki* compilation focuses on a similar situation, with the unearthly creatures "in the guise of cranes." The mortal who accidentally sees them is possessed by the longing to get hold of one of their robes and instructs his dog to snatch the precious garment away on his behalf. The man is then entitled to marry "the robeless maiden who, after bearing him four children," regains the stolen garb and returns to her celestial abode (p. 43).

A further variation on the popular yarn, known as "'Shrine of Nagu,' concerns a heavenly maiden who descends to earth with seven companions to bathe at a spring" and is forcefully adopted by a human couple. The creature brings her foster parents great prosperity by "brewing a magical rice wine (*sake*) that cures physical ailments" but is callously forsaken by her mortal family and roams the land until she reaches the village of Nagu, there to become "the local deity" (p. 44). This finale recalls the heroine's fate of exile and eventual redemption recounted in the closing part of the Grimms' *Rapunzel*. A popular variant of *The Tale of the Bamboo-Cutter* is *The Robe of Feathers* (in Ashliman, D. L. 1998–2008a; original source: Hadland Davis), where a fisherman finds a magnificent feathered array and resolves to hold onto this unexpected treasure at any price. Confronted by the heavenly maiden to whom the robe once belonged and without which she is powerless to return to her home in the sky, the man finally agrees to surrender the garment on condition that she will dance for him. The creature obliges and crowns her otherworldly performance with a glorious ascent into the dawn-wreathed heavens amid her radiant robe's iridescent aura.

Nowadays, the best known and most commonly recounted version of the tale is the so-called *Taketori* narrative. In this particular variant, an old and childless bamboo cutter named Taketori no Okina discovers a baby the size of his thumb within a shining bamboo stalk, takes her home, deeming her as preternaturally beautiful as a fairy, and raises her with his wife as if she were their own child. Named Kaguya Hime ("Radiant Night Princess"), the unusual creature rewards her benefactors by quietly ensuring that whenever Taketori chops off a bamboo stalk, he will find a small nugget of gold hidden within. As the girl's beauty grows preternaturally year after year, her foster father seeks to protect her from importunate attentions but five royal suitors eventually beg for her hand in marriage. Kaguya Hime responds by asking each prince to accomplish an impossible task. One by one, all five suitors meet with dismal failure in the pursuit of their unattainable goals. Kaguya Hime's next suitor is none other than the Mikado himself, the Emperor of Japan, but is tersely rejected on the pretext that the girl does not belong to his country. She does, however, agree, to keep in touch with this unprecedentedly eminent petitioner for her hand. Eventually, the heroine reveals that she is not of this world and has no choice but to return to Tsuki no Miyako (the "Capital of the Moon") where she comes from and her people reside. (Some versions propose that the Princess was relegated to the human domain as a punishment for some unspecified transgression, whereas others claim that her temporary exile resulted from the Moon people's desire to keep the precious creature out of trouble in the course of a fierce heavenly conflict.)

Although on the day designated for Kaguya Hime's departure the Mikado surrounds her human home with mighty guards intended to prevent what he sees as her unjust abduction by the lunar retinue, the Princess' fate is sealed and her ascent to heaven is therefore inevitable. (In some renditions of the story, the Emperor is not portrayed as a suitor but said to offer his assistance to old Taketori out of deep admiration for the maiden's filial devotion to her mortal guardians.) Following Kaguya Hime's departure, the girl's foster parents fall grievously ill, unable to cope with their bereavement. The Mikado, for his part, instructs his men to burn both the letter and the jar of elixir of life bestowed upon him by Kaguya Hime as farewell presents atop the highest mountain in the region, hoping that his signal might reach the heavenly kingdom to which his beloved has returned. Immortality (*fuji*), the illusory gift which the Emperor has no wish to endure in the absence of the cherished one, is reputed to have led to the current denomination of Mount Fuji and the incineration rite to lie behind the mountain's volcanic activity: the wreath of smoke curling up from its sacred summit is supposedly a bridge to the utopian world of Tsuki no Miyako.

According to Okada, it is vital to appreciate the symbolic significance of the bamboo grove itself as a setting endowed with a unique *genius loci* of supernatural caliber: that is to say, "a sacred topos appropriate for engendering otherworldly figures." Despite its mythological resonance, the location is nonetheless steeped in social reality, for it also serves to remind the reader that the old bamboo-cutter, thanks to his "privileged access to the hallowed space," stands as a representative of "a class of craftsmen marginal yet necessary to court society" — that is to say, those gentle and innocent souls "who can 'see' and 'know' such alien creatures" (p. 54). The emphasis traditionally placed by Japanese aesthetics on the creative value of artisanal talent as a quality in no way inferior to artistic excellence proclaims itself with economical elegance throughout the story. As a topos associated with ultramundane agencies and realms, the bamboo grove effectively operates as a dystopian reality to the extent that it is capable of initiating a deviation from the norms, expectations and objectives shaping ordinary reality. The "dys" prefix, in this instance, does not unequivocally connote a negative distortion but rather a radical reorientation of life-altering proportions.

Thus, the tale can be seen to engage assiduously, albeit elliptically, with issues of cultural identity and power relations while also enthroning the natural environment as the wellhead of its mythical infrastructure. At the same time, as Okada contends, in modeling Kaguya Hime's suitors upon actual historical personages and lending those figures humorous and even downright uncomplimentary connotations, the story performs an audacious "reappropriation of 'history'" (p. 60). The first of the princes is portrayed as lazy, the second as mendacious, the third as risibly naive (or unlucky), the fourth as impetuous and selfish, and the fifth as a downright coward. By mocking the people responsible for the erection of the political, ideological and hierarchical systems of the time by means of a narrative that utilizes the emerging vernacular and script, the story implicitly destabilizes not solely the civil foundations of the culture whence it stems but also its language, its rhetoric and its texts — namely, the scholarly legacy associated with the patriarchal domain of Chinese letters.

Satire of this kind is also found, through transcultural investigation, in Andrew Lang's *Prince Prigio*. Deploying the familiar motif of the royal christening and its uninvited fairy (here also addressed in Chapter 3), the story pivots on a prince cursed with excessive cleverness. Victim of his intellectual zeal and hence prone to conceitedness, the titular character rejects the magical phenomena around him and flatly denies the existence of the monster known as "the Firedrake" who threatens his country's welfare. Hence, he refuses to obey the King's request that he confront the creature in accordance with his standing as "the oldest" of his sons. The humor, in this tale, emanates primarily from Prigio's sophistic rhetoric and from Lang's self-reflexive metacommentary on the fairy tale's conventions. "Thanks to the education that your majesty has given me," he argues, "I have learned that the Firedrake, like the siren, the fairy, and so forth, is a fabulous animal which does not exist. But even granting, for the sake of argument, that there is a Firedrake, your majesty is well aware that there is no use in sending *me*. It is always the eldest son who goes out first, and comes to grief on these occasions, and it is always the third son that succeeds. Send Alphonso (this was the youngest brother), and *he* will do the trick at once" (Lang 2008, pp. 16–18).

Returning to the *Taketori* narrative, it is crucial to appreciate that this fairy tale, by challenging scholarly tradition, "enacts two gestures: first, as it seeks to install itself as a legitimate mode of discourse it harks back to another discursive moment in history and mimes its movements; and second, it adopts a definite stance toward the figures appearing in the earlier texts, appropriating them for its own linguistic and narrative ploys"

(Okada, p. 60). In assessing the story's attitude to discourse, it is also noteworthy that considerable attention is devoted to the text-dominated nature of the relationship between Kaguya Hime and the Mikado. Epistolary dialogue, in this instance, operates as a replacement for physical contact, with the written word itself cast in the role of a fetishistic substitute for the sender's actual body and soul. Concomitantly, as Okada maintains, the written word is instrumental in the orchestration of a structure of deferral: "The princess twice defers her departure and the putting on of the robe of feathers," first by composing a message for the old bamboo-cutter in which she expresses her desire not to leave the earth, and then by writing a letter to the Mikado oozing with sadness and regret. Even when, having donned the sacred garment, drunk the water of forgetfulness and ascended heavenward with her ample entourage, the heroine would seem to have relinquished the human world for good, the story "is still not over" (p. 77). These narrative complications indicate that "words" only have the power to "forestall" but are not "able actually to present any 'thing.'" Therefore, "the *Taketori* text operates as if in full knowledge of the ultimate impossibility for words to produce either oral or scriptive 'presence'" (p. 79). From a narrative point of view, the *Taketori* text's greatest strength indubitably lies with its flair for emplotment, whereby each prince's respective quest is accorded the space and details appropriate to a fairy tale in its own right, while nonetheless maintaining a logical connection with the broader narrative framework predicated on Kaguya Hime's preposterous requests.

Feathers — the visual detail distinguishing not only the *Taketori*'s protagonist but also its overarching iconographic structure — play a pivotal ceremonial role in numerous traditions and cultures. Frequently utilized as healing implements, feathers are believed to harbor talismanic capacities and esoteric affiliations with the spirit realm. In the specific context of Japanese lore, it is noteworthy that the tree creatures knows as *tengu*, who are responsible for guarding the woodlands and can assume the form of any animal, are equipped with feathered wings. Ivan Morris describes the creatures as "hideous red-faced dwellers of the hills and forests who were equipped with noses of inordinate length and wings and who, rather incongruously, were in the habit of carrying feather fans" (Morris, p. 130). Commenting on their function as ceremonial tools of global significance, Susannah Marriott observes that feathers are also employed "in divination rituals" and that in the context of Zanzibar, in particular, they are even held to "confer invisibility if plucked from the neck of a black chicken" (Marriott, p. 86).

An imaginative interpretation of the relationship between feathers and Faërie is offered by the fairy fashion volume *Faerie-ality: The Fashion Collection from the House of Ellwand* through a style that firmly rejects the syrupy version of the fairy found in many forms of modern popular culture. (The book as a whole is discussed in the preceding chapter in relation to the creativity topos.) Feathers are accorded unrivaled centrality by the designs for the costumes created by the House of Ellwand specifically for "the Cotillion of the Pheasant" held "at the First Full Moon After the Bluebells Bloom" and hosted by the Fairy Queen herself (Bird, Downton and Ellwand, p. 9). Stunning full-page photocollages of feathers from different birds provide the context for the display of the Cotillion collection itself. This includes gowns designed to match their wearers' personalities — with a simple pheasant feather dress complemented by "a bay underskirt and obi" for the "quiet beauty," for example, a flamboyant number where the pheasant feather skirt is accompanied by a shiny "beech leaf bodice" and "Chinese lantern puff leaves" for the eccentric, and a bold piece combining a "bodice of oak leaves" with a skirt in which the obligatory pheasant feathers are interleaved with "a trend-setting touch of parrot" for the "fashionista who's always looking for an edge to cut" (foldout inset, pp. 14–15).

Queen Gloriana's own gown is so spectacular as to deserve separate display on a card protected by an onion-skin envelope that stands out as an object of undeniable aesthetic worth unto itself. The costume evinces a magnetic juxtaposition of a "stargazer lily bodice with a royal poppy starburst atop a wild mélange of feathers, petals, leaves," and a royal crown consisting of a "cypress cone pierced by a single, majestic parrot feather." It is therefore hardly surprising to hear that "It's charisma plus quality that leave her [Gloriana] standing alone" (p. 13). Elliptically inspired by Shakespeare's depiction of Titania in *A Midsummer Night's Dream*, this mighty fairy's robe is likewise unforgettable in its "skin-tingling" admixture of "pigeon (the skirt), and pheasant (the sleeves) with a constricted snakeskin bodice" (p. 19). Pheasant feathers are likewise prominent in the design of the "bell-bottoms and not-so-scruffy scuffs" featuring among the friskier casual wear items (p. 77). The House of Ellwand's catalogue enthrones feathers no less conspicuously in its hat collection, as showcased by items such as "The Pheasant Tailwind" and "The Parrot Mad Hatter" (pp. 28–29). This stylistic trend reaches a climax in the volume's climactic section, which is devoted to a high-class fairy wedding, and particularly in the costumes designed for the Mother of the Bride, where "duck" and "goose" feathers prevailed with thinly veiled ironical intent, the Groom, whose prismatic personality is captured through the juxtaposition of exotic touches of "parrot" and "peacock," and the Maid of Honor, where a skirt uniting "silky crow feathers and a single green parrot feather" evoke a "touch-me velveteen look" of "spellbinding" power (pp. 99–104).

An especially dazzling — and amusing — interpretation of the feather motif can be found in the swimsuit collection "Bathing Beauties," and particularly in the design for the "Mae," where "Lush crow and owl feathers" meet "bottlebrush and honesty seeds," and the "Mata Hari," where "mysterious pheasant" is contrasted with "pink rosebuds and pheasant straps" (p. 58). Feathers become even more essential a presence in David Ellwand's companion volume *Fairie-ality Style: A Sourcebook of Inspirations from Nature* as the key medium in the execution not only of delicate clothes but also tapestries, wall-hangings and rugs ideally designed to furnish Faërie's abodes and simultaneously to remind us all of nature's awesome creativity as a prime source of stimulation for fairies and mortals alike. As the examples offered above hopefully demonstrate, the *Faerie-ality* books exhibit an alternately ironical and debunking attitude toward the vapidly romanticized notion of the feathery fairy promoted by artists and illustrators keen on domesticating the creature's ominous connotations. The fairies envisioned by the House of Ellwand are being who — ethereal, graceful and regal as they may seem — are nonetheless also down-to-earth consumers and fun-lovers with little or no time for conventional ethical considerations and are endowed, in fact, with an exuberant appetite for spectacle, revelry and dalliance.

The fairy tale tradition's relationship with the concept of dystopia as described earlier vis-à-vis *The Tale of the Bamboo-Cutter* — i.e., as a twisting, inversion or destabilization of the ordinary and the ordained — manifests itself in various guises. One of its most powerful ploys is the enlisting of fairy figures and their ghoulishly protean universe to the expression of unconscious and repressed materials. These consist of the fantasies, longings and fears censored by human society as fanciful or even morally unsound in the service of the iron dictates of rationality, common sense and productivity. A resplendent case in point is supplied by fairy painting — and art generally — in the Victorian era. Flourishing between 1840 and 1870 to leave its traces in the artifacts of later periods, this represents, as Christopher Wood indicates, a conscious effort to transcend "the intolerable reality of living in an unromantic, materialistic and scientific age" (Wood, p. 8). Like fairy art of the Victorian age, the anime examined in this chapter harness salient aspects of the fairy tale tradition to the exposure of the vast reservoir of affects and aspirations which society suppresses in the name of so-called progress — only to become, paradoxically, more and more dehumanized, tyrannical and estranged from itself. Rekindling in allegorical form the fairy tale tradition is thus emplaced as means of awakening dormant facets of the psyche in order to imbue that stultifying reality with salubriously inquisitive drives and, ideally, by and by foster its intellectual and spiritual renewal. The emphasis laid by the shows on the ubiquity of chaos and discord intimates that such a process is inevitably labyrinthine and beset by apparently insurmountable obstacles. Yet, the fairy tale dimension itself serves to imbue the quest with a tenacious sense of hope. Furthermore, by depicting their dystopian worlds with studious attention to the minutest detail, the anime accomplish a synthesis of reality and fantasy of eerie and, at times, truly disquieting intensity. The fantastic component gains density from its systematic infusion with realistic attributes and the realistic element, in turn, accrues defamiliarizing potentialities from its displacement onto the fantastic.

While echoing fairy art of the Victorian period along the lines described above, the anime here discussed also hark back to another important manifestation of the fairy tale tradition in the same epoch: its unmatched prominence in "the theatre" at the diverse levels of "plays, ballet, opera and pantomime" (p. 42). This cultural phenomenon is implicated with the concept of dystopia in two ways. On the one hand, the stage can be seen as a means of containing the unruly world of Faërie — an ideal task in the case of the pointedly delimiting type of stage prevalent in the West during the nineteenth century. On the other hand, it provides a niche within the boundaries of supposedly civilized and orderly human dispensations for the emergence of patently non-human presences saturated with disturbing, menacing and transgressive energies, irrespective of the volume of evanescent gauze and filigree lace in which they are garbed. Thus, the utopia of a luminously rational and intelligible universe is punctured by the dystopian shadow of impenetrable otherworldliness. In the anime themselves, a markedly theatrical atmosphere if elegantly conveyed by settings in which the stylistic proclivities characteristic of indigenous scroll painting, Gothic art and classic science fiction varyingly collude to evoke a definite sense of sculptural mass. This impression, in turn, is enriched by the deft juxtaposition of light and shadow and by a punctilious dedication to architectural fixtures and props.

The anime's thespian dimension is further underlined by their eminently antimimetic sensibility — an aesthetic preference that finds paradigmatic expression through non-realistic creatures combining disparate life forms and through the presentation of putatively actual events in a distorted, crooked or aberrant fashion. This helps them stand out as particularly apposite heirs to the fairy tale tradition in contemporary culture. In this respect, the shows could also be said to bear witness to their medium's involvement in a broader aesthetic trend, which Max Lüthi has beautifully delineated as follows: "The grownup, still under the influence of the Enlightenment and realism, quickly turns away from the fairy tale with a feeling of contempt. But in modern art, fascination with the fairy tale is everywhere evident. The turning away from descriptive realism, from the mere description of external reality in itself, implies an approach to the fairy tale. The same can be said of the fantastic mixtures of human, animal, vegetable, and mineral, which, like the fairy tale, bring all things into relationship with one another" (Lüthi 1976, pp. 145–146).

It is also vital to remember, in studying the anime themselves through the lenses of the fairy tale tradition, that this fabulous domain's embroilment with the notion of dystopia is largely a corollary of the pervasive mood of darkness and strife infusing numerous folk beliefs about the meaning, origins and intent of fairies. These creatures are sometimes regarded as manifestations of departed souls, as borne out most explicitly by stories in which fairies are virtually indistinguishable from specters: the Chinese tale *A Shiver of Ghosts*, discussed later in this chapter, exemplifies this trend. Another popular view holds that fairies are devils associated with witchcraft and necromancy. At several points in history, fairies and witches have been seen as so intimately related to each other as to be virtually coterminous. This is not entirely surprising when one takes into consideration the intensely multiaccentual connotations invested on both figures over the centuries. At the same time, it entails the advantage of rebalancing certain conventional perspectives on both types by intimating that fairies cannot be automatically conceived of as childlike playthings and witches, for their part, should not be presumed to personify undilutedly malign — let alone physically repulsive — agencies. The ongoing cultural hold of the fairy's connection with the witch — and, by extension, all manner of regional sorceresses and enchantresses — is attested to by a crossword clue used by the Azed puzzle No. 1,985 published in *The Observer* on 13 June 2010, the solution to which is supposed to be the word "fairy": namely, "13 (Across). Female magician, excellent with young around" (Azed No. 1,985).

A seemingly more romantic but still perturbing thesis posits fairies as demoted angels caught in an interstitial space between heaven's gates and the unholy outside when the rebel angels were ostracized. A further belief permeated by a grievous apprehension of conflict and loss describes fairies as lilliputian beings driven into hiding by human invaders and thus relegated to subterranean realms, remote and shadowy hillsides, cemeteries or legendary lands across the sea. Closely related is the view according to which fairies were once honored deities forced to survive as pale, dwindled and marginal vestiges of their former selves by the ascendancy of Christianity. This does not, however, unproblematically render them powerless: rather, it entails their potentially anarchic cultivation of customs and standards independent of human laws. As Kimie Imura observes, "If Christianity is the brilliant world of Logos, they reside in the dusky world of Mythos" (in Amano, p. 76). According to Diane Purkiss, fairies are post-antiquity variations on diverse creatures from the ancient world likewise endowed with ambiguous connotations — e.g., nymphs, satyrs, fauns, centaurs — or else depicted as downright pernicious — e.g., gorgons, demonic children and mothers, child-killing monsters and vampiric hybrids. Those archaic beings were able to survive "unchanged to lie comfortably alongside Christianity," argues Purkiss, for the reason that "they were not official; they did not attract attention. They did not have big, visible shrines and priests and holy texts of their own. They were oral, popular." Hence, they were also capable of "mingling promiscuously with the new, Christian-speaking dead, the saints, the angels, and creating new stories and meanings" (Purkiss, p. 52). As a result, narratives about fairies colluded with saints' legends, chivalric romances, tales about witchcraft and witch trials. In this process of alacritous cross-pollination, the ancient entities and their latter-day mutations were able to retain their universal fascination as incarnations of our deepest anxieties and longings about the darkness marking death and birth alike.

Iain Zaczek pursues a germane argument with his comments regarding pictorial production in the Victorian era. Throughout this period, it became increasingly common for images of "fairies, angels, cupids and cherubs" to coexist within "the walls of exhibition galleries and museums." In principle, such paintings ought to "have been very different, as they stemmed from fields that hardly seemed compatible — Christianity, pagan mythology and fantasy. In practice, though, it was just as acceptable to place a fairy on top of a Christmas tree as it was to use an angel; and in pantomimes, the fairy godmother had become the popular equivalent of a guardian angel" (Zaczek, p. 180). Thus, as Peter Narváez contends, even though "official Christian clergy have often denounced fairies and fairy beliefs as being evil and satanic," in actuality, "the relations of folk religion and official religion have been associative rather than antithetical, an established church absorbing and integrating aspects of fairylore rather than eliminating them" (Narváez, p. 197). This syncretic approach finds a direct parallel in Japanese culture's well-documented tendency to synthesize diverse mythical and ritual sources in its elaboration of indigenous belief systems, as explicitly borne out by Shinto.

On a broader plane, fairy-related beliefs could be seen as a latently transgressive agency, capable of puncturing from within formally sanctioned doctrines and the political systems devoted to those doctrines' hegemonic hold. This hypothesis proves most tantalizing when it is assessed with reference to contrasting interpretations of the social significance of myth. The functionalist perspective advocates that the fundamental role of myth is to foster social cohesion. This position is paradigmatically encapsulated by Bronislaw Malinowski's assertion that "Myth fulfils in primitive culture an indispensable function: it expresses, enhances, and codifies belief; it safeguards and enforces morality; it vouches for the efficiency of ritual and contains practical rules for the guidance of man" (Malinowski, p. 79). While this approach is no doubt relevant to numerous social situations, it does not, as Narváez points out, account satisfactorily for "conflict within a society and social change in general," which actually indicate that "some traditional expressive behaviors may serve resistant, aggressive, combative ends that are more socially divisive than cohesive" (Narváez, p. 299). Neither myth in general nor fairy beliefs specifically can ever be presumed to serve a single or unequivocal purpose and there is always a possibility, therefore, that even a body of lore normally dedicated to the preservation of societal equilibrium and ethical boundaries will at some point seek to question the system it is intended to bolster and, in so doing, destabilize its utopian aspirations to unbreachable harmony.

If the mystery enveloping the provenance of fairies is enough to warrant the fairy tale tradition's dystopian dimension, we should not ignore the substantial extent to which this is consolidated by much folklore surrounding fairyland and its denizens. As remarked at various junctures in this book, it is not uncommon for stories, anecdotes and rumors about fairies to emphasize their inherent malice and minatory disposition. Such propensities are deemed capable, as also noted, of triggering both relatively innocuous mishaps or delusions and momentous calamities, and acquire especially sinister connotations in stories concerning the abduction of humans (both as infants and as adults) by fairy folk. The felling of a fairy tree or the penetration of one of the fairies' secret haunts may also unleash great misfortunes. In addition, it is wise to beware of fairy gold since it invariably turns out to amount to totally useless objects such as gingerbread cakes or even leaves and gorse blossom. As shown in Chapter 2: Alterity, fairies have also been frequently invoked as incarnations of deep-seated cultural anxieties and thereby exploited as convenient scapegoats, immolated by human society in order to exorcize what it dreads most acutely about itself. In the late nineteenth century, for example, it was common for social groups and phenomena which the Victorian world picture deemed incompatible with its notions of decorum and stability to be embodied in fairies. As Carole G. Silver argues, categories and concepts as disparate as political unrest and mental imbalance, women and their quest for emancipation, the disenfranchised masses and ethnic minorities rank high among the fears displaced by Victorians onto fairies. The Little People, in this purview, stand as the dystopian underside of Victorian society's utopian self-idealization as an era of peerless moral excellence and societal concord.

A further factor fueling the dystopian atmosphere of uncertainty surrounding Faërie and its people has to do with the creatures' disquietingly nebulous — and hence uncategorizable — nature. Narváez attributes this ontological haziness to the fact that "in collecting extraordinary and anomalous folklore," one encounters multiple "levels of belief and disbelief, the humorous and the solemn, empirical truth and cultural truth." The body of "knowledge" surrounding fairies is often as "interstitial" in nature as the times and places traditionally associated with their manifestations insofar as it cannot be decisively situated on either side of those conceptual pairings but actually inhabits an elusive borderline, a mobile threshold (Narváez, p. 3). This pervasive sense of uncertainty and inconclusiveness has impelled innumerable anthropologists, sociologists and psychologists — as well as scientists, visionaries and amateurs — to formulate convincing theories regarding the provenance of fairies and, in the process, arrive at evidence for their existence. A few instances of such fervid theorizing are here worthy of inspection for the sake of contextual breadth.

As Silver explains, some folklorists have sought to prove the existence of fairies by invoking "physical phenomena and artifacts or tokens," such as "fairy bolts" and "fairy pipes" (Silver, p. 36). However, the most pervasive and influential theories on the subject have tended to polarize inconclusively around two incompatible sets of people: those who have regarded the Fair Folk as Spirit — e.g., Theosophists, Rosicrucians, Spiritualists and Christians of various denominations) — and those who have classified it as Matter — e.g., schools of thought of a primarily anthropological stamp positing fairies as surviving specimens of extinct primitive races or species. An especially intriguing contribution to the spiritual theory is provided by Franz Hartmann's article "Some Remarks about the Spirits of Nature," where the traditional conception of fairies as elemental entities is imaginatively redefined to suggest that they possess not merely physical but also — and more significantly — psychological powers that enable them to mold our dispositions. Hartmann argues that "the spirits of nature have their dwellings within us as well as outside of us, and no man is perfectly master over himself unless he thoroughly knows his own nature and its inhabitants" (Hartmann, p. 29). Thus, becoming acquainted with fairies is here posited as a precondition of that vital quality — self-understanding — without which we can barely call ourselves human. Hartmann's position also anticipates the view that all human beings harbor unconscious realities — what our forefathers would at times conceive of as possessing spirits — and that they need to know and embrace those realities in order to function as anything other than soulless puppets.

Promulgators of the materialist theory, conversely, often maintain that fairies, alongside many other fantastic beings, are a product of language — or, to be more precise, of the metaphors deployed by ancient civilizations in order to define various aspects of the natural environment and cosmic phenomena utterly beyond their comprehension. What is thought of as a category of actual creatures, according to this approach, is in fact a linguistic event grounded in the logic of mythopoeic thinking. George W. Cox promotes this view in *An Introduction to the Comparative Science of Mythology and Folklore*, showing that "the fairy queens who tempt Tannhäuser and True Thomas to their caves," for instance, are actually tropes designating "the beauty of the night, cloudless and still" (Cox, p. 156). As this example of materialist reasoning indicates, its promoters are themselves perfectly capable of employing some highly evocative lyrical language. Other theorists in the same camp inspired by Sir Edward Burnett Tylor explain fairies as issues of the union of animistic beliefs and survival mechanisms. Thus, the stories invented by primitive societies in which nature is seen to be pervaded by animate agencies are held to have endured among traditional rural communities and contributed significantly to the shaping of folklore all over the planet. This standpoint has played a major part in the dissipation of the damning shadow enfolding so-called superstitions, contending that supposedly irrational fears and rituals associated with the more traditional strata of the population are culturally meaningful and impactful and should be neither derided nor dismissed as evidence of barbarism.

It is also noteworthy that the reality of fairies was defended by various Victorian scholars who did not wish to either idealize the creatures in quasi-religious terms or debunk their mystery and dislocating power but rather sought to take cognizance of the species at a pragmatic level by recourse to science. Sophia Morrison, for example, proposes that "there is nothing supernatural" about fairies insofar as "what used to be so called is something that we do not understand at present.... Our forefathers would have thought the X-rays, and wireless telegraphy ... 'supernatural'" (in Evans-Wentz, p. 119). Alfred Russell Wallace, likewise championing a scientific perspective on fairies, argues that these entities can be regarded as "preterhuman discarnate beings" (in Oppenheim, p. 326) who coexist with humanity within the same world. Emma Hardinge-Britten advocates a cognate position by suggesting that fairies are comparable to "*embryonic* states for the soul, as well as for the body ... realms of gestation for spiritual, as well as for material, forms" (Hardinge-Britten, p. 382). Relatedly, fairies are portrayed by Walter Yeeling Evans-Wentz as "a distinct race between our own and that of spirits" (Evans-Wentz, p. 47).

One of the most comprehensive and aesthetically enticing explanations of fairies' essential nature on scientific grounds is supplied by Edward Gardner, Secretary of the Theosophical Society, who contends that fairies are spirits responsible for the "growth" of plants by acting as transmitters of the sun's "stimulating energy" to the "raw material" provided by "seed" and "soil" (in Conan Doyle, p. 124). Imbuing his discourse with truly poetical verve, Gardner also maintains that spirits secure "the evolution of beautiful and responsive forms" (p. 129), as some specialized kinds of fairies create and assemble the different cells due to form flowers and roots, while others deal with a plant's overall shape and color. In light of these views, Cicely Mary Barker's "Flower Fairies" suddenly acquire some unexpected connotations. Most importantly, both Gardner's theories and Barker's pictures vividly remind us of a crucial — and globally treasured — aspect of fairy lore: the belief that the Good Folk is responsible for looking after all imaginable forms of vegetation. Even within the boundaries of an urban habitation, fairies are known to take care of house plants during their active seasons and to guard them by sleeping in them or in their vicinity during phases of dormancy or rest.

This idea strikes its roots in animistic religions according to which every plant, river, mountain — indeed, even the lowliest of rocks — has its own guardian spirit. Japan's Shinto still embraces this view today. In many other cultures, however, animism has vanished or, at any rate, been relegated to the very margins of tradition, and several of the beliefs associated with it have been transferred to the province of fairy lore. Hence, popular adages such as "fairy folks are in old oaks" are ultimately grounded in a deeply ingrained heritage. Fairies' animistic connection with woods, specifically, is evocatively conveyed by Ralph Waldo Emerson's recollections: "A lady with whom I was riding in the forest said to me that the woods always seemed to her to wait, as if the genii who inhabit them suspended their deeds until the wayfarer had passed onward; a thought which poetry has celebrated in the dance of the fairies, which breaks off the approach of human feet" (Emerson). It should also be noted, on this point, that studious self-disguise as plants and flowers is said to be one of fairies' most efficient means of hiding from humans while concurrently blending with the mortal world. Their garments can be fashioned to look like common types of vegetation and chromatically adapted throughout the year to reflect seasonal variations. Fairies' movements abet their camouflage, emulating the motion of petals caressed by a barmy springtime breeze or of leaves swirling in the squally wind of late autumn.

The sense of dystopian uncertainty enveloping the origins of fairies is reinforced by the ambiguity of the creatures' ontological status in the contemporary world. As Narváez comments, "for centuries there have been reports of fading fairy traditions," maintaining that people have ceased to believe in fairies, even though there are indications that fairy faith is, in fact, still widespread in many cultures. This suggests that "the idea of the fairies' disappearance itself is part of the fairylore belief complex" (Narváez, p. xii). According to Silver, ancient beliefs have not vanished but been projected onto other categories of being such as extraterrestrial or alien creatures and related phenomena. Thus, "While the more traditional fairies show signs of continuing life in Ireland and Scotland ... new and different elfin species are continually being invented or discovered.... Believers are already speculating that the recent mysterious computer viruses are new, submicroscopic species of the elfin world" (Silver, p. 210). This view is akin to the idea, held by Jeffrey Sconce, that novel forms of a spiritual and incorporeal kind unrelentingly evolve in conjunction with changing technologies and corresponding channels of information and communication. Both traditional and contemporary media are indeed inhabited by phantasmatic forces, or cryptopresences, and the internet itself could be regarded as a prime artificer of impalpable, fairy-like entities comparable to techno-ectoplasms. Technology's collusion with the otherworldly domain can be traced back to early Spiritualism and its experiments with telegraphy and photography. Since that time, according to Sconce, Western — and most notably American — societies have remained "intrigued by the capacity of electronic media to create sovereign yet displaced, absent and parallel worlds" (Sconce, p. 25). The main reason for this abiding cultural propensity would seem to be an inveterate urge to "ascribe mystical powers to what are ultimately very material technologies" (p. 6), and hence endow their tools and procedures with a modicum of aliveness and animation. Moreover, Silver reminds us, it is not uncommon for UFO experts and enthusiasts to maintain that "the fairies really *are* the little green men — alien creatures from outer space who have come to join us" (Silver, p. 210).

It is nonetheless undeniable that since the late eighteenth century, rampant urbanization, the erosion or domestication of wild spaces, and the sanitization of fairy tales for moralistic purposes have been ineluctably conducive to the attenuation — and, in some pockets of society, even the total demise — of fairy faith. Nineteenth-century children's literature, in particular, served to accelerate the Fair Folk's extinction by unleashing a plethora of expurgated, straitlaced and honeyed narratives that generally tended to neglect or deform genuine fairy lore. These stories were largely responsible for divulging the notion that fairies themselves were puerile and that belief in their existence was the sole prerogative of kids. As an entire tradition of trivialization and utopianization burgeoned, once feared and respected beings came to be lumped together with cute toys and Christmas decorations. The cultural manipulation of fairies was abetted by the famous case of the Cottingley photographs — images of graceful, tiny and winged creatures putatively taken by Frances Griffiths, aged eleven, and her cousin Elsie Wright, aged sixteen, in 1917. These intriguing pictures attracted enormous attention when published, and gained Sir Arthur Conan Doyle's undiluted support (Conan Doyle himself being a Spiritualist). The girls' secret was revealed when Frances eventually admitted — notably, not until 1983 — that the images were the result of a rather primitive but undeniably ingenious form of collage or compositing. Despite their artificiality, the images had a lasting effect on the public's perception of fairy folk as diminutive, charming and doll-like entities. "Ironically," as Silver puts it, "the photographs, the ostensible proof of the actual existence of fairies, deprived the elfin people of their grandeur and status. In general terms, denuding the fairies of the invisibility that made them powerful and frightening diminished them" (Silver, p. 190).

If the term dystopia is taken to connote, as proposed earlier in this chapter, not a straightforwardly "bad" dimension, which is the idea intrinsic in the dys- prefix, but a warped or dislocated reality, then it could be assumed that with the passage of time, fairies have resiliently relinquished their traditional anchors to survive—and indeed renew themselves—on alternate planes. The interdependence of survival and self-regeneration is vital to the anime plots under scrutiny, insofar as no dystopia ever leaves out the hopeful possibility of a new beginning. In this perspective, contemporary cultural products like the anime discussed in this context can be approached precisely as adaptive relocations of the fairy tale tradition onto fresh expressive territory. In other words, just as fairies rely on their protean adaptability to the changing requirements and expectations of different epochs, the fairy tale tradition as a whole analogously mutates over the centuries in order to emblematize ever-shifting social and ideological constellations. The specific media, forms and genres though which the fairy tale tradition—and, via this discourse, fairies themselves—find expression within the compass of distinctive milieux and at particular moments in history can be regarded as the contingent semiotic channels through which both the fairy tale tradition and fairies announce their tenacious survival instincts and prismatic versatility.

In his introduction to *Italian Folktales*, a collection of traditional stories painstakingly assembled and edited over a period of two years and requiring undiluted dedication, Italo Calvino maintains that during the time of his engagement in the project, the entire world acquired the flavor of fairyland, inducing him to sense charms, enchantments and metamorphoses at the heart of even the most prosaic workaday events, and to perceive fairylike attitudes and traits in every human he met. It is from this experience that Calvino came fully to recognize the profound relevance of Faërie to real life as an allegorical explanation of reality (Calvino 2009). This lesson is indubitably vital to the world picture proposed in this book as a whole but gains special urgency in the treatment of dystopias. Indeed, it is in the face of warped, deviant and displaced realities—and of the attendant injunction to understand and negotiate their vicissitudes—that we are most likely to benefit from a preparedness to confront the unfamiliar with eyes unclouded and not fret in the presence of seemingly unredeemable contradictions. One of the most potent tropes deployed by the fairy tale tradition to evoke a disconcerting atmosphere of spatial, psychological and emotive unanchoring consists of magical transformations. This motif enables a fairy tale to bring forth within the mortal domain something that clearly belongs to Faërie and ought not, in strictly logical terms, be allowed to spill beyond its boundaries. Fairies frequently rely on invisibility to move around our world at leisure and maximize the mischievous impact of some of their ruses, inducing fear by making their presence known only through elusive signs such as the jingle of hidden bells, the rustle of impalpable silk, floating melodies or heady aromas. More spectacular still, however, is their abrupt transition from one form to another, which may include gender switches and incarnations in animal guise.

In this fluid universe, language operates as a comparable means of dislocation, as attested to by the fact that fairies are not to be referred to explicitly by name — hence the widespread adoption in numerous contexts (including this book) of epithets such as Little People, Fair Folk, Good Folk, Hill Folk, Wee Folk, Green Children, People of Peace, Good Ladies or Gentry. Furthermore, the fairy tale tradition persistently shows that the creatures themselves tend to employ secret names permeated with magical or sacred attributes, and are bound to retain their powers only as long as these esoteric designations are left undisclosed. Therefore, the ultimate enigma embedded in human language itself as a system averse to transparent communication and more likely, in fact, to capitalize on the unsaid and the half-stated, the ambiguous and the equivocal, finds a resonant allegorical equivalent in the language of Faërie and its tendency to dissever what is said from what is meant and, in turn, meaning from utterance. According to J. C. Cooper, the taboo associated with "the Power of the Name" underlying the "prohibition against using the names" in the case of fairy folk strikes its roots in "the universal belief in the creative force of sound: 'In the beginning was the Word ... and the Word was God.'" The ritualistic significance of names must also be taken into account in assessing the interdiction against naming fairies directly and the profusion of aliases commended as tactful alternatives to their actual appellations, insofar as a "name is also a powerful means of exorcism and is the basis of incantation in which 'words of power' can compel elemental forces and open doors magically, as Ali Baba's 'Open sesame.'" In addition, the use of a person's or a spiritual entity's "true name" is held in many traditions to procure "magic power over the soul" (Cooper, p. 64). As A. M. Hocart states, in this respect, "A man's name is commonly treated as part of his person. In Babylon what had no name did not exist" (Hocart; cited in Cooper, p. 64).

One of the most beautiful descriptions of fairy folk ever recorded that faithfully captures the species' baffling elusiveness without any concessions to either sensationalist or picturesque leanings is offered by Walter de la Mare in *Broomsticks*: "If you can imagine a figure — even now I cannot tell how tall she was — that seems to be made of the light of rainbows, and yet with every feature in its flaxen-framed face as clearly marked as a cherub's cut in stone; and if you can imagine a voice coming to you, close into your ear, without you being able to say exactly where it is coming *from — that* was what I saw and heard" (de la Mare, p. 66). As Katharine Briggs aptly comments, "There is no whimsy here, but the careful building up, touch by touch, of what almost becomes a personal experience" (Briggs, p. 257). While the fairy's undeniable beauty makes her endearing and unthreatening, her association with inhuman sounds proclaims her imponderable alienness.

The anime here addressed draw inspiration from a transcultural narrative corpus that capitalizes on an unbalancing sense of dislocation as a means of interrogating, with often subversive undertones, the establishment of particular power structures in human (or posthuman) societies. They thereby engage with the iniquitous processes through which those structures come to provide validation for the advancement of distinctive cultural identities and corresponding perceptions of history and its recording, while also taking care to highlight the dire extent to which natural rhythms are bound to be impaired — sometimes irredeemably — in the process. The fairy-related actors brought into play in the elaboration of these issues are not, despite the anime's dystopian emphasis, univocally or uniformly malevolent, devious or corrupt. Nor are they aesthetically repulsive. In fact, although cuteness is not exactly an obvious facet of their mien, they undoubtedly exude a sense of charisma akin to an awe-inspiring otherworldly aura. The dramatic functions deployed in tandem with such figures feature the performative dimension as a major component of all three shows due to the prominence of ebullient action sequences and adventure-oriented complications. At the same time, the shows judiciously rely — without, by and large, any patronizing concessions to didacticism — on the explanatory modality in order to elucidate their plots' relevance to societal illnesses of global magnitude. Hence, the anime also offer apposite objects of study with reference to approaches to the fairy tale tradition operating within educational, cautionary and interrogative frames of reference.

In *Basilisk* (TV series; dir. Fumitomo Kizaki, 2005), the fairy tale tradition's dimension finds epic formulation in the chronicling of the struggle between two ninja clans, the Iga and Kouga, in the year 1614. Animosity, vindictiveness and ancient grudges have been temporarily kept at bay by a precarious non-hostilities pact but this is abruptly suspended when the Tokugawa Shogunate finds itself confronted by a grave succession issue. At this point, each of the two rival factions resolves to back its own representative in the race for the assumption of the title of shogun when the current ruler steps down, and a new leader must therefore inherit the poisoned chalice of power. The contest is choreographed in accordance with strict rules of chivalric resonance around the images of two identical scrolls upon which the leader of each clan has inscribed the names of its most skillful ninjas. The tribe able to vanquish all ten of its rival warriors and to gain possession of the scroll that bears their names will be declared victorious. It will also, as an added bonus, become automatically entitled to the maintenance of a prestigious position for one thousand years to come. Despite the anime's historical underpinnings, strengthened by the provision of a detailed background to the current state of affairs, the scrolls clearly operate as talismanic, quasi-magical entities redolent of the sorts of objects typically deployed by the fairy tale tradition to trigger a quest and sustain a character's motivation throughout the adventure.

The fairy tale dimension comes most prominently into the limelight with the articulation of the saga's romantic dimension. This revolves around the two warring clans' young heirs, Gennosuke and Oboro, whose ordeal as classic star-crossed lovers brings to mind Romeo and Juliet's timelessly captivating tragedy. Thrust onto opposing sides by a feud for which they hold no responsibility and in which they would rather have no involvement, the two characters are forced to face the eternally thorny choice between love and duty. Not all viewers enjoy period sagas punctuated by bouts of blood-spilling that come across as unquestionably sensational, though neither realistic nor especially disturbing due to their blatantly artificial (Tarantinesque) acting style and mise-en-scène. However, even audiences that do not feel instinctively drawn to the type of adventure dramatized in *Basilisk* will feasibly recognize the ingeniousness and dexterity of the martial techniques displayed in its action sequences. These capitalize on an imaginative blend of elements drawn from both actual and fictionalized versions of indigenous history and fairy tale conventions of global appeal. Some skills, accordingly, are faithful reflections of talents traditionally ascribed to ninja and particularly their agility, stealth and flair for disguise and camouflage — bearing in mind, of course, that ninja themselves are creatures whose historical credentials are overlaid with myriad legends of often fairytalish temper. Other abilities exhibited by *Basilisk*'s fighters seem to have sprung straight out of fairy lore: for instance, the power to create pink butterflies out of thin air.

A significant proportion of *Basilisk*'s characters can be approached as fairy types because of their possession not only of gravity-defying martial skills but also of an uncompromising ruthlessness and very peculiar somatic attributes. The latter bring to mind some of the most formidable — and least romanticized — fairy figures by starkly opposing the saccharine images prevalent in Western popular culture since the nineteenth century and in Japan itself since at least the 1980s. Whereas (as also noted elsewhere in this study) those images capitalize on traits such as gossamer wings and cute costumes, the bellicose and vengeful fairy types presented in *Basilisk* repeatedly exhibit grotesque or even repulsive variations on the graphic themes of deformity and disfigurement. Even the visuals' occasional concessions to graphic elegance are quick to give way to the macabre, and flourishes of linear brilliance to take a careening plunge into horror. They thus place sobering emphasis on the most unpalatable elements of cruelty, capriciousness, belligerence and ugliness coursing the Faërie realm at its rawest and coarsest. These factors have been varyingly documented by numerous critics over the centuries. Ronald Macdonald Robertson's 1791 account of his visit to the Isle of man, as cited by W. W. Gill, stresses that alongside "playful and benignant" fairies, there exist many "sullen and vindictive" characters (Gill, p. 233). Morrison likewise remarks that many of the "Little People," whom she posits not as "the tiny creatures with wings who flutter about in many English fairy tales" but actual "small persons," tend to be "mischievous and spiteful, and that is why they are called by such good names, in case they should be listening!" (in Evans-Wentz, pp. v–vi).

Furthermore, *Basilisk*'s baleful fairy figures will not typically hesitate to endure agonizing deaths for the sake of their kinspeople but evince no trace of reverence, generosity or conviviality toward the rest of the human species. They will readily leave those who do not stand in their way alone but will as swiftly annihilate anybody they perceive as a real, or even just potential, obstacle. In this respect, those characters mirror some traditional fairies whose ethical principles, as Briggs explains, are tenuous to say the least: "So far as respect for human goods is concerned, honesty means nothing to the fairies. They consider that they have a right to whatever they need or fancy, including the human beings themselves. On the whole it may be said that if they are suitably propitiated and treated with respect, allowed to take what they fancy and feed where they like, unmolested in their revellings and unhindered in their journeys, the fairies have a kindly feeling toward mankind, will help them if they can, and enjoy their companionship" (Briggs, pp. 134–135).

If *Basilisk*'s take on dystopia is fundamentally retrospective, *Ergo Proxy* (TV series; dir. Shuko Murase, 2006) adopts a futuristic approach to the concept, taking us into a post-apocalyptic world where the only inhabitable place appears to be the domed city called Romdo. Constructed in the aftermath of a nuclear holocaust conducive to worldwide ecological collapse in order to accommodate both humans and their android servants, the AutoReivs, the city passes itself off as a veritable Eden. This does not mean, however, that Romdo is the perfect utopia: Ri-l Mayer, the anime's heroine, unceremoniously describes it as a "boring paradise" and maintains that the sole thing the city truly "desires" is "a dull face." Moreover, the domed metropolis actually depends for its survival on a harsh management system designed to ensure that feelings and emotions have no place within its boundaries, that the government council is in a position to control the lives of its citizens down to the minutest detail and that crime is no longer conceivable. Since Romdo's human inhabitants are harvested in artificial wombs, the maintenance of this state of affairs is unlikely to suffer any serious threat. Romdo's illusorily paradisal reality comes abruptly to an end with a chain of inexplicable murders ostensibly connected with a phenomenon known as "Awakening." This occurs when AutoReivs become infected with a virus dubbed "Cogito" that enables them to be conscious of their own existence and embark on voyages of self-exploration. The androids are automatically held responsible for all of the murders but it soon transpires that the truth behind those bizarre crimes is far more unpalatable as the existence of a hitherto unknown creature is disclosed: namely, a prodigy dubbed "Proxy" resulting from secret government-sponsored experimentation, conducted within a nefarious web of manipulation and intrigue.

The Proxies are actually "Agents of the Creator," the architect-architech behind the anime's dystopia, and are meant to be completing his task — i.e., effecting the restoration of the human race by changing its form. The culmination of this process is intended to be the annihilation of humanity as we know it. In carrying out their mission, the Proxies are not endowed with unlimited powers but are actually bound to the plan designed for them by the Creator. Ironically, even though they are pivotal to his scheme, once they have accomplished their goal, they are destined to become superfluous and be perceived simply as monsters or evil demons. The "Pulse of Awakening," or "Proxy Destruction Program," is held to commence as soon as humanity has awakened and restored itself. It should be noted, however, that this idea — like many of the concepts underpinning the anime's concurrently science fictional and philosophical mentality, remains open to interpretation and that both *Ergo Proxy*'s human characters and the Proxies themselves retain an aura of indissoluble ambiguity just as fairyland's inhabitants infamously do. Matters are further complicated by the fact that through their exposure to humans, Proxies have come to experience sorrow and compassion and have ended up loving the very species they are meant to erase. The show's finale offers a reparative gesture by proposing that the world has finally reached the point where it can begin to heal itself, as humankind can once again face its connection to the earth after millennia of self-estrangement from the natural domain. A long and onerous struggle awaits the survivors but the challenge they confront is the key to redemption not solely for humans but for life itself.

While the series derives its kinetic momentum from the adventures spawned by the imperative to ascertain the Proxy's origins and intended function, its most interesting component lies with its speculative propensities. These come to the fore as the awakened creatures are forced to confront a seemingly intractable dilemma: whether the virus that has endowed them with self-awareness is what gives them their identity or whether they have acquired an identity through their experiences. The creatures' conundrum reflects metaphorically our own efforts as humans — vain and insistent in equal measures — to establish whether we become who we are as a result of environmental influences or because of innate qualities. Given the show's existentialist preoccupations, it may seem hardly surprising that the androids should bear the names of illustrious philosophers such as Berkeley, Husserl, Derrida, Kristeva, Deleuze, Guattari and Lacan. Moreover, the title of each installment is preceded by the tag "*meditatio,*" which can be read as an echo of one of Descartes' principal works, *Meditations on First Philosophy* (1641). Other philosophical allusions to Descartes are the title itself and the name of the virus supposed to affect the AutoReivs, both of which are indebted to the philosopher's famous dictum "*Cogito, ergo sum.*" The denomination chosen for one of the main Proxy specimens, Monad, derives from the systems elaborated by Spinoza and Leibniz. At the same time, however, the series incorporates discreet hints at both mythology and the fairy tale tradition itself through names such as

Daedalus (a clear Classical reference), Pino (short for Pinocchio) and Rabbit (an homage to *Alice in Wonderland*). Although *Ergo Proxy's* dystopia comes across as emphatically futuristic, especially in comparison with a series like *Basilisk*, it actually relies with remarkable and often haunting consistency on the iconographic and symbolic powers of a complex array of allusions to Renaissance, Baroque and Neoclassical art — most palpably, in the architectural and sculptural arenas.

A fundamental component of *Ergo Proxy's* ideation of a consummately dystopian society lies with its enterprising approach to worldbuilding, conducive to the detailed mapping of an entire speculative universe. Some of the major locations indigenous solely to the anime deserve some consideration in this context but it must first be noted that *Ergo Proxy's* spatial richness mirrors the stunning variety of fairy realms accommodated within the fairy tale tradition itself— a multiverse so copious as to induce a sense of dislocation or disorientation akin to the unsettling power of dystopia. (This term is again employed, in this regard, as connotative of an unstable and displaced reality and not of a "bad" or "ugly" world as the prefix "dys" might suggest if taken at face value.) The sheer conceptual diversity of the worlds encompassed by the fairy tale tradition may be enough unto itself to produce a marginal feeling of bafflement in a reader, listener or viewer suddenly exposed to several of those domains in rapid succession. If, however, we move past the plane of abstract concepts and agree to embark on an exploratory journey of the kind fairy tales so often encourage, mild confusion could easily escalate into vertigo. Even a person least passionate about Faërie and its sprawling reality will feasibly be surprised by the cornucopian profusion of its realms, by their countless folds, pockets and detours and by the dark revelations issuing from their Pandora's Box. Commenting merely on the fairies of the British Isles, Briggs argues that these "are of different sizes, dispositions and kinds" and that this diversity is tangibly confirmed by the impressive range of "habitations in different places" with which each category is traditionally associated (Briggs, p. 14). Thus, the Wee Folk may be encountered — ideally by legitimate invitation rather than by stealth or deceit — in subterranean corridors or underwater palaces, stone circles and mounds in secluded meadows, barrows, natural hillocks, holes in the sides of a hill, tiny streams coursing between clumps of ivy and ferns, ancient hollow trees, abandoned barns and lily pads — and this list is by no means exhaustive. If one were imaginatively to multiply the diversity highlighted by Briggs in relation to a rather limited cultural-geographical area to account for the variety of fairy realms one might expect to find across the globe, an astronomical figure could well be the outcome of the exercise.

With its dexterously twisted interpretation of Faërie's multiple dimensions, *Ergo Proxy* tenaciously endeavors to throw into relief their more alarming facets, especially by means of realistic images of frozen or barren wastelands and crumbling cities scattered across the planet. The anime's version of Faërie hence reveals deep sensitivity to its web of delusions and illusions. In so doing, *Ergo Proxy* offers an unobtrusive allegorical commentary on a dark cultural reality of great relevance not only to its own dystopian domain but also to the world we quotidianly inhabit. What is thereby frankly exposed is the extent to which human beings themselves live essentially delusory and illusory lives, consciously or subliminally ignoring their dependence on masks designed to promulgate a social image — costumes that ultimately turn out to conceal not a truth or reality but rather the blinding absence of both truth and reality behind the covers themselves. Concomitantly, *Ergo Proxy* is eager to give expression, in an appropriately adapted figurative fashion, to fairyland's imbrication with baleful energies which no edulcorated or lace-bedecked depiction could ever presume to domesticate with conclusive finality. On the technical plane, those forces are effectively foregrounded by the consistent use of dramatic lighting and chromatic palettes designed to communicate a ubiquitous sense of tension and unease, alongside nightmarish juxtapositions of forms that ought to be logically incompatible and yet convey an eerie impression of balance and harmony. The Proxies themselves, in their extravagant grotesqueness, should evoke undilutedly negative feelings of dread or revulsion, yet come across as enchantingly weird rather than hideous. Where lighting is specifically concerned, it is noteworthy that although most scenes are pervaded by gloom, the central figures often appear to radiate an inner dazzling glow reminiscent of nineteenth-century gaslight — and tangentially suggestive of fairies' auric emanations.

Ergo Proxy's multiple dimensions are progressively brought to the fore by the adventures undertaken by the protagonists in disparate locations. The character of Vincent Law plays a particularly important role in enabling the anime's action to shift from one space to the next, in contrasting the distinctive atmospheres yielded by those settings, and in either integrating or flinging into collision their disparate world views. Vincent is also key to the drama by virtue of his special connection with the Proxies: an aspect of his personality that is incrementally elucidated as the story progresses to reach a sensational, yet elegantly staged, climax with the revelation that he is actually the principal Proxy — i.e., Ergo Proxy. An immigrant employed by Romdo's AutoReiv Control Division, the department responsible for disposing of infected AutoReivs, Vincent is haunted by a traumatic past and a crippling amnesia. He flees from the city, hounded down by the authorities due to his presumed implication in the Proxy-related crisis afflicting their society and ventures into the inhospitable outside world in the company of Pino — an infected AutoReiv previously owned by a childless couple as a surrogate daughter and then supplanted by the advent of a human baby. Equipped with the mind of a child, yet mature well beyond her age, Pino could be said to function as a highly unusual variation on the theme of the fairy godmother, showing Vincent how to escape from Romdo and abetting his arduous quest each step of the way. *Ergo Proxy*'s special worldbuilding flair is borne out by all of the successive stages in Vincent and Pino's odyssey.

Each city in the series' world, we discover, corresponds to a Proxy, and three hundred entities of this kind are said to have been generated in the aftermath of the ecological disaster leading to the current state of affairs. Beside Romdo, *Ergo Proxy*'s reality encompasses the Commune, a settlement just outside Romdo's boundaries whose occupants live off the refuse discarded by the metropolis; the domed city of Mosque, which hosts a chamber wherein Ergo Proxy's memories are encoded and could therefore be said to function as the drama's symbolic kernel, while also holding crucial significance for Vincent himself given his standing as a personality forged from Ergo Proxy's edited mnemonic bank; Halos Dome City (originally joined to the city of Asura in a Sun-Moon pairing), a world beset by chaos and ceaseless warfare where a facility known as WombSys produces artificial warriors; City Lights Bookstore (possibly an homage to the real venue of that name in San Francisco), where Vincent discovers who he and Ergo Proxy truly are and volumes storing information that could repair his memory are kept; and Ophelia Dome City, one of the most intriguing locations in the whole show from an aesthetic point of view: its dense patterns of streets form a conical shape reaching down toward a lake placed at the hub of a nature reserve, revealed to be its Proxy's lair.

In the presentation of its characters' often precipitous and traumatic travels across the anime's dystopian map, *Ergo Proxy* communicates a radically dislocated sense of time. Although, on the whole, it is quite possible to surmise the actual time scales entailed in each adventure, the overall impression evoked by the flow of events is that time is, quite simply, out of joint. On this point, the series echoes a vast tradition of fairy tales in which humans are temporarily allowed admission to an alternate reality but must then pay a heavy penalty for their departure from the familiar world. In the most sinister instances, they are condemned to dissolve into dust shortly after returning to the mortal domain. More frequently, however, they are subject to bizarre time warps, compressions or elongations. Humans may spend whole decades in an alternate reality and yet reenter the normal world at the very instant they left it. Alternately, they may visit Faërie for no more than the twinkling of an eye and yet find that their homeland has undergone radical transformation upon their return. The tale of *Visu the Woodsman and the Old Priest*, referred to in Chapter 3, exemplifies the latter narrative modality.

The topos of temporal distortion is an especially apposite vehicle for the articulation of dystopian societies. Moreover, it carries incontrovertible transcultural resonance, its popularity within the most disparate traditions being arguably unmatched by any other recurrent theme. In the context of Japanese lore, that motif finds its best known formulation in the story of *Urashima Taro*, the indigenous equivalent of the *Rip Van Winkle* and *Ossian* narratives. In this tale, a man who saves a turtle from a band of abusive children is rewarded with a visit to a kingdom under the sea where he is treated to splendid feasts and luxurious entertainment. Upon returning to his village, the character discovers that he has been away for decades and that all his relatives and friends have gone, which sentences him to a peculiar punishment: a lonely existence as an outsider in his own home (in Lang 1967).

If *Basilisk* and *Ergo Proxy* represent the retrospective and the futuristic poles of anime's engagement with the topos of dystopia, *Wolf's Rain* (TV series; dir. Tensai Okamura, 2003) could be said to bridge the two typologies by focusing on a post-apocalyptic habitat which, however, harks back to a relatively primitive phase of human civilization due to its state of advanced — even irreparable — environmental depletion. *Wolf's Rain* occasionally professes its connection with the fairy tale tradition quite explicitly. For instance, the belief that wolves are the only creatures capable of finding paradise when the human world finally comes to an end, even though wolves are supposed to have been extinct for two hundred years, is derisively dismissed by one character as being "just a kids' tale," while another character warns that it would be foolish to underestimate the significance of fairy tales for the simple reason that they always contain a grain of "truth." Sure enough, we soon discover that wolves have not totally vanished but rather assumed human form and that they still perceive other members of their species as wolves. In addition, the cryptic drama surrounding the character of Cheza, a preternaturally beautiful girl abiding in what seems to be suspended animation within a laboratory tank, is compared to a fairy tale unfolding in defiance of all known scientific rules.

The fairy tale dimension is reinforced by the story's symbolic emphasis on the quest for a superior dimension, capable of transcending the terrors of the dominant dystopia. As the show's prologue states, people commonly "say there's no such place as paradise. Even if you search to the ends of the Earth, there's nothing there." Nevertheless, the protagonist, Kiba, is "driven to find it" at the behest of an inner voice encouraging him to go on searching. It is this indefatigably pursued objective that fortuitously draws Kiba to Cheza — who is indeed said to have evinced the first signs of life in response to the smell of wolf's blood and to be associated with "lunar flowers" symbolic of an ultramundane reality. It is here worth mentioning that the emblematic bond linking a mysterious female character with a preternatural plant is a motif also deployed to great dramatic effect in *Blue Seed* (TV series; dir. Jun Kamiya, 1994–1995) and *Texhnolyze* (TV series; dir. Hiroshi Hamazaki, 2003). The yearning to reach paradise also binds Kiba to three more members of his species in a shared quest fraught with violence and menace, yet bolstered by loyalty, courage and perseverance — that is to say, qualities commended by many fairy tales over the centuries and also, no less crucially, axial to Japan's traditional ethics. *Wolf's Rain*, in its adventurous reconceptualization of the fairy tale tradition, brings to mind Angela Carter's subversive assessment of the lupine figure — advanced specifically with reference to the tale of *Little Red Riding Hood* in the short story "The Company of Wolves" — as a symbolic agent of revelation, awakening and growth, capable of catalyzing formative experiences of self-discovery and self-understanding in unsettling and utterly unpredictable fashions (Carter 1998).

As a creature radically displaced by forces beyond her control onto a liminal reality plane, and coveted for her supposedly special powers, Cheza brings to mind the changelings so frequently found in the fairy tale tradition: human babies stolen by the fairies, normally due to their desirability as a means of improving fairy stock by enhancing its beauty, and the mocking preternatural replacements left by the abductors in the human babies' cradles. Whereas the human children seized by the fairies are normally blessed with comely physiognomies, their substitutes are unseemly or even downright repulsive — either because they have been intentionally picked from the ranks of failing fairies, such as babies unable to thrive on fairy milk and hoary fairies approaching senility, or because they are simply not alive but actually consist of pieces of wood or golem-like lumps of earth endowed with no more than an ephemeral illusion of motility. Cheza's enchanting charm would seem to make her more akin to a stolen human child than to a fairy substitute. Yet, the esoteric knowledge which the girl is held to possess draws her closer to the province of fairy folk endowed by age and experience with special — even burdensome — wisdom. The girl's otherworldliness is underscored from an early stage in the story by the assertion, put forward by one of the main scientists responsible for monitoring her responses, that Cheza defies any known scientific law, transcending the boundaries of both reason and logic with humbling, though seemingly unintentional, obstinacy.

Like *Ergo Proxy*, *Wolf's Rain* culminates with an uplifting prospective scenario of purification and rebirth. When the world freezes over, the sole vestige of life being the seeds left in her wake by Cheza as her mortal form dissolves, nothing seems likely to relieve the mournful mood of desolation enveloping the landscape and the fading images of the valiant men-wolves that have sacrificed their lives in the show's climactic confrontation. Nevertheless, as the seeds germinate and disclose glorious specimens of the lunar flower with which the fairy girl has been emblematically associated throughout the anime, and more plants gradually proliferate until the entire vista has been restored to its pre-apocalyptic beauty, there are intimations that the human world is ready at last to experience the blessings not only of ecological renewal but also of resurrection. This possibility would appear to find fruition in the wordless sequence, flooded by a stirring aria allusive to the emergence of new energies, in which the main characters make brief appearances in full possession of their pristine vitality amid the hustle and bustle of a busy contemporary metropolis. Luckily, the series refrains from any facile concession to the clichéd vision of an idyllic utopia with which several dystopian narratives culminate (the finale of Steven Spielberg's 2002 movie *Minority Report* is a case in point). Accordingly, the atmosphere of sheer bliss summoned by the sequences focusing on the planet's regeneration is ironically ruptured by the presentation of the hectic city as a grey and smoky space soaked in insistent rain, even though resilient moon flowers manage to flourish among the garbage infesting the murky alleys.

Wolf's Rain joins forces with one of the most inveterate aspects of global lore in its articulation of a widespread narrative curve: that of the pilgrimage to a promised land. However, had this been the sole or most conspicuous facet which the anime shared with the prism of storytelling, and particularly with the fairy tale tradition, its discussion would have logically belonged with this book's third chapter. In fact, what proclaims far more incisively the series' affiliation with the fairy tale tradition is its imaginary inscription of that time-honored motif in the constellation of a consummately dystopian reality — the term dystopian, here as elsewhere in this chapter, connoting a gesture of radical displacement. Accordingly, the topos of the journey gains dramatic resonance not so much from the chronicling of an odyssey of discovery, significant though this theme no doubt is to the show's diegesis, as from the painstaking construction of a dislocated universe. It is, moreover, from this narrative project that *Wolf's Rain* derives the strength and momentum to weave together into an original whole a bundle of well-tested elements. These include both some common ingredients of the fairy tale tradition — as such ancient castles, snow-cloaked wastelands, evil noblemen — and images embedded in the related realm of science fiction — derelict urban conglomerates, cutting-edge technology, hypothetical life forms. Yet, the displacement factor capable of synthesizing these motifs into a coherent ensemble resides entirely with the anime's own narrative invention: that is to say, the proposition that its current reality originates in a two-hundred-year old mystery that cannot be obviously traced back to any generic predecessor, even though it may reverberate with echoes from myth and legend, but is in fact indigenous to *Wolf's Rain* per se.

The atmosphere of rampant dislocation is intensified by the anime's method of characterization. On the one hand, the main actors might seem to conform to conventional typologies: e.g., the prey, the hunter, the leader, the outsider, the clown and the child. On the other hand, such formulae pale to near insignificance when compared with the psychologically nuanced constitution of virtually every member of the cast. This applies both to the central characters of the wolves, each of whom perceives his identity as both a wolf and a human quite differently and accordingly harbors a distinctive attitude to humanity itself, and to the supporting personae — most notably, among the latter, the wolf-obsessed sheriff Quent and his peculiar dog Blue; the scientist investigating Cheza's enigmatic existence, Cher; her husband Hubb, a keen detective; and the formidable Nobles pursuing paradise for their own sinister reasons, Darcia and Jaguara. The characters' richness is reinforced throughout by the anime's dramatization of their singular back-stories as dystopian narratives in their own right. As the show's technovisionary dimension coalesces with its timelessly epic thrust in a story of undying hope and haunting despair, the fairy tale tradition's darker subtexts come to the fore with dispassionate frankness. The wilderness in which several memorable sequences are set is thereby presented as a condition affecting the soul — human and lupine alike — no less than the blighted environment itself. Thus, the anime's marvelous and mystical connotations never obscure its allegorical significance as a study of the harsher realities of political iniquity and monomaniacal self-aggrandizement. In fact, it is precisely by recourse to its fabulous materials that *Wolf's Rain* elaborates most effectively its intrinsically credible drama. This irony is enabled by the fantasy's defamiliarizing powers: the audience is led in a methodical and discreet fashion to acknowledge, and to reflect upon, the story's underlying realism by being compelled to look for it beneath its prodigious elements. It is most likely that if the realistic component had been dished out for our instant consumption as a documentary report, it would have proved far less impactful — and, in any case, appeared tied to a specific context, which would have impaired the anime's transcultural import. In this matter, the show corroborates Marina Warner's contention that the "enchantments" pervading the fairy tale as a practice and art serve to "universalize the narrative setting, encipher concerns, beliefs and desires in brilliant, seductive images that are themselves a form of camouflage, making it possible to utter harsh truths, to say what you dare" (Warner 1995, p. xvii).

In the anime examined in this chapter, the issue of cultural identity is so axial as to shape the dramatic unfolding of the three shows from start to finish. It is actually hard to conceive of any of these series independently of its articulation of the multifarious processes through which their characters constellate, perpetuate and periodically reassess their roles in relation to specific cultural formations — and, by implication, distinctive power dynamics, attitudes to the relationship between human society and the natural habitat and perceptions of the temporal trajectories in which they are incessantly inscribed. Thus, *Basilisk*'s entire cast is defined by the tribal allegiances and obligations of each of its members, on the basis of which the identities of individuals and clans alike are forged and their respective histories are recorded. Both *Ergo Proxy* and *Wolf's Rain* posit cataclysmic ecological damage as the hostile substratum upon which their societies have been post-apocalyptically fashioned and against which, concomitantly, these societies have had to protect themselves through the erection of strict power structures and subject positions. The worlds portrayed by *Ergo Proxy* and *Wolf's Rain* could never seek legitimation and ultimately subsist, as dystopian civilizations in anime format, without recourse to an implied historiographical web of unknown tomes encoding those momentous cultural developments. Indeed, the identities of both singular individuals and the alternate-history domains in which those are embedded depend vitally on successive instantiations and disruptions of official accounts of events. These hypothetical texts inevitably partake, given their shadowy and impalpable substance, of the alternate reality of fairy tales even though the cultures they underpin may appear to emblematize either the apotheosis of reason (*Ergo Proxy*) or the pit of disenchantment (*Wolf's Rain*).

Anime's dystopian appropriation of the fairy tale tradition could be said to strike its roots in the dark substratum of many old narratives predating their manipulation by censors, moralists and educators. A survey of even the most selective sample of stories in their ancestral forms will soon reveal that they abound with instances of cruel behavior and with physically and ethically repugnant beings. Relatedly, their yarns incessantly engage with all manner of unpalatable themes and events, including murder, torture, mutilation, exposure, starvation, cannibalism, incest, rape, infanticide, child abuse, gory revenge, brutal punishments, satanic pacts and gross humiliations. These elements typically function as vehicles for voicing the perverse fantasies, fears and emotional lacerations of whole communities, as either lucidly acknowledged or repressed realities. Of the anime here studied, *Basilisk* is no doubt the one that dwells most persistently on lurid portrayals of humankind's most destructive and savage propensities, whereas *Wolf's Rain* tends to engage more quietly with the concepts of violation and abuse — even though it unquestionably exhibits its own fair share of bloodiness. In *Ergo Proxy*, virtually the entire catalogue of the fairy tale tradition's murkiest ingredients comes into view through a dispassionate dissection of the atrocities and indignities poisoning the anime's dystopia that aptly relies on monstrosity as a visual metonym for a broad social reality. The monsters themselves are depicted in such a way as to epitomize the specific culture in which they manifest (i.e., de*mon*strate) their ascendancy. As a result, much as they echo archetypal forms to be found in previous manifestations of the fairy tale tradition all over the globe, they cannot be viewed entirely as expressions of universal and timeless structures of signification. First, their portrayal is influenced by the codes and conventions of anime itself as an art form and, beyond anime as such, by he representational registers established by the distinctively Japanese genre of the *daikaiju* ("giant monster") movie. Second, they are shaped by the ideological climate of the particular dystopia forged by *Ergo*

Proxy as both its setting and its axial topos. This is most effectively attested to by the climactic sequences in which the Proxies subtly morph before our eyes and thus alert us to their intrinsically protean nature as entities that belong to the intended order of things, on the one hand, but are incompatible with its prospective evolution on the other. This duplicity is palpably notable as the Proxies shift from their human to their preternatural configurations, and vice versa, at times acquiring transitional physiognomies that seem more than human due the aura of numinous authority they emanate, yet less than monstrous due to the tantalizing aesthetic excellence they incarnate. These dexterously modulated iconographic details are largely responsible for the creatures' dramatic caliber as products of a very distinctive culture rather than free-floating archetypes. The psychological dynamics of the conflict between the two Proxies central to the anime's climax further augments the action's prismatic impact, while also obliquely inviting us to ponder the affective tensions tearing *Ergo Proxy*'s whole world grievously apart.

In Japan's fairy tale tradition, dystopian realities are often alluded to through a pervasive emphasis on social, ethical and broadly cultural decline, as typically evinced by the tale of *Benkei and the Bell* (in Griffis). Pivotal to the narrative is a magical object deprived of its powers by human greed and mindless violation. The dystopian perspective finds an uplifting counterpart in indigenous stories devoted to the celebration of the powers of fantasy and play. *How the Jelly-Fish Lost His Shell* and its sequel, *Lord Cuttle-Fish's Concert* (in Griffis), illustrate this idea by highlighting with carnivalesque irreverence the risible limitations of science in the face of nature-guided magic. Thus, while no human medicine is capable of curing the queen's long illness, the unexpected sight of a grotesque animal festival instantly replenishes the royal lady's body and spirit. An analogous atmosphere is communicated by the tale of *Little Silver's Dream* (in Griffis). In this narrative, a moral of the kind one might expect to encounter in a Western tale of the sanitized variety is circuitously reached and self-restraint is accordingly upheld as the prime virtue to which any respectable person should aspire. Yet, it is couched in terms that deliberately cause it to come across as so flimsily formulaic as to fade into virtual insignificance when compared to the unbridled exuberance of the heroine's oneiric ride. Pervaded by a conception of the natural order as a reality in excess of social mores, the tale discloses a demonic world of unrestrained reveling that abides in memory as a veritable treasurehouse of indigenous beliefs interlaced with baleful visions of sea ghosts. This particular image strikes its roots in one of the most distinctive areas of Japanese lore: the body of legends inspired by the belief that the spirits of humans that have perished at sea can return aboard spectral vessels.

As Michiko Iwasaka and Barre Toelken explain, these spirits "often demand that a ladle or bucket be passed to them, but careful Japanese fishermen and seafaring people know that you must supply only a bucket without a bottom; otherwise the ghosts will use it to fill your ship with water until it sinks. The subject of such encounters need not be guilty of any particular offense against the dead, but are simply victims of the residual *goryou* of unburied and unritualized people" (Iwasaka and Toelken, p. 103). (Please note that the term "*goryou*," commonly translated as "ghost," combines the words "honorable" and "spirit" or "soul.") A stunning interpretation of this material, abetted by exceptionally stylish design and mise-en-scène, can be found in the anime series *Mononoke* (dir. Kenji Nakamura, 2007). With their exuberant taste for the ludic, both *Lord Cuttle-Fish's Concert* and *Little Silver's Dream* transculturally foreshadow the distinctive mood later enthroned by Maurice Sendak's *The Wild Things*.

The aforementioned Chinese tale *A Shiver of Ghosts* (in Birch) likewise depicts a sea voyage culminating in the crew's arrival at the "Country of Ghosts": a verdant, peaceful and prosperous land. Upon visiting the capital, a pleasant city harboring a magnificent royal palace, the men partake of a splendid banquet held at its court of puppet-like specters, laid out just for their benefit and replete with sumptuous dishes and exquisite beverages. Its purpose is to secure the mortal visitors' amicable departure from the land, since their presence among the ghostly population is bound to be eventually conducive to discomfort or even sickness — as attested to by the local king's temporary collapse when the head of the crew approaches him too closely and causes him to be overwhelmed by the breath of a living creature. This logical inversion of the classic kiss-of-death motif, where the victim is invariably human and the agent of misfortune a spirit or demon, is in itself amusing. Thus, the tale conveys its dystopian perspective through the portrayal of a radically displaced reality in which the boundary between life and death is by no means sacrosanct. The plot as a whole, moreover, evinces a humorously matter-of-fact approach to the thorny issues of spectrality and haunting, thus reflecting an important facet of indigenous lore that itself thrives on the logic of displacement — in this case, of an ethical rather than spatial kind. Hence, it states in the most factual tone imaginable that ghosts have an easier time than living beings when it comes to food and drink provision, and that as long as they have a dark and gloomy house or grave-mound as accommodation, they neither need nor seek anything else. The story also warns us not to fear ghosts unnecessarily, maintaining that this is precisely what invests them with a power they do not normally pursue of their own accord, while also conceding, however, that many a wrongdoer have very good reason to be terrified of justice-seeking specters. Most importantly, the tale emphasizes the importance of respecting Faërie's independence, and hence its right not to be interfered with by nosy humans — a topos already noted in Chapter 2 vis-à-vis *The Grateful Crane* and its metamorphic heroine

The tale of *The Firefly*, also centered on a shape-shifting lady, further alerts us to the incommensurability of the human and spirit realms. It does so by proffering a delicately economical warning not treat any creature disrespectfully out of sheer carelessness because we can never be truly certain with whom we might be dealing (in Ashliman, D. L. 1998–2008a; original source: Hadland Davis). An analogous message is conveyed by the Celtic tale *November Eve* (i.e., Hallowe'en): a terse reminder that there are times when mortals would do well to leave fairies in peace without presuming to meddle in their affairs. The story revolves around Hugh, an ordinary human who is ridiculed and chastised by the fairies for disturbing their Halloween revelries on the grounds that this is the "one night of all the year when the dead can leave their graves and dance in the moonlight on the hill, and mortals should stay at home and never dare to look on them." The protagonist's punishment consists of a trip to a very unusual fair, attended both by members of the Fair Folk — including the formidable King Finvarra and his spouse Onagh — and by temporarily resurrected humans whom Hugh is appalled to recognize as having been long dead. Whereas the clumsy mortals presented in the Chinese tale are allowed to leave the Country of Ghosts scot-free, their Celtic relative must pay a price for his gross violation of fairy privacy. Thus, the following morning he awakens "within the old stone circle by the fairy rath" to find that "his arms" are "all black with the touch of the hands of the dead" (in Marriott, p. 149; original source: Wilde).

An especially harrowing dystopian perspective is offered by the fairy tale *Willow Wife* with a focus on a world so hell-bent on progress as to have completely lost touch with its roots in the natural domain (in Ashliman, D. L. 1998–2008a; original sources: Hadland Davis and Gordon Smith). In dramatizing the inseparability of the protagonist's bride from a venerable willow tree, and hence the interdependence of the two entities' souls, the story depicts a distinctively Shintoist reality predicated on the fluidity of individual boundaries. It is here also worth noting that in several traditions, willow fairies are reputed to be endowed with special powers and to emblematize eternal life. Where *The Snow Bride* and *The Vampire Cat*, here addressed in Chapter 2, epitomize romantic lore at its most sinister, the story of *Willow Wife* resonates with wrenchingly melancholy tones that typify an unmistakably Japanese aesthetic sensibility. The shamanic world picture evoked by *Willow Wife* also finds expression in *The Princess Peony* (in Ashliman, D. L. 1998–2008a; original source: Gordon Smith). As narratives such as *The Vampire Cat* and *Willow Wife* indicate, the metamorphic creatures portrayed in Japanese lore are generally female. *The Princess Peony* supplies an intriguing inversion of the established motif by focusing on a youth who, vainly loved by a maiden facing an arranged marriage, assumes the shape of a gorgeous peony and remains faithfully by the hapless girl's side until her wedding day, when the flower sadly withers for loss of hope. In this story, the dystopian ethos is communicated by the exposure of the utter vulnerability which unsullied beauty and innocence must endure in a world dominated by the soulless imperatives of political advancement and financial gain.

In contrast with the tales discussed in the previous paragraph, *The White Butterfly* (in Ashliman, D. L. 1998–2008a; original source: Hadland Davis) celebrates the positive repercussions of a commodious approach to nature and to the preternatural energies that dwell in its inscrutable folds. One of Japan's most cherished fairy tales, *The White Butterfly* pivots on an ancient and dying man named Takahama, who has devoted his life to the memory of his former betrothed Akiko, killed by consumption shortly before the wedding. As Takahama approaches his final hour, Akiko returns to him in the guise of a white butterfly symbolizing her unwaveringly loyal soul. Butterflies have been deployed as symbols of transformation and regeneration in countless traditions for time immemorial. Concomitantly, they have been frequently cited as paradigmatic incarnations of the transience of pleasure and beauty. Japanese poetry has indeed often invoked the image of the butterfly as an effective metonym for the irretrievability of the past and its delights (actual or imagined as these may be), in consonance with the aesthetic principle of *mono no aware*. Roughly translatable as the "sadness of things," this phrase is beautifully expounded by Motoori Norinaga (1730–1801), who describes it as a multifaceted response to disparate situations. These embrace "things both public and private, the best of things interesting, splendid, or awesome; there are also such things as flowers, birds, the moon, and the snow, appealingly described according to the season.... When the heart is heavy, then especially do the sight of the sky, the colors of the trees and grass, act to produce *aware*" (Norinaga, p. 203). Since "Nothing is felt more deeply by the human heart than love," the scholar avers, it is hardly surprising that *aware* should be "experienced particularly profoundly, indeed unendurably, most often in love" (p. 213).

As Chris Eisenbraun observes in the entry of his online dictionary of symbols devoted to butterflies, "There is a line of Japanese poetry expressing sorrow over the lost pleasures of the past, a response to the maxim, 'The fallen blossom never returns to the branch'; 'I thought that the blossom had returned to the branch — alas, it was only a butterfly'" (Eisenbraun). Unlike the phoenix, whose transformations and periodic transitions between death and rebirth are regarded as ceaseless processes, the butterfly represents the overwhelming ephemerality of the fleeting moment. In ancient Greece, the butterfly was equated to *psyche*, the "soul." In several other cultures, relatedly, it is held to symbolize the metamorphoses undergone by the spiritual core of both human beings and other animals throughout their life cycles and possibly beyond. The butterfly's transience is also typically linked with the alternate reality of Faërie, as evinced by the pictorial representation of various specimens of pixies, elves and even goblins as beings endowed with magic wings.

Whereas butterfly wings are now almost automatically regarded as one of the fairy's most characteristic attributes, it must be noted that these only established themselves as key iconographic traits relatively late in history. Magic wands, incidentally, are another visual feature ubiquitous in modern representations of fairies that bear no direct connection with traditional beliefs. Warwick Goble (1862–1943) tersely underscores the artificiality of the wing motif in visual representations of the Fair Folk with the picture "The fairies came flying in at the window," where a gaggle of diminutive fairies are busy fitting a pair of glorious butterfly wings to a young girl's back. Over the cumulative history of fairy lore, disconcerting attributes such as disproportionate limbs, asymmetrical physiognomies, unruly manes and webbed feet have, in fact, been far more pervasive than butterfly appendages or starry batons. This is not to deny that fairies, like butterflies, have been repeatedly associated with prospects of spiritual transformation and with the soul — and specifically, as epitomized by *The White Butterfly*, with the soul of the departed. However, wings may well be an effect of a fairy's luminous aura rather than physical attributes. On a more facetious note, Marriott reminds us, the "'butter' element ... relates to fairy lore" to the extent that fairies "are always associated with cows, milk and cream" (Marriott, p. 90). According to D. J. Conway, wings are not a general fairy attribute but rather "collections of massed energy" characteristic of the "subspecies of faery" which she refers to as "Small Folk" (Conway, p. 73) on the basis of their diminutive size and lesser status. The superior species of the "Fay," held to be "the most intelligent" and "the closest to humans in appearance and body type" (p. 49), does not sport any fluttery appendages.

What should not be ignored, for the sake of documentary accuracy, is that modern visualizations of fairies strike their roots in the specific conception of the figure promoted by nineteenth-century painters and draftsmen who imagined it, as Marriott observes, as an essentially "theatrical confection of frothy tulle, gossamer, insect wings, and ballet slippers" (Marriott, p. 84). According to Purkiss, this kind of imagery still plays a significant role in today's collective imaginary — the difference between the nineteenth-century scenario depicted by Mariott and the contemporary one being that nowadays, "one sees middle-class mothers and children in toy stores, tussling over frilly fairy skirts. Surprisingly, it is often the daughter who wants to wear the fairy costume and the post-feminist mother who would be more comfortable with a tomboy in pirate costume" (Purkiss, p. 3). The delicate fairies populating the pages alluded to by Marriott were tersely — indeed frighteningly — displaced by the Romantic visions of Faërie imagined by Goethe, Coleridge and Keats. Yet, they resurfaced as a potent cultural dominant in Victorian times through the association of fairies with natural innocence, gracefulness and juvenile charm. Ironically, these beings were commonly publicized by means of theatrical artifice and related stage machinery and special effects — in other words, something neither natural nor airily elegant. In addition, although fairies' association with innocence was meant to make them akin to totally inexperienced children, the actual children involved in the cultural construction of the Good Folk were stage laborers employed to play stereotypical fairy roles. In the paradoxical logic of the Victorian stage, therefore, fairies became the creatures supposed to epitomize precisely what their real-life enactors were *not*.

As appropriations of the fairy tale tradition in a contemporary medium, the anime explored in this chapter put their darker dramatic elements to optimum effect in order to emphasize the ongoing and serious import of fairy tales in present-day societies. In other words, they deploy their technical novelty and their sensitivity to historical and cultural crisis in tandem with a keen perception of the fairy tale tradition as a discourse uniquely equipped to sustain their own artistic visions. In the process, we are invited to transcend the stultifying strictures of "relevance" and "reality" as the ultimate yardsticks against which the fairy tale's place in today's world should be measured. As Elizabeth Cook maintains, people who typically promote those criteria believe that "a good children's story has to be about children and adults who wear the same clothes, go to the same schools and do the same jobs as the children in the audience and their parents: they must worry about the identical economic and ethical problems, and must not care about any of the ambitions or distresses that could touch a prince or an artist in the middle ages and will not literally call for decision in the life of a shop steward today" (Cook, p. xii). These are the sorts of people who, as attested to by the case of a "headmaster chosen in a B.B.C. programme to defend modern primary education," claimed not to "see what 'relevance' Napoleon could possibly have for a child living in Bermondsey" (p. xiii).

This crudely utilitarian attitude should not be mistaken as a plea for innovation, as an invitation to focus on the needs of present generations by marginalizing the authority of the past. In fact, it amounts to a repressive disciplinary strategy designed to guarantee each subject's maximum utility and productivity within the contingent boundaries of the here-and-now by deadening any external stimulus with the potential to galvanize the imagination. What is thereby discouraged is the very desire to speculate about the past, in both its historiographical reconstructions and its fictive configurations, and about the future as the multidimensional ensemble of as yet untapped hypotheses. This desire to wonder — not solely *about* the past and the future but also *at* their promises and their puzzles — is precisely what the anime here examined seek to foster. They do so by harnessing their creative vision to the ideation of spaces defined by a pervasive sense of displacement and disorientation, and hence in an ideal position to ignite the imagination by challenging us to find a route through these contemporary equivalents of the fairy tale's forests of thorns.

Filmography

Primary Titles

Basilisk (2005). Original Title: *Basilisk — Kouga Ninpou Chou.* Status: TV series (24 episodes). Episode Length: 24 minutes. Director: Fuminori Kizaki. Series Composition: Yasuyuki Muto. Scenario: Muto Music: Kou Nakagawa. Character Designer: Michinori Chiba Art Director: Shigemi Ikeda. Chief Animation Director: Chiba Original Novel: Futaroh Yamada. Sound Director: Yoku Shioya. Director of Photography: Kenji Fujita. Executive producer: Koji Kajita. Producers: Hidemasa Arai, Hideyuki Nanba. Color Designer: Takae Iijima. Special Effects: Miyako Hoshi. Animation Production: Gonzo. Music Production: Future Vision Music.

Le Chevalier D'Eon (2006-2007). Original Title: *Le Chevalier D'Eon.* Status: TV series (24 episodes). Episode Length: 25 minutes. Director: Kazuhiro Furuhashi. Series Composition: Tow Ubukata. Music: Michiru Oshima. Original Story: Tow Ubukata. Character Designer: Tomomi Ozaki. Art Director: Hiroshi Ohno. Sound Director: Hozumi Gouda. Director of Photography: Jun Yanai. Producers: Daisuke Katagiri, Hisao Iizuka, Katsuji Morishita, Mariko Seto. Chief Editor: Junichi Uematsu. Color Designer: Izumi Hirose. Costume Designer: Kiriko Yumeji. Digital Effects

Animator: Masaya Suzuki. Historical Research: Masahiro Kawashima. Sound Effects: Naoto Yamatani. Special Effects: Masahiro Murakami. Animation Production: Production I.G.

La Corda d'Oro — Primo Passo (2005-2006). Original Title: *Kin-iro no Corda — primo passo.* Status: TV series (26 episodes). Episode Length: 25 minutes. Director: Koujin Ochi. Series Composition: Reiko Yoshida. Music: Mitsutaka Tajiri. Original Manga: Yuki Kure. Character Designer: Maki Fujioka. Art Director: Chikako Shibata. Chief Animation Director: Fujioka. Sound Director: Hiromi Kikuta. Director of Photography: Shinya Matsuzaki. Apparel Designer: Rie Nishimura. Color Setting: Rieko Sakai, Yukiko Ario, Yuuko Satou. Editing: Seiji Morita, Yuri Tamura. Photography: Satoshi Shimizu, Tetsuya Enomoto, Tomoyuki Shimizu. Special Effects: Tomomi Ishihara. Animation Production: Yumeta Company.

La Corda d'Oro — Secondo Passo (2009). Original Title: *Kin-iro no Corda — secondo passo.* Status: Special (2 episodes). Episode Length: 25 minutes. Director: Ochi. Screenplay: Reiko Yoshida. Original Manga: Yuki Kure. Character Design: Maki Fujioka. Chief Animation Director: Fujioka. Production: Aniplex.

Earl and Fairy (2008). Original Title: *Hakushaku to Yousei*. Status: TV series (12 episodes). Episode Length: 24 minutes. Director: Kouichirou Sohtome. Original Creator: Mizue Tani. Series Composition: Noriko Nagao. Screenplay: Nagao. Music: Takehiko Gokita. Original Character Designer: Asako Takaboshi. Character Designer: Maki Fujii. Art Directors: Mitsuharu Miyamae, Yoichi Yajima. Animation Directors: Miyamae, Fujii, Takafumi Shiokawa. Producers: Asuka Yamazaki, Masafumi Takatori, Rika Sasaki. Background Art: Masao Ichitani, Takayuki Kotani. Editing: Hideaki Murai. Sound Effects: Noriko Izumo. Special Effects: Naomi Kaneko. Color Designer: Rika Nishio. Animation Production: Artland.

Ergo Proxy (2006). Original Title: *Ergo Proxy*. Status: TV series (23 episodes). Episode Length: 30 minutes. Director: Shuko Murase. Music: Yoshihiro Ike. Character Designer: Naoyuki Onda. Art Director: Kazumasa Satou, Toshiyuki Yamashita. Chief Animation Director: Hideto Komori. Sound Director: Keiichi Momose. Director of Photography: Kazuhiro Yamada. Producers: Akio Matsuda, Michiko Suzuki, Takashi Kochiyama. Color Designer: Kiyomi Yamazaki. Digital Special Effects: Toshio Hasegawa. Editing: Tomoki Nagasaka. Special Effects: Daisuke Imai, Nobutaka Murakami. Animation Production: Manglobe.

Honey and Clover (2005). Original Title: *Hachimitsu to Clover*. Status: TV series (26 episodes). Episode Length: 25 minutes. Director: Ken'ichi Kasai. Script: Yousuke Kuroda. Music: Yuzo Hayashi. Original Manga: Chika Umino. Character Designer: Shuichi Shimamura. Art Director: Chikako Shibata. Chief Animation Director: Takahiko Yoshida.

Sound Director: Jin Aketagawa. Director of Photography: Yutaka Kurosawa. Producers: Atsuya Takase, Hiroaki Nakane, Masarou Toyoshima, Nobuhiro Osawa. Clothing Supervision: Kazuki Kuraishi. Editing: Shigeru Nishiyama. Food Designer: Mitsuyo Sakuma. Sound Effects: Katsuhiro Nakano. Animation Production: J.C. Staff.

Kino's Journey (2003). Original Title: *Kino no Tabi—The Beautiful World*. Status: TV series (13 episodes). Episode Length: 24 minutes. Director: Ryuutarou Nakamura. Script: Sadayuki Murai. Music: Ryo Sakai. Original creator: Keiichi Sigsawa (novel). Original Character Designer: Kouhaku Kuroboshi. Character Designer: Shigeyuki Suga. Art Director: Masayoshi Banno. Sound Director: Yota Tsuruoka. Director of Photography: Naoyuki Ohba. Producer: Nobuhiro Osawa. Editing: Tsuyoshi Imai. Animation Production: Studio Wombat.

Last Exile (2003). Original Title: *Last Exile*. Status: TV series (26 episodes). Episode Length: 23 minutes. Director: Koichi Chigira. Music: Dolce Triade, Hitomi Kuroishi. Art Directors: Hiromasa Ogura, Keiichi Oku. Animation Director: Hiroyuki Okuno. Animation Character Designer: Minoru Murao, Osamu Horiuchi, Yuichi Tanaka. Character Conceptual Designer: Range Murata. 3D Director: Yasufumi Soejima. Producers: Hiroyuki Orukawa, Shinji Nakashima, Takashi Imamoto. Chief Cinematographer: Takashi Horiuchi. Color Scheme Designer: Keiko Goto. Editing: Fumi Hida, Kengo Shigemura. Visual Director: Hiromasa Ogura. Animation Production: Gonzo. Music Production: TV Tokyo Music, Victor Entertainment.

Nodame Cantabile (2007). Original Title: *Nodame Cantabile*. Status: TV series (23 episodes). Episode Length: 25 minutes. Director: Ken'ichi Kasai. Series Composition: Tomoko Konparu. Music: Suguru Matsutani. Original Creator: Tomoko Ninomiya. Character Designer: Shuichi Shimamura. Art Director: Shichiro Kobayashi. Sound Director: Jin Aketagawa. Director of Photography: Yoshio Ookouchi. Producers: Atsuya Takase, Kouji Yamamoto, Nobuhiro Osawa, Yukihiro Ito. Color Designer: Mayumi Tanahashi. Digital Special Effects: Atsushi Sato. Editing: Shigeru Nishiyama. Sound Effects: Katsuhiro Nakano, Masafumi Watanabe, Masahiro Nakano. Sound Production: Rie Tanaka. Animation Production: J.C. Staff.

Paradise Kiss (2005). Original Title: *Paradise Kiss*. Status: TV series (12 episodes). Episode Length: 23 minutes. Director: Osamu Kobayashi. Series Composition: Kobayashi. Script: Kobayashi. Music: NARASAKI from COALTAR OF DEEPERS, THE BABYS. Original Manga: Ai Yazawa. Character Designer: Nobuteru Yuki. Art Directors: Asami Kiyokawa, Shinichi Uehara. Sound Director: Masafumi Mima. Director of Photography: Seiichi Morishita. Producers: Kouji Yamamoto, Masao Maruyama, Ryo Oyama, Tetsuya Watanabe, Yoko Matsusaki, Yukihiro Ito. Chief Editor: Yoshiko Kimura. Clothing Designer: Atsuro Tayama. Color Designer: Yoshinori Horikawa. Digital Art: Rei Kawano. Digital Effects: Shinichi Igarashi. Sound Effects: Shizuo Kurahashi. Special Effects: Ayumi Arahata, Kumiko Taniguchi, Tomoe Ikeda, Toyohiko Sakakibara. Texture Art: Yuichi Suehiro. Animation Production: Madhouse Studios.

Petite Cossette (2004). Original Title: *Cossette no Shouzou*. Status: OVA series (3 episodes). Episode Length: 38 minutes. Director: Akiyuki Shinbo. Screen-

play: Mayori Sekijima. Music: Hitoshi Konno (Violin), Yuki Kajiura, Yuriko Kaida (Vocals). Original Manga: Asuka Katsura. Character Designer: Hirofumi Suzuki. Art Director: Easter Himegumi. Animation Directors: Hirofumi Suzuki, Takahiro Chiba. Art Designers: Junichi Azuma, Toshiharu Iijima. Sound Director: Toshiki Kameyama. Director of Photography: Junichi Watanabe, Koji Tanaka. Producers: Ai Abe, Masatoshi Fujimoto, Takeshi Anzai. Color Designer: Keiko Shibuya. Editing: Kazuhiko Seki. Sound Effects: Minoru Yamada. Animation Production: Daume.

Someday's Dreamers: Summer Skies (2008). Original Title: *Mahou Tsukai ni Taisetsu na Koto: Natsu no Sora*. Status: TV series (12 episodes). Episode Length: 24 minutes. Director: Osamu Kobayashi. Screenplay: Norie Yamada. Music: Takefumi Haketa. Original Creator: Norie Yamada. Original Character Designer: Kumichi Yoshizuki. Art Director: Toshiharu Iijima. Animation Directors: Kenyoshi Hori, Kobayashi. Animation Character Designer: Yusuke Yoshigaki. Sound Director: Yukio Nagasaki. Director of Photography: Hiroshi Yoshida. Animation Production: Hal Film Maker.

The Story of Saiunkoku (2006-2007). Original Title: *Saiunkoku Monogatari*. Status: TV series (39 episodes). Episode Length: 25 minutes. Director: Jun Shishido. Series Composition: Reiko Yoshida. Script: Ayuna Fujisaki, Kurasumi Sunayama, Reiko Yoshida. Music: Kunihiko Ryo. Original Creator: Sai Yukino (novel). Original Character Designer: Kairi Yura (novel illustration). Character Designer: Miwa Oshima. Art Director: Chikara Nishikura. Sound Director: Fusanobu Fujiyama. Director of Photography: Shinya Matsui. Producers: Ikuko Shimogawara, Yuji Shibata. Color

Designer: Chiharu Tanaka. Conceptual Designer: Kazuo Watanabe. Editing: Kashiko Kimura. Sound Effects: Shoji Kato. Animation Production: Madhouse Studio.

Tokyo Godfathers (2003). Original Title: *Tokyo Godfathers*. Status: movie. Length: 92 minutes. Director: Satoshi Kon. Screenplay: Keiko Nobumoto, Kon. Music: Keiichi Suzuki. Original Story: Kon. Character Designers: Kenichi Konishi, Kon. Art Director: Nobutaka Ike. Animation Director: Konishi. Sound Director: Masafumi Mima. Director of Photography: Katsutoshi Sugai. Producer: Masao Maruyama. Chief Animator: Konishi. Color Designer: Kazunori Hashimoto. Editing: Takeshi Seyama. Animation Production: Madhouse Studios.

Wolf's Rain (2003). Original Title: *Wolf's Rain*. Status: TV series (26 episodes). Episode Length: 30 minutes. Director: Tensai Okamura. Script: Keiko Nobumoto. Original Creator: Nobumoto. Character Designer: Toshihiro Kawamoto. Art Director: Atsushi Morikawa. Mechanical Designer: Shinji Aramaki. Art Designers: Shingo Takeba, Tomoaki Okada. Sound Director: Kazuhiro Wakabayashi. Director of Photography: Kosuke Arakawa. Producers: Go Haruna, Masahiko Minami, Minoru Takanashi. Color Designer: Nobuko Mizuta. Sound Effects: Shizuo Kurahashi. Animation Production: BONES.

Ancillary Titles

Andersen Stories (TV series; dir. Masami Hata, 1971)

Aria the Animation (TV series; dir. Junichi Sato, 2005)

Aria the Natural (TV series; dir. Junichi Sato, 2006)

Aria the Origination (TV series; dir. Junichi Sato, 2008)

Aria the OVA ~Arietta~ (OVA; dir. Junichi Sato, 2007)

Blue Seed (TV series; dir. Jun Kamiya, 1994-1995)

Cinderella (TV series; dir. Hiroshi Sasagawa, 1996)

Fate/stay Night (TV series; dir. Yuji Yamaguchi, 2006)

FLCL (OVA series; dir. Kazuya Tsurumaki, 2000)

Gilgamesh (TV series; dir. Masahiko Murata, 2003-2004)

Gunbuster 2 (OVA series; dir. Kazuya Tsurumaki, 2004–2006)

Hell Girl (TV series; dir. Akiyuki Shinbo, 2005-2006)

Hell Girl Second Cage (TV series; dir. Akiyuki Shinbo, 2006-2007)

Hell Girl: Cauldron of Three (TV series; dir. Akiyuki Shinbo, 2008)

Honey and Clover II (TV series; dir. Tatsuyuki Nagai, 2006)

Howl's Moving Castle (movie; dir. Hayao Miyazaki, 2004)

Jin-Roh: The Wolf Brigade (movie; dir. Hiroyuki Okiura, 1998)

Kanon (TV series; dir. Tatsuya Ishihara, 2006-2007)

Mermaid's Forest (TV series; dir. Masaharu Okuwaki, 2003)

Minority Report (movie; dir. Steven Spielberg, 2002)

Mononoke (TV series; dir. Kenji Nakamura, 2007)

Nodame Cantabile: Finale (TV series; dir. Chiaki Kon, 2010)

Nodame Cantabile: Paris (TV series; dir. Chiaki Kon, 2008)

Peter Pan (movie; dirs. Clyde Geronimi, Wilfred Jackson and Hamilton Luske, 1953)

Ponyo on the Cliff by the Sea (movie; dir. Hayao Miyazaki, 2008)

Puss in Boots (movie; dir. Kimio Yabuki, 1969)

The Snow Queen (TV series; dir. Osamu Dezaki, 2005-2006)

Star Wars (movie; dir. George Lucas, 1977)

Tales from Earthsea (movie; dir. Goro Miyazaki, 2006)

Texhnolyze (TV series; dir. Hiroshi Hamazaki, 2003)

This Ugly Yet Beautiful World (TV series; dir. Shouji Saeki, 2004)

Touka Gettan (TV series; dir. Yuji Yamaguchi, 2007)

Tsubasa: RESERVoir CHRoNiCLE (TV series; first season: dir. Koichi Mashimo, 2005; second season: dirs. Mashimo and Hiroshi Morioka, 2006)

Zoku Natsume Yuujinchou (TV series; dir. Takahiro Ohmori, 2009)

Bibliography

The anonymous fairy tales cited in the book are referenced as follows:

- by editor — e.g., the reference for *The Fire-Fly's Lovers* is "(in Griffis)";
- by editor and original source if the tale is attributed to a specific original source by the editor of the text in which it features — e.g., the reference for *The Snow Bride* is "(in Ashliman, D. L. 1998–2008a; original source: Hadland Davis)."

Amano, Y. 2006. *Fairies*. Trans. C. Nieh. Milwaukee, OR: Dark Horse.

Andersen, H. C. 2004. *Tales of Hans Christian Andersen*. Trans. N. Lewis. Illustrations by J. Stewart. London: Walker.

Argueta, M. 1998. *Little Red Riding Hood in the Red Light District*. New York: Curbstone.

Ashliman, D. L. 1998–2008a. *Japanese Legends about Supernatural Sweethearts*. http://www.pitt.edu/~dash/japanlove.html.

Ashliman, D. L. 1998–2008b. *Folktales from Japan*. http://www.pitt.edu/~dash/japan.html.

Azed No. 1,985. 2010. *The Observer*, 13 June.

Bacchilega, C. 2008. "Extrapolating from Nalo Hopkinson's *Skin Folk*: Reflections on Transformation and Recent English-Language Fairy-Tale Fiction by Women." In *Contemporary Fiction and the Fairy Tale*, edited by S. Benson. Detroit: Wayne State University Press.

Barthes, R. 1990. *The Pleasure of the Text*. Trans. R. Miller. Oxford: Basil Blackwell.

Bertoli, J. 1977. *The Grateful Crane*. Illustrations by K. Shimizumi. Morton Grove, IL: Albert Whitman.

Bettelheim, B. [1976.] 1991. *The Uses of Enchantment: The Meaning and Importance of Fairy Tales*. London: Penguin.

Birch, C. 2000. *Tales from China*. Oxford: Oxford University Press.

Bird, E., Downton, D., and Ellwand, D. 2006. *Fairie-ality: The Fashion Collection from the House of Ellwand*. Somerville, MA: Candlewick.

Briggs, K. 2002. *The Fairies in Tradition and Literature*. London: Routledge.

Buckley, A. B. 1879. "How to Enter It; How to Use It; and How to Enjoy It." In *The Fairy-Land of Science*. http://www.mainlesson.com/display.php?author=buckley&book=fairyland&story=enter.

Calvino, I. 1988. *Sulla Fiaba*. Turin: Giulio Einaudi.

Calvino, I. 1996. *Six Memos for the Next Millennium*. Trans. P. Creagh. London: Vintage.

Calvino, I. [1956.] 2009. *Italian Folktales*. Trans. G. Martin. London: Penguin.

Campbell, J. 1988. *The Power of Myth*. New York: Doubleday.

Carter, A. 1990. *The Virago Books of Fairy Tales*. London: Virago.

Carter, A. [1998.] 2006. *Burning Your Boats*. London: Vintage.

Cavallaro, D. 2010. *The Mind of Italo Calvino*. Jefferson, NC, and London: McFarland.

Cavalli-Sforza, L. 2004. *L'evoluzione della cultura: Proposte concrete per studi futuri*. Turin: Codice.

Chambers, R. 1826. *Popular Rhymes of Scotland*. Edinburgh: W. Hunter.

Chesterton, G. K. 1908/1915. *All Things Considered*. Extract. In "G. K. Chesterton's Fairy Tales." *SurLaLune*. http://www.surlalunefairytales.com/introduction/gkchesterton.html.

Conan Doyle, A. 1922. *The Coming of the Fairies*. London: Hodder and Stoughton.

Conway, D. J. 2005. *The Ancient Art of Faery Magick*. Berkeley, CA: Crossing Press.

Cook, E. 1976. *The Ordinary and the Fabulous — An Introfuction to Myths, Legends and Fairy Tales*, Second Edition. Cambridge, London, New York and Melbourne: Cambridge University Press.

Cooper, J. C. 1983. *Fairy Tales: Allegories of the Inner Life — Archetypal Patterns and Symbols in Classic Fairy Stories*. Wellingborough, Northamptonshire: Aquarian.

Cox, G. W. 1881. *An Introduction to the Comparative Science of Mythology and Folklore*. London: C. K. Paul.

Cross, G. 1990. *Wolf*. London: Puffin.

Curie, M. *Brainy Quote*. http://www.brainyquote.com/quotes/keywords/fairy.html.

Darnton, R. 1984. "Peasants Tell Tales: The Meaning of Mother Goose." In *The Great Cat Massacre and Other Episodes in French Cultural History*. New York: Basic.

Davis, J. K. 2009. "Modern Versions of Little Red Riding Hood Contemporary Novels of the Classic Fairy Tale." *Suite 101*. http://folktales.suite101.com/article.cfm/little_red_riding_hood_modern_versions.

de la Mare, W. 1925. *Broomsticks*. London: Faber.

de Lint, C. *The Quote Garden*. http://www.quotegarden.com/fairies.html.

Derrida, J. 1998. *Of Grammatology*. Trans. G. C. Spivak. Baltimore: The Johns Hopkins University Press.

Dickens, C. 1852–1853. *Bleak House*. *Classic Bookshelf Electronic Library*. http://www.classicbookshelf.com/library/charles_dickens/bleak_house/21/.

Einstein, A. *SurLaLune Quotations*. http://www.surlalunefairytales.com/introduction/quotes.html.

Eisenbraun, C. "Butterflys." *The Symbols One Word at a Time*. http://www.scootermydaisyheads.com/fine_art/symbol_dictionary/butterfly.html.

Ellwand, D. 2009. *Fairie-ality Style: A Sourcebook of Inspirations from Nature*. London: Walker.

Emerson, R. W. 2003. *Nature and Selected Essays*. London: Penguin. Extract: http://www.monadnock.net/emerson/history.html.

Evans-Wentz, W. Y. 1966. *The Fairy-Faith in Celtic Countries*. London: University.

"Fairy tale." *Wikipedia — The Free Encyclopedia*. http://en.wikipedia.org/wiki/Fairy_tale.

Feyerabend, P. *All Great Quotes*. http://www.allgreatquotes.com/fairy_quotes.shtml.

Field, N. 1987. *The Splendor of Longing in The Tale of Genji*. Princeton, NJ: Princeton University Press.

Frazer, J. G. [1913–1920.] 1992. *The Golden Bough: A Study in Magic and Religion*, Third Edition. New York: Macmillan. Electronic Edition: Bartleby.com. 2000. http://www.bartleby.com/196.

Froud, B. 2000. *Good Faeries/Bad Faeries*. London: Pavilion.

Gaiman, N. *The Quote Garden*. http://www.quotegarden.com/fairies.html.

Gibbings, W. W. 1889. *Folk-Lore and Legends, Scotland*. London: W. W. Gibbings.

Gilbert, S. M., and Gubar, S. 1979. *The Madwoman in the Attic: The Woman Writer and the Nineteenth-Century Literary Imagination*. New Haven, CT: Yale University Press.

Gill, W. W. 1932. *A Manx Scrapbook*. London and Bristol: Arrowsmith.

Gordon Smith, R. 1908. *Ancient Tales and Folk-Lore of Japan*. London: A. and C. Black.

Griffis, W. E. [1908.] 2008. *Fairy Tales of Old Japan — Illustrated Edition*. Gloucester: Dodo.

Grimm, J., and Grimm, W. [1812/1814/1822.] 2000. *Grimm's Fairy Tales*. London: Folio Society. (Based on *Grimm's Fairy Tales*. 1909. Trans. E. Lucas. London: Constable.)

Grimm, J., and Grimm, W. 1884. *Household Tales*, vol. 2. Trans. M. Hunt. London: George Bell.

Hadland Davis, F. 1913. *Myths and Legends of Japan*. London: G. G. Harrap.

Hardinge-Britten, E. 1884. "Irish Folk-Tales." *Folk-Lore Journal* 2.

Hartmann, F. 1911. "Some Remarks about the Spirits of Nature." *Occult Review* 14, pt. 2, July–December.

Hearn, L. 1905. *Chin Chin Kobakama*.

Extracts: *The Art Bin*. http://artbin.com/art/ohearn1.html.

Hewlett, M. 1913. *Lore of Proserpine*. New York: Charles Scribner's Sons.

Heyden, L. 2008. "Christmas Fairies." *Suite 101*. http://paganismwicca.suite101.com/article.cfm/christmas_fairies.

Hocart, A. M. 1933. *The Progress of Man*. London: Methuen.

Ikeda, H. 1963. *The Introduction of Foreign Influences on Japanese Children's Literature through Grimm's Household Tales*. In *Brüder Grimm Gedenken*. Marburg: Elwert.

Iwasaka, M., and Toelken, B. 1994. *Ghosts and the Japanese: Cultural Experience in Japanese Death Legends*. Logan: Utah State University Press.

James, G. 1910. *Green Willow and other Japanese Fairy Tales*. Illustrations by W. Goble. London: MacMillan.

"Japan Smitten by Love of Cute." 2006. http://www.theage.com.au/news/people/cool-or-infantile/2006/06/18/1150569208424.html.

Jerrold, D. *Quotes Junction*. http://www.quotesjunction.com/fairies-quotes-and-sayings/.

Jungman, A. 2005. *Lucy And The Big Bad Wolf*. London: Barn Owl.

Kawai, H. 1988. *The Japanese Psyche, Major Motifs in the Fairy Tales of Japan*. Dallas: Spring.

Kawai, H. 1995. *Dreams, Myths and Fairy Tales in Japan*. Einsiedeln, Switzerland: Daimon.

King, S. 1995. *Rose Madder*. London: New English Library.

Kirk, R. [1691.] 1976. *The Secret Commonwealth of Elves and Fairies*, edited by S. Sanderson. Cambridge: Cambridge University Press.

Kready, L. 1916. *A Study of Fairy Tales*. Boston: Houghton Mifflin. http://www.sacred-texts.com/etc/sft/sft01.htm.

Lane, M. 1993. *Picturing the Rose: A Way of Looking at Fairy Tales.* New York: H. W. Wilson.

Lang, A. [1895.] 2008. *My Own Fairy Book: Namely, Certain Chronicles.* Whitefish, MT: Kessinger.

Lang, A. [1897.] 1967. *The Pink Fairy Book.* New York: Dover.

Lang, L. 1903. *The Crimson Fairy Book.* London: Longmans, Green.

Lee, D. 2005. "Inside Look at Japanese Cute Culture." *Uniorb.* http://uniorb. com/ATREND/Japanwatch/cute.htm.

Lennon, J. *Brainy Quote.* http://www. brainyquote.com/quotes/quotes/j/jo hnlennon167353.html.

Lonsdale, S. 2001. *Japanese Style.* London: Carlton.

Lüthi, M. 1976. *Once Upon a Time: On the Nature of Fairy Tales.* Trans. L. Chadeayne and P. Gottwald. Bloomington: Indiana University Press.

Lüthi, M. 1984. *The Fairy Tale as Art Form and Portrait of Man.* Trans. J. Erickson. Bloomington: Indiana University Press.

Malinowski, B., and Redfield, R. 1948. *Magic, Science and Religion and Other Essays.* Boston: Beacon.

Marriott, S. 2006. *The Ultimate Fairy Handbook.* London: MQP.

McCaughrean, G. 1999. *One Thousand and One Arabian Nights.* Oxford: Oxford University Press.

Mitford, A. B. 1871. *Tales of Old Japan.* London: Macmillan & Co.

Morris, I. 1994. *The World of the Shining Prince: Court Life in Ancient Japan.* New York, Tokyo and London: Kodansha International.

Murakami, H. 1999. *The Wind-Up Bird Chronicle.* London: Vintage.

Nagatomo, S. 2006. "Japanese Zen Buddhist Philosophy." *Stanford Encyclopedia of Philosophy.* http://plato.stanford.edu/entries/japanese-zen/.

Narváez, P. 1991. *The Good People: New Fairylore Essays.* Garland Reference Library of the Humanities, vol. 1376. New York: Garland.

Nesbit, E. 1901. *Nine Unlikely Tales for Children.* London: Unwin.

Norinaga, M. 1969. *Gengi Monogatari Tama no Ogushi. Motoori Norinaga Zenshuu,* edited by S. Ohno, vol. 4. Tokyo: Chikuma Shobo.

Okada, H. R. 1991. *Figures of Resistance: Language, Poetry, and Narrating in The Tale of the Genji and Other Mid-Heian Texts.* Durham, NC: Duke University Press.

Oppenheim, H. 1985. *The Other World: Spiritualism and Psychical Research in England, 1850–1914.* Cambridge: Cambridge University Press.

Orenstein, C. 2002. *Little Red Riding Hood Uncloaked: Sex, Morality, and the Evolution of a Fairy Tale.* New York: Basic.

Ozaki, Y. T. 2008. *Japanese Fairy Tales.* Gloucester: Dodo.

Peirce Williston, T. 1911. *Japanese Fairy Tales — Second Series.* http://www. sacred-texts.com/shi/jft2/index.htm.

Perrault, C. [1697.] 2000. *Perrault's Fairy Tales.* London: Folio Society. (Based on *The Sleeping Beauty and Other Fairy Tales from the Old French.* 1912. Retold by Sir. A. Quiller-Couch. London: Hodder & Stoughton; and *Histories, or Tales of Past Times, By M. Perrault.* 1729. Trans. R. Samber.)

Propp, V. [1928]. 1969. *Morphology of the Folk Tale.* Austin: University of Texas Press.

Puette, W. J. 1983. *Tale of Genji: A Reader's Guide.* Tokyo, Rutland, VT, and Singapore: Tuttle.

Purkiss, D. 2000. *Troublesome Things — A History of Fairies and Fairy Stories.* London: Penguin.

Reeve, J. 2006. *Japanese Art in Detail.* London: The British Museum Press.

Rosten, L. *All Great Quotes.* http://www.allgreatquotes.com/fairy_quotes.shtml.

Ruskin, J. *SurLaLune Quotations.* http://www.surlalunefairytales.com/introduction/quotes.html.

Saint-Exupéry, A. de. [1943.] 1991. *The Little Prince.* Trans. K. Woods. London: Egmont.

Schmitz, A. 1998. *Darkest Desire: The Wolf's Own Tale.* London: Ecco.

Sconce, J. 2000. *Haunted Media: Electronic Presence from Telegraphy to Television.* Durham, NC: Duke University Press.

Scott, W. *SurLaLune Quotations.* http://www.surlalunefairytales.com/introduction/quotes.html.

Seifert, L. C. 1996. *Fairy Tales, Sexuality, and Gender in France 1690–1715.* New York: Cambridge University Press.

Seki, K. 1978–1980. *Nippon Mukashibanashi Taisei* (Collection of Japanese Fairy Tales). Tokyo: Kadokawa Shoten, vols. 1–12.

Sendak, M. 2000. *Where the Wild Things Are.* New York: Red.

Shirane, H. 1987. *The Bridge of Dreams: A Poetics of The Tale of Genji.* Stanford, CA: Stanford University Press.

Silver, C. G. 2000. *Strange and Secret Peoples: Fairies and Victorian Consciousness.* Oxford and New York: Oxford University Press.

Snyder, M. 2008. "The Swan Maiden's Feathered Robe (page 1)." *The Endicott Studio Journal of Mythic Arts—Farewell Issue.* http://www.endicott-studio.com/rdrm/rrSwan.html.

Solzhenitsyn, A. 1970. "Nobel Lecture in Literature 1970," *Nobelprize.org.* http://nobelprize.org/nobel_prizes/literature/laureates/1970/solzhenitsynlecture.htm.

Tanizaki, J. [1933.] 2001. *In Praise of Shadows.* Trans. T. J. Harper and E. G. Seidensticker. London: Vintage.

Tatar, M. [1987.] 2003. *The Hard Facts of the Grimms' Fairy Tales,* Expanded Edition. Princeton and Oxford: Princeton University Press.

Tolkien, J. R. R. 1965. *Tree and Leaf.* Extract. In "What Is a Fairy Tale?" *SurLaLune.* http://www.surlalunefairytales.com/introduction/ftdefinition.html.

Tuan, Y. 2004. *Place, Art, and Self.* Center for American Arts and Columbia College Chicago.

van Gennep, A. 1960. *The Rites of Passage.* Chicago: Chicago University Press.

Viguie, D. 2004. *Scarlet Moon.* New York: Simon Pulse.

von Franz, M.-L. 1996. *The Interpretation of Fairy Tales.* Boston: Shambhala.

von Schiller, F. [1800.] 2008. *Die Piccolomini.* Charleston: BiblioBazaar.

Warner, M. 1995. *From the Beast to the Blonde: On Fairy Tales and Their Tellers.* London: Vintage.

Warner, M. 2000. *No Go the Bogeyman.* London: Vintage.

Wilde, Lady F. S. [1887.] 2007. *Ancient Legends, Mystic Charms, and Superstitions of Ireland.* Forgotten.

Wood, C. 2007. *Fairies in Victorian Art.* Woodbridge, Suffolk: Antique Collectors' Club, New Edition.

"Yuki-onna." *Wikipedia—The Free Encyclopedia.* http://en.wikipedia.org/wiki/Yuki_onna.

Zaczek, I. 2005. *Fairy Art: Artists & Inspirations.* London: Star Fire.

Zipes, J. 1991. *Fairy Tales and the Art of Subversion.* New York: Routledge.

Zipes, J. 2006. *Why Fairy Tales Stick—The Evolution and Relevance of a Genre.* New York: Routledge.

Index

LaVergne, TN USA
03 February 2011
214975LV00004B/1/P